# PRACTICAL
# EVALUATION
*for*
# EDUCATORS

# PRACTICAL
# EVALUATION
## *for*
# EDUCATORS

**FINDING WHAT WORKS AND WHAT DOESN'T**

ROGER KAUFMAN
INGRID GUERRA
WILLIAM A. PLATT

**CORWIN PRESS**
A SAGE Publications Company
Thousand Oaks, California

Roger Kaufman
*Florida State University*
*Sonora Institute of Technology*
*Roger Kaufman & Associates*

Ingrid J. Guerra
*Wayne State University*

William A. Platt
*Concurrent Technologies Corporation*

*For information:*

Corwin Press
A Sage Publications Company
2455 Teller Road
Thousand Oaks, California 91320
www.corwinpress.com

Sage Publications Ltd.
1 Oliver's Yard
55 City Road
London EC1Y 1SP
United Kingdom

Sage Publications India Pvt. Ltd.
B-42, Panchsheel Enclave
Post Box 4109
New Delhi 110 017  India

Printed in the United States of America

*Library of Congress Cataloging-in-Publication Data*

Kaufman, Roger
Practical evaluation for educators: Finding what works and what doesn't/
Roger Kaufman, Ingrid Guerra, William A. Platt.
    p. cm.
Includes bibliographical references and index.
ISBN 0-7619-3197-X (cloth) – ISBN 0-7619-3198-8 (pbk.)
    1. Educational evaluation. I. Guerra, Ingrid J. II. Platt, William A. III. Title.
LB2822.75.K37 2006
379.1′58—dc22                                                    2005005358

This book is printed on acid-free paper.

05   06   07   08   09   10   9   8   7   6   5   4   3   2   1

| | |
|---|---|
| *Acquisitions Editor:* | Rachel Livsey |
| *Editorial Assistant:* | Phyllis Cappello |
| *Production Editor:* | Beth A. Bernstein |
| *Copy Editor:* | Carla Freeman |
| *Typesetter:* | C&M Digitals (P) Ltd. |
| *Proofreader:* | Sue Irwin |
| *Indexer:* | Teri Greenberg |
| *Cover Designer:* | Michael Dubowe |

# Contents

# Preface

## ANOTHER BOOK ON EVALUATION! WHY?

Because we care about education adding value for our learners and for our educational partners, evaluation is worth doing. But it must be done well. And that is where this book comes in. Only by using a sensible and sensitive approach to evaluation will we be able to know what is working, what is not, and what to change as well as what to keep. We can do educational evaluation to create a positive and productive learning environment that delivers worthy results and avoids the *wrong things.* We want evaluation data that lead to good decisions. As professionals, we know that good evaluation helps us take responsibility for what we do and for the consequences of our actions.

Educational evaluation is so important that it has become a discipline that has expanded—some might say "exploded"—over the past several decades. With growth have come diverse concepts, arguments, and strong opinions. There is even a bit of nonsense! A flood of writing on the subject has yielded some major advances in thinking and a fair share of controversy on both peripheral and core issues. Educational evaluation as a field has been served by the advances and the arguments, but at the same time has lost the straightforward, if basic, nature that once stood as viable evaluation practice. Educational evaluators now face a daunting array of confusing choices, terminology, and agendas for planning and conducting evaluative inquiry. It does not have to be thus, and should not be. This book is designed to meet this challenge and to help all of us through the barbed wire of confusing jargon in this field.

## WHO SHOULD READ THIS BOOK?

To get beyond the clatter in the field, we define evaluation in clear terms that meet educational requirements for adding measurable value and for knowing what works and what does not. Evaluation is comparing our results with our intentions. Educational evaluation may look at individual learning programs, improvement initiatives, school and district organization and reorganization, and community contributions. In particular, we have designed this book for the following people:

Decision makers or anyone concerned with making sure that education adds value for learners, educators, parents, and citizens.

Principals and assistant principals, to help guide progress toward success; they can find out what is working and what isn't and what to change and what to keep.

Superintendents and assistant superintendents, to help them determine progress and recommend to boards what is working, what isn't, what to keep, and what to change—all on the basis of results and solid data.

Curriculum consultants, to make sense of what is getting presented, what should be presented, and what might be eliminated or revised.

School improvement teams who are charged with helping education to continuously improve. . . . They must ask and answer the right educational questions so their recommendations will deliver measurable results.

Evaluation teams and specialists, to help them ask and answer the "right" educational questions and know what data to collect, why it should be collected, and how it should be presented to those responsible for educational accomplishments.

Teachers, to help them find out what works and what doesn't for their learners in terms of what was mastered that was worth learning and what was not successful.

Concerned citizens, so that they can become contributing partners in improving educational results and contributions.

This book on evaluation fits snugly with new initiatives in education—both federal and state—where results based on solid data must be collected and reported. Funding will increasingly be based on solid evidence of the value educators add for learners, faculty, administrators, parents, communities, and school boards: solid data. Important results.

## WHAT IS OUR APPROACH, AND WHY DOES IT MATTER?

Education is about learners: their success in school and in later life. Useful education goes beyond texts, courses, teachers, and activities. Education must add value for all stakeholders and should do it in a way that results and value can be proven. No fuzzy words, no glittering generalizations. Just facts and the measurable value added to all stakeholders.

Money no longer flows for simply stated good intentions. *No Child Left Behind* and other initiatives are increasingly concerned with what useful results are delivered. Being responsive to that kind of *results-based* planning, doing, developing, implementing, and results—and this will accelerate in the future—provides the key role for evaluation: finding what works and what doesn't. And using that results-based and value-added base for responsive and responsible education is what this book, if followed, will provide.

Useful evaluation will tell educators and the community alike what should be kept and what should be improved. Without asking and answering the right evaluation questions, there can be no rational defense of what we are doing, nor can there be any rational response to possible arbitrary and capricious demands on us. Without sensible and sensitive evaluation, we have no sound basis for deciding what to change and what to continue.

## GOOD EVALUATION IS THE SAFETY TOOL WE CAN USE

We believe there is logic to useful educational evaluation, which leads to well-grounded professional practice for individuals, organizations, and our shared society. This logic is based on the purpose of educational systems to serve the needs of society to add value to all stakeholders. Our approach to evaluation requires a wide view that embraces the fabric of societal and organizational context, not just teaching and learning alone.

Practical evaluation is interrelated to other organizational activities, which include: Needs Assessment, Strategic Thinking and Planning, Program Development, Program Execution and Management, and Continuous Improvement.

Our conception of program evaluation is simplified into four clear phases as a "phased action plan" (PAP). We emphasize the importance of asking the right questions to structure evaluation inquiry. To this end, each phase of the plan has a prime question that sets the stage for that phase. We will use this action plan to structure the topics in this book in the sequence in which they are relevant to conducting an evaluation study. We also provide background on several models of evaluation and the historical context of the emerging field so you can make some sense of it and do evaluation that is useful to all.

*Clear thinking and clear evaluation:* Rigor and discipline are key elements to our conception of useful educational evaluation. We also maintain that evaluation makes the most sense when it is used to assess educational

**Figure FM.1** Phased Action Plan for Evaluation

| Alignment & Direction | Observation | Results | Action & Adjustment |
|---|---|---|---|
| Tools & Concepts | Program Events | Results– Products, Outputs, & Outcomes | Societal Expectations & Value Added |
| Organizational Plans & Programs | Observations & Data Collection | Data Analysis | Plans Updated |
| Needs From Mega | | Trends & Issues | Evaluation Reports |
| | Process Data | | Continued Program Management |
| Questions | Product Data  Issue Data | Recommendations | |

results and the appropriateness of educational processes as a function of the results they are to deliver: to get means and ends properly related. Results may be good or inappropriate depending on the effectiveness of the programs. And programs may be good or bad depending on how well the program is responsive to meeting the needs of society. Education systems that do add value to meeting the needs of society link effective teaching and learning methodologies with valid goals and objectives to generate desirable results. Evaluation can be the vehicle by which educators show the value they add to the enterprise and to our shared world. Showing results trumps endless discourse about our intentions and processes.

## WHAT'S IN IT FOR ME?

Why should you bother? Evaluation can be troublesome, tiring, and time-consuming. There are lots of books on evaluation—why use this one? This book is different. It is based on the solid definition of the context of education in our shared society, and it requires us to plan and deliver in ensuring that our learners will be successful both in school and in life. Both! This book gets very explicit about defining educational results and consequences in and for our shared society, defining this in measurable terms so that planning and delivery will be successful. And the evaluation that follows this societal focus ensures that we successfully align everything we use, do, produce, and deliver in terms of measurable success in school and in life.

Doing this is the safest approach you can take, an approach that is supported by data, results, facts, and clear reporting to yourself and others about what worked and what did not. Well-grounded evaluation findings will provide all stakeholders a reasonable basis for their actions and decisions. Lack of such information opens the way for irrational argument and wrong choices. Our approach to evaluation will clearly define the value added by each component of the school system When you use this approach, you will see just how important it can and will be in meeting the needs of learners, educators, parents, and the community. *Evaluation will never be arbitrary* when evaluation criteria are tied to valid goals and objectives of both the school and society.

## WHAT ARE THE CONTENTS?

This book integrates the tools, concepts, and methods for practical educational evaluation. We provide practical examples, scenarios from believable educational realities, and some rules of the road and guides for educational evaluation so you can discover what works and what doesn't.

- The structure of the book is based on the actions that are required to implement a real and useful evaluation study.
- The logic of the book starts with the valid education–related needs of society and shows how evaluation can support decision making based on the goals and objectives that flow from valid needs.
- A four-phased approach is provided: Alignment and Direction, Observation, Analysis, and Action.
- Methodological descriptions provide criteria for use and examples of typical settings in which each method is appropriate.
- Practical examples are provided in the scenarios.
- Evaluation traps and errors are exposed.
- Rules of the road for doing evaluation are provided.
- Guidance on management and decision making is provided.
- Guidance on contracting for evaluation services is provided.

What don't we do? *We don't repeat all of the statistical concepts and tools that are so well covered in other educational books. These are easy to find and are written by credible authors. We don't provide an educational evaluation cookbook, because we are convinced that "one size fits all" doesn't work very well with clothes and won't work with evaluation either. Every educational evaluation opportunity is different, and we want to provide you with the basic concepts and tools to "custom fit" what you use and do to that specific reality.*

*Why the scenarios?* In this book, moving from chapter to chapter as we provide more evaluation concepts and tools, we develop "scenarios" so you can relate the concepts and tools in the book to a simulated educational example. While these cases in point might not be exactly like your immediate situation, you should see how "it all works in real educational life." Why don't you use your actual situation to apply the concepts and tools to your realities? The scenarios in each part section show you how.

## ACKNOWLEDGMENTS

No book or professional work is really the unique contribution of its authors. This one is no exception. We give special thanks to the many colleagues and students who have helped us to understand the importance of evaluation, which really allows one to find out what worked and what didn't—and that fear should have no part in evaluation.

We appreciate the publishers of our previous works, which we build on here, providing some of the bedrock of what we share in this book.

We thank Corwin Press for inviting this book and providing it, as well as to Rachel Livsey for working with us, and her patience as we went through Hurricanes Charley, Frances, Ivan, and Jeanne: nature's conspiracy to make us spend more and more time past our original deadlines. Thanks to Carla Freeman and Beth Bernstein for sensitive and sensible editing.

Finally, we thank you, the reader, for considering this approach to evaluation and putting it to good use to measurably improve what education uses, does, produces, and delivers to our shared world.

# About the Authors

 **Roger Kaufman** is Professor Emeritus, Florida State University, and Director of Roger Kaufman & Associates. He is also Distinguished Research Professor at the Sonora Institute of Technology. His PhD is in communications from New York University. He consults with public and private organizations in the United States, Canada, Australia, New Zealand, Latin America, and Europe. He is a Certified Performance Technologist and a Diplomate in School Psychology and a Fellow in Educational Psychology of the American Psychological Association. He has been recognized by the ASTD for Distinguished Contribution to Workplace Learning and Performance.

Dr. Kaufman has published 36 books and more than 235 articles on strategic planning, performance improvement, quality management and continuous improvement, needs assessment, management, and evaluation.

 **Ingrid J. Guerra** is Assistant Professor at Wayne State University in Detroit, Michigan, and Research Associate Professor at the Sonora Institute of Technology in Sonora, Mexico. Previously, she was an assistant professor at the University of Michigan–Dearborn, where she taught across two graduate programs, Performance Improvement & Instructional Design, and Public Administration. She is also a private consultant for private and public organizations nationally and internationally and a professional member of Roger Kaufman & Associates. She has served as Chair of Needs Assessment TIG for the American Evaluation Association and Chair of the Research Committee for the International Society for Performance Improvement. In addition, she has published articles in journals such as *International Public Management Review*, *International Journal for Educational Reform*, *Performance Improvement Quarterly*, *Performance Improvement Journal*, *Human Resource Development Quarterly*, *Educational Technology*, and

*Quarterly Review of Distance Education,* among others. Ingrid received her PhD and MA in Instructional Systems and her bachelor's in Psychology from Florida State University.

 **William A. Platt** is currently a Principle Instructional Designer for Concurrent Technologies Corporation in Johnstown, Pennsylvania, and was previously the Program Manager for Evaluation in the Office of Technical Training and Evaluation in the Veterans Benefits Administration. He is a member of the American Evaluation Association. He has consulted for the defense industry in the area of simulation and training and has presented professional papers on task analysis and instructional design. He was a Branch Head with the Naval Training Systems Center in charge of Land Warfare Training Analysis. His PhD is in Instructional Technology from Indiana University. He served as member of the Adjunct Faculty at the Marine Corps Service Support Schools and has served as a training advisor for Marine Corps training commands. He retired at the rank of Lieutenant Colonel.

# A Short
# Self-Assessment
# of Evaluation

W e want this book to be practical and useful. This short assessment is designed to find out what you believe you and your organization should include in an evaluation. We cover several areas that an evaluation should or could include in its scope.

We ask you to take this self-assessment twice: once now, and once after you finish the book. If you keep a record of your responses now so you can compare them with your perceptions at the finish of the book, you can evaluate any changes in what you believe you and your organization should include in an evaluation.

## HOW YOUR ORGANIZATION "SEES" EVALUATION

Evaluation is essential to the success of learners, the educational system, and the citizens who pay for it. Please rate your organization on these questions. Note that as we move through the material in this book, we will be covering these critical elements of successful educational evaluation and ensure we have the "right" data for useful decisions and results.

For each item, first check each item in the *What Is* column that best describes your educational organization as it *currently* views evaluation. Then, in the *What Should Be* column, check each item for how you think your educational organization *should* view evaluation.

This exercise is a demonstration on how evaluation can help you decide what works and what doesn't, what to change and what to keep.

We suggest that your repeat this assessment at the end of the book so you can see for yourself the extent to which you have shifted from your entry assessment after going through the materials and concepts in the book. You may see how your views about evaluation have shifted from *What Is* to *What Should Be.*

# A Short Self-Assessment of Evaluation Readiness

For each item, check the item that best describes your educational organization, both for What Is and What Should Be.

| 1 = Strongly Disagree | 5 = Agree |
|---|---|
| 2 = Disagree | 6 = Strongly Agree |
| 3 = Somewhat Disagree | 7 = Not Applicable |
| 4 = Somewhat Agree | |

**WHAT IS** — Describes how you see your organization *currently* operating.

**WHAT SHOULD BE** — Describes how you think your organization *should be* operating.

## HOW YOUR ORGANIZATION SEES EVALUATION

| WHAT IS | | | | | | | Item | WHAT SHOULD BE | | | | | | |
|---|---|---|---|---|---|---|---|---|---|---|---|---|---|---|
| 1 | 2 | 3 | 4 | 5 | 6 | 7 | 1. Concerned about results for individual performance accomplishment | 1 | 2 | 3 | 4 | 5 | 6 | 7 |
| 1 | 2 | 3 | 4 | 5 | 6 | 7 | 2. Concerned about results for small groups | 1 | 2 | 3 | 4 | 5 | 6 | 7 |
| 1 | 2 | 3 | 4 | 5 | 6 | 7 | 3. Concerned about results for a department | 1 | 2 | 3 | 4 | 5 | 6 | 7 |
| 1 | 2 | 3 | 4 | 5 | 6 | 7 | 4. Concerned about results for the entire organization | 1 | 2 | 3 | 4 | 5 | 6 | 7 |
| 1 | 2 | 3 | 4 | 5 | 6 | 7 | 5. Concerned with the impact the educational agency has on learners upon graduation or completion | 1 | 2 | 3 | 4 | 5 | 6 | 7 |
| 1 | 2 | 3 | 4 | 5 | 6 | 7 | 6. Concerned with the impact of the learners after they leave school in terms of their contributions to our shared society | 1 | 2 | 3 | 4 | 5 | 6 | 7 |
| 1 | 2 | 3 | 4 | 5 | 6 | 7 | 7. Weak in terms of formal evaluation because of time restraints | 1 | 2 | 3 | 4 | 5 | 6 | 7 |
| 1 | 2 | 3 | 4 | 5 | 6 | 7 | 8. Weak in terms of formal evaluation because of lack of evaluation abilities | 1 | 2 | 3 | 4 | 5 | 6 | 7 |
| 1 | 2 | 3 | 4 | 5 | 6 | 7 | 9. Weak in terms of formal evaluation because of not knowing what to do with the evaluation data | 1 | 2 | 3 | 4 | 5 | 6 | 7 |
| 1 | 2 | 3 | 4 | 5 | 6 | 7 | 10. Management is focused on results | 1 | 2 | 3 | 4 | 5 | 6 | 7 |
| 1 | 2 | 3 | 4 | 5 | 6 | 7 | 11. Staff is focused on results | 1 | 2 | 3 | 4 | 5 | 6 | 7 |
| 1 | 2 | 3 | 4 | 5 | 6 | 7 | 12. Our culture is results focused | 1 | 2 | 3 | 4 | 5 | 6 | 7 |
| 1 | 2 | 3 | 4 | 5 | 6 | 7 | 13. Evaluation is seen as comparing results with intentions | 1 | 2 | 3 | 4 | 5 | 6 | 7 |

*(Continued)*

| WHAT IS<br>Describes how you see your organization *currently* operating. | | | | | | | | WHAT SHOULD BE<br>Describes how you think your organization *should be* operating. | | | | | | |
|---|---|---|---|---|---|---|---|---|---|---|---|---|---|---|
| | | | | | | | **1 = Strongly Disagree**    **5 = Agree**<br>**2 = Disagree**    **6 = Strongly Agree**<br>**3 = Somewhat Disagree**    **7 = Not Applicable**<br>**4 = Somewhat Agree** | | | | | | | |
| 1 2 3 4 5 6 7 | | | | | | | 14. Evaluation is seen as comparing results with intentions and deciding what to stop, what to continue, what to modify | 1 2 3 4 5 6 7 | | | | | | |
| 1 2 3 4 5 6 7 | | | | | | | 15. Evaluation functions are included in planning | 1 2 3 4 5 6 7 | | | | | | |
| 1 2 3 4 5 6 7 | | | | | | | 16. Evaluation results are shared with all internal partners (include parents and learners) | 1 2 3 4 5 6 7 | | | | | | |

### HOW YOUR ORGANIZATION GOES ABOUT EVALUATION

| WHAT IS | | | | | | | | WHAT SHOULD BE | | | | | | |
|---|---|---|---|---|---|---|---|---|---|---|---|---|---|---|
| 1 2 3 4 5 6 7 | | | | | | | 17. Collects "hard"[1] performance data | 1 2 3 4 5 6 7 | | | | | | |
| 1 2 3 4 5 6 7 | | | | | | | 18. Collects "hard" performance data for impact on society or community | 1 2 3 4 5 6 7 | | | | | | |
| 1 2 3 4 5 6 7 | | | | | | | 19. Collects "soft"[2] (perception) performance-related data | 1 2 3 4 5 6 7 | | | | | | |
| 1 2 3 4 5 6 7 | | | | | | | 20. Collects "soft (perception)" performance-related data for impact on society or community | 1 2 3 4 5 6 7 | | | | | | |
| 1 2 3 4 5 6 7 | | | | | | | 21. Uses both "hard" and "soft" data for assessing needs | 1 2 3 4 5 6 7 | | | | | | |
| 1 2 3 4 5 6 7 | | | | | | | 22. Involves internal partners (staff) in setting objectives | 1 2 3 4 5 6 7 | | | | | | |
| 1 2 3 4 5 6 7 | | | | | | | 23. Involves external partners (parents and community members) in setting objectives | 1 2 3 4 5 6 7 | | | | | | |
| 1 2 3 4 5 6 7 | | | | | | | 24. Formally evaluates results external to the organization | 1 2 3 4 5 6 7 | | | | | | |
| 1 2 3 4 5 6 7 | | | | | | | 25. Formally evaluates results within the organization | 1 2 3 4 5 6 7 | | | | | | |
| 1 2 3 4 5 6 7 | | | | | | | 26. Prepares measurable objectives that state both what result is to be accomplished and how the accomplishment will be measured | 1 2 3 4 5 6 7 | | | | | | |

*(Continued)*

| WHAT IS — Describes how you see your organization *currently* operating. | | | | | | | THE BASIS FOR EVALUATION CRITERIA | WHAT SHOULD BE — Describes how you think your organization *should be* operating. | | | | | | |
|---|---|---|---|---|---|---|---|---|---|---|---|---|---|---|
| | | | | | | | 1 = Strongly Disagree   5 = Agree<br>2 = Disagree   6 = Strongly Agree<br>3 = Somewhat Disagree   7 = Not Applicable<br>4 = Somewhat Agree | | | | | | | |
| 1 2 3 4 5 6 7 | | | | | | | 27. Plans on the basis of ends | 1 2 3 4 5 6 7 | | | | | | |
| 1 2 3 4 5 6 7 | | | | | | | 28. Plans on the basis of consequences of results for society and community | 1 2 3 4 5 6 7 | | | | | | |
| 1 2 3 4 5 6 7 | | | | | | | 29. Plans only on the basis of individual performance | 1 2 3 4 5 6 7 | | | | | | |
| 1 2 3 4 5 6 7 | | | | | | | 30. Plans only on the basis of resources | 1 2 3 4 5 6 7 | | | | | | |
| 1 2 3 4 5 6 7 | | | | | | | 31. Plans only on the basis of activities, programs, projects | 1 2 3 4 5 6 7 | | | | | | |
| 1 2 3 4 5 6 7 | | | | | | | 32. Plans on the basis of results for society and community | 1 2 3 4 5 6 7 | | | | | | |
| 1 2 3 4 5 6 7 | | | | | | | 33. Plans to link resources to activities, programs, projects | 1 2 3 4 5 6 7 | | | | | | |
| 1 2 3 4 5 6 7 | | | | | | | 34. Plans to link resources to results that add value for clients and clients' clients | 1 2 3 4 5 6 7 | | | | | | |
| 1 2 3 4 5 6 7 | | | | | | | 35. Plans only on the basis of activities, programs, projects | 1 2 3 4 5 6 7 | | | | | | |
| 1 2 3 4 5 6 7 | | | | | | | 36. Choose means and resources (e.g., technology, curriculum, in-service training, restructuring, layoffs) without first identifying results to be achieved | 1 2 3 4 5 6 7 | | | | | | |
| 1 2 3 4 5 6 7 | | | | | | | 37. Defines and uses needs assessment for identifying gaps in results for impact on external clients and society | 1 2 3 4 5 6 7 | | | | | | |

*(Continued)*

| WHAT IS — Describes how you see your organization *currently* operating. | Scale | Item | WHAT SHOULD BE — Describes how you think your organization *should be* operating. |
|---|---|---|---|
| 1 2 3 4 5 6 7 | 1 = Strongly Disagree  2 = Disagree  3 = Somewhat Disagree  4 = Somewhat Agree  5 = Agree  6 = Strongly Agree  7 = Not Applicable | 39. Plans only on the basis of activities, programs, projects | 1 2 3 4 5 6 7 |
| 1 2 3 4 5 6 7 | | 40. Defines needs assessment for identifying gaps in results for impact on individual operations or tasks. | 1 2 3 4 5 6 7 |
| 1 2 3 4 5 6 7 | | 41. Rank orders needs on the basis of the costs to meet the needs as compared to the costs of ignoring them. Using Evaluation Data | 1 2 3 4 5 6 7 |
| 1 2 3 4 5 6 7 | | 42. Uses data from a needs assessment to set objectives | 1 2 3 4 5 6 7 |
| | | **USING EVALUATION DATA** | |
| 1 2 3 4 5 6 7 | | 43. Use evaluation data for improvement | 1 2 3 4 5 6 7 |
| 1 2 3 4 5 6 7 | | 44. Use evaluation data for punishing | 1 2 3 4 5 6 7 |
| 1 2 3 4 5 6 7 | | 45. Compares accomplishments with objectives established at the beginning of the project | 1 2 3 4 5 6 7 |
| 1 2 3 4 5 6 7 | | 46. Compare accomplishments to the payoffs for those accomplishments for individual projects | 1 2 3 4 5 6 7 |

1. "Hard" data are results that are independently verifiable, such as completion rate, test scores, employment, and income level.
2. "Soft" data are results that are personal and not independently verifiable, such as perceptions, opinions, and feelings.

# Introduction 1

The chapters of many texts can be read out of order, but that is not true with our text. We have taken special pains to put our chapters in the order that makes sense according to a logic of evaluation that we hope you will embrace and use in your own evaluation studies. You can start by shedding any fear of evaluation. One should not fear evaluation either as the evaluator or any other educational partner when going under the magnifying glass. This book provides a professional and comprehensive set of concepts guidelines for conducting evaluation studies that are useful for improving the educational enterprise. Our approach is results centered. We avoid reliance on fringe movements in evaluation in favor of building on the solid and proven core concepts and methods.

This is not your "standard" educational evaluation book. This one focuses on asking and then answering useful educational questions in order to make sensible and justifiable data-driven decisions.

Our approach will introduce you to some powerful yet commonsense evaluation tools for planning and doing evaluation. Some traditional topics like testing, measuring, and statistics are placed in the proper perspective so that they serve the purpose of evaluation rather than control you. We stress that in any evaluation, you must carefully first decide on what to evaluate and why, and then design and carry out the evaluation to answer a set of critical evaluation questions.

> Evaluation, at its core, is simple and useful: Finding what works and what doesn't.

Evaluation compares our results to our intentions. Sensible? We think so. We also know that evaluation is a large field with its share of pitfalls. We will point out some traps and problems associated with the conventional practice and language of evaluation in order to make our approach clear. And practical. We place a primary emphasis on results, as well as on collecting and using relevant and useful data.

We start with some commonsense ideas.

Whenever we do anything, especially when it involves the future of our learners, it is practical to ask, "How did we do?" We spend the time of our learners, our teachers, and our educators to help them master that which will be useful. Education is about learners and the future: their future as well as ours. We should all care enough to find out whether we helped or hindered. Evaluation, then, helps us to find out what works and what should be modified, changed, or stopped.

> Evaluation data, therefore, must be used for improving and never for blaming.

The value of results is related to individual, organizational, and societal goals, objectives, and expectations that must be treated as a whole system (rather than just looking at pieces and parts and hoping the whole thing will go together).

To usefully evaluate practices and programs to improve education, it is vital to collect and use data in a sensitive, practical, and efficient manner. To do this, we put ourselves in the business of asking and then answering the right questions.

With common sense as our premise, we suggest that the best way to convey a useful framework for providing our approach to collecting and using important data is in four distinct phases. We consider these phases a useful framework that you can build on to conduct an evaluation. We call this framework the Evaluation Action Plan (EAP). We fully expect that the EAP will guide you as you design, develop, and conduct successful evaluations. The plan is reflected in the organization of this book to support planning and doing. The plan simplifies the often overly complex models of evaluation yet emphasizes the major considerations and tasks involved in collecting useful data; based on the right questions, it

**Five Principles of Evaluation:**

Systematic Inquiry

Competence

Integrity and Honesty

Respect for People

Responsibility for General and Public Welfare

will allow you to design, develop, and implement valuations, as well as act on findings to improve the educational enterprise. We also think it is important to adhere to the ethical and professional guidelines set forth in the five principles published by the American Evaluation Association (AEA).

## PHASES OF THE EVALUATION ACTION PLAN (EAP)

Sound evaluation starts by asking the right questions. We build on the proposition that the value of an educational program is based on how well that program meets the needs—gaps in results and consequences—of society. For an evaluation finding to be useful, meaningful, relevant,

**Figure 1.1**    The Four Phases of the Evaluation Action Plan (EAP)

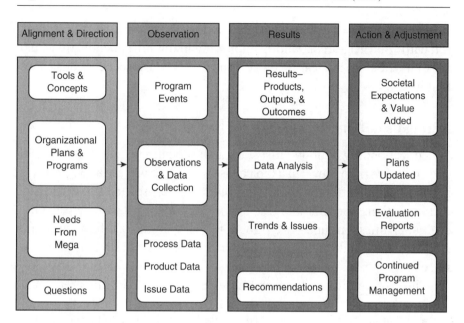

unambiguous, and acceptable, you must start with some fundamental and essential planning that examines the basis of the educational enterprise. This planning will guide your evaluative inquiry. At each phase of our plan, there are some prime questions to be answered (see Figure 1.1).

*Alignment and Direction:* Making sure the evaluation questions we ask and answer are useful. To be useful, we ask questions not only about the intended results of educational programs but also about the legitimacy of the results as well. The prime question for *alignment and direction* asks whether the goals and objectives of school programs are based on valid needs—important gaps in results—of society. The consequence of the alignment and direction phase is a set of useful questions to guide the evaluation inquiry. Having that in hand, we can proceed to determine the information required to answer each question. We look for those answers in the observation phase.

*Observations:* Application of tools and methods to collect valid and useful data. The prime questions for the *observation phase* are: What information will answer the evaluation question set, and what methods will collect the required data?

*Results:* Comparing what we accomplished with what we wanted to accomplish. The prime questions in the *results phase* are: Did we accomplish what we set out to accomplish, and if not, why not?

*Action and Adjustment:* Using the data for appropriate decisions on what to keep and what to change. The prime questions for the *action phase* are: What do we report to stakeholders and decision makers, and what should we keep or change in programs to bring them into alignment with the needs of society?

Each phase of this plan will equip you to move to the next by providing you with knowledge, tools, and examples, but in this introduction, we would like to set the stage by clearing away some myths and misconceptions about evaluation.

## Asking Useful Questions

Educational evaluation must start with educational questions—useful questions. We have provided a typical list below. You will see as we progress in the action plan that data can be collected and used to answer each of these questions. We will stress the importance of the relation between the evaluation questions and the type of data that will support the answer and be both reliable and valid. There are four sets of prime questions that set the stage for each phase of the action plan.

The prime questions for each phase relate to the following areas:

- *Alignment and Direction.* Are the valid needs of society reflected in the results produced by the organizational- and program-level set of solutions? In other words, do educational programs cause students to learn, and are they learning the right things in order to be successful in school and in life? The primary questions yield a host of related supporting questions, each relating to the specific concerns of the evaluation study being planned. This set of questions becomes the focus for inquiry activities, including observation and data collection.
- *Observation.* What information must be gathered to answer the general set of questions? What methods will best gather that information? What support tools are required?
- *Results.* Are the observed results the intended results? What Process factors contributed to the observed results? What issues and trends become apparent over time?
- *Action and Adjustment.* What should be kept, adjusted, or discarded to start new?

You will be pleased when you see how powerful this approach can be. You will also note that building your observation plan will become easier as you look for ways to answer the questions, instead of picking a methodology and then limiting your study to the data that method gathers. A host of study-defining evaluation questions will flow from the primary set of evaluation questions.

Here is an example set:

- What objectives in our educational mission did we achieve?
- Did these objectives add value to our communities and shared society?
- What did learners master?
- Was what the learners mastered worth mastering? In what ways?
- Are methods, tools, materials, and activities effective? Efficient?
- What should we change?
- What should we keep?
- What should we stop?
- What value did we add for all internal and external stakeholders?
- What results justify our continued programs, projects, and activities?
- Do the educational programs have unintended consequences?
- What should we do next?

By asking and answering these vital educational evaluation questions, we can prove our worth to ourselves, our financial backers, and our stakeholders. Is this not all very sensible? We think so, because the questions ultimately define the scope of the evaluation study. The question set must keep us focused on the core purpose at hand. In fact, those fundamental evaluation questions will shape reality, as they will limit our range and scope of the data that help us answer them.

Useful educational questions come from asking, "What it is we want to accomplish in our educational enterprise, and why?" It is also important that this procedure be collaborative and representative of the full population of stakeholders. Their contributions will provide insights otherwise missed by a narrow evaluation team, and their participation will begin a sense of ownership and buy-in required for using the evaluation results to create the required change.

In this book, we will share with you some frameworks and guidelines for (1) asking the right questions and (2) making sure that your questions are correctly targeted toward really knowing what results were accomplished as well as (3) the usefulness of those results and how to define and get valid data. This entire book is designed so you will be successful at educational evaluation.

## Ensuring Commitment

It is vital to establish the "ownership" of education by those who receive and deliver it as well as define its contributions so that we create a lasting partnership for success. Trust, understanding, and agreement on a common destination—results to be achieved—are all key to a successful educational enterprise. If we don't have the commitment and participation of all stakeholders, our success might be less than it could be.

Evaluation data can sometimes be scary to both educators and stakeholders alike. If there is good news, it should be trustworthy. If there is bad news, it is best provided in an environment of trust and the common purpose of continuous improvement and based on real and justifiable data. We should never withhold disappointments, but we best make certain that our successes and shortfalls are based on solid evidence.

> *Fear Builders:* Actions on the part of the evaluator or evaluation team that cause stakeholders to fear evaluation.

Thus this book is based on asking and answering the right questions and collecting the realistic and trustworthy data for comparing our educational objectives with our actual accomplishments. Trust, common purpose, and shared destiny are key to getting and maintaining commitment. We want you to avoid instilling fear in favor of building trust. From time to time, we will point out evaluation behavior that does both.

Creating the partnership for education also hinges on seriously involving all stakeholders, but also listening to them. Really listening. While it might be tempting to move ahead with educational plans and evaluations without the stakeholders' involvement and commitment, doing so risks them later seeing your worthwhile efforts as deceptive or worse.

> *Trust Builders:* Behavior on the part of the evaluator or evaluation team that builds trust among stakeholders.

Peter Drucker (1973) had good advice when he suggested we ensure "transfer of ownership" to our stakeholders; people see what is done as their own rather than belonging to someone else. And the best way to ensure the transfer is to involve the educational partners in setting the objectives and sharing with them the results of our educational successes and shortfalls. Look for ways to build trust, and your evaluation study will prove not only to be easier, but your recommendation and findings will have more impact and stand a better chance of leading to meaningful change.

Evaluation provides us the opportunity to have an open and honest relationship with our stakeholders based on performance data, and not just rumors, misunderstandings, and biases. Involving them is the best way to ensure that what we do and deliver is considered in the light of the value we add to learners and our shared communities.

## Involving Key Stakeholders in Useful Educational Evaluation

We invite our key stakeholders—our partners in educational accomplishment—to contribute to asking and answering these "right questions."

Key evaluation stakeholders include:

- Learners
- Teachers
- Parents
- Administrators
- Educational staff
- Future employers
- The community (society) in which we live.

The stakeholders we invite to join us should be representative of the communities we serve. They should be seen as a sample of everyone in the educational service area, and they should be seen by their peers as appropriate and representing them. Though as humans we all have individual interests and concerns, as much as it is possible, do not select stakeholders to help us define useful educational objectives and evaluation criteria—and review our progress—who have axes to grind, who have special "single issues," or who represent a powerful lobby.

A vital challenge for the stakeholders who will help us all be successful is to keep them focused on results and consequences, not on means, activities, resources, or politics. Single-issue politics from both within and outside of our schools has a chilling effect on defining our objectives, selecting the best curriculum and means, and using our results for improvement only.

## Clarifying the Purpose and Nature of Evaluation

Before you start to plan, before you collect data, and before you grapple with our chapters, ask yourself why you are doing evaluation. Is this your initiative, or were you directed to evaluate? What is the motivation for the study? What are you looking to accomplish and contribute as a result of this evaluation? We hope it derives from an outside-in, shared view of societal well-being, which we refer to as "Mega planning." The aim is to reach an "Ideal Vision," where the educational programs are an integrated and efficient means to reaching valid societal ends—societal ends that we agree on, not those that are imposed arbitrarily by one group or another.

However, we know that societal/community-referenced evaluation is not always the case. Consider some traditional reasons evaluations are carried out:

- Evaluation to see whether a solution to a problem is working
- Evaluation to discover the cause of a problem
- Evaluation to confirm compliance with a mandate

- Evaluation to sort out a mess
- Evaluation to bring about a change in social consciousness
- Evaluation to provide feedback to control a program
- Evaluation to satisfy the requirements of law

With careful attention to detailed planning, each of these can be made to be compatible with our data-driven and results-oriented action approach to evaluation. But if taken too narrowly—in isolation and without proper context—each of these has its own narrow set of problems, blind spots, and special data generation and collection troubles. What we are saying is that the way you perceive the evaluation purpose can shape and limit the data that are observed (or not observed), collected or (not collected), and interpreted or ignored. We have taken pains to provide guidance that will help you avoid pitfalls, stick to the right questions, and remain relevant. But the most important understanding that we want to convey in this book is that the value in evaluation stems from a societal view of right and wrong actions as they relate to an Ideal Vision.

We enthusiastically believe that evaluation must directly face the issues that follow from this point: Education is a means to societal ends, and thus adding measurable value to our shared society is critical.

Some evaluations are merely descriptions without judgments of worth, especially value added to our shared society. Such an approach misses the point. We think evaluation practice must confront this issue. This is fundamental to building coherent meaning and integrity in this fractured field.

Our conception of this approach is summed up in the term *Mega*.

## WHAT IS MEGA, AND WHY IS IT A PRACTICAL APPROACH?

The concept of Mega is a view of society based on consensus and agreement on how we see and interact with the world. It is a focus on the things we can agree are good and desirable. It avoids the peripheral areas of discordant beliefs that can sidetrack both evaluators and the program actions that lead to societal well-being. It is based on common sense that we all use in our daily lives. In fact, most people around the globe use it for their families and themselves to make daily decisions about their lives and well-being.

For example, here are some guiding principles of Mega thinking, planning, and evaluating:

1. Every time I deal with others, I expect them to treat me the way I treat them. I commit to do no physical, psychological, or financial harm and expect others to do the same.

2. When I do business with anyone—fly on an airline, eat in a restaurant, drive in a car, go to the dentist and physician, buy items in a supermarket or pharmacy—I expect them to put my health, safety, and well-being as the first thing on their "to do" list. No exceptions. I do the same in everything that I use, do, and deliver.

3. If you agree with the above, then you are "acting Mega."

Let's see what that means as we define Mega and put the idea into action. When you think and act Mega, you commit to add value—real measurable value—to those you deal with as well as to our shared society. This means you don't cause deadly pollution, you don't physically hurt yourself or others with dangerous goods and services, and you don't kill, maim, or poison others. You do what billions of people across the globe do as parents: You ensure the self-sufficiency, self-reliance, and positive quality of life for others.

So what's so difficult to understand about this? Sociologists call doing so—being Mega—*the social contract*, and it is the basis of much that exists in our shared world:

- The basic and conventional religions around the world
- Rotary and other social service groups
- The Ten Commandments

These all provide guidelines for Mega thinking and doing, and even if you are not a person of formal faith, being Mega oriented is ethical. It is also practical: Why would you want to harm others when such harm might in turn be visited upon you?

In business, the medical Hippocratic oath also is worth adherence: "Do no harm." Why would you want to harm your clients? Kill them? Injure them? Why make an unsafe or deadly airplane or car or food or medicine? Do so, and you best get out of business and likely also out of the country. Short-term thinking is long-term failure.

Mega does not mean superimposing your (or anyone else's) values or procedures on others. It is what is agreed upon by all social partners. And Mega is not code for "really big" or "really important." Mega means adding measurable value to all, including society.

> Mega thinking, planning, and doing is both practical and ethical: Treat others as you would have them treat you for health, safety, and well-being.

A few years ago, with some help, Kaufman asked people from around the world and in very diverse cultures, "What kind of world would you want to help create for tomorrow's child?" They were asked to speak to ends, and not to means, resources, programs, projects, politics, or activities—just

**Figure 1.2**    An Ideal Vision

---

**BASIC IDEAL VISION: The world we
want to help create for tomorrow's child**

There will be no losses of life nor elimination or reduction of levels of well-being, survival, self-sufficiency, quality of life, from any source including (but not limited to):

➢ war and/or riot

➢ unintended human-caused changes to the environment including permanent destruction of the environment and/or rendering it non-renewable

➢ murder, rape, or crimes of violence, robbery, or destruction to property

➢ substance abuse

➢ disease

➢ pollution

➢ starvation and/or malnutrition

➢ destructive behavior (including child, partner, spouse, self, elder, others)

➢ accidents, including transportation, home, and business/workplace

➢ discrimination based on irrelevant variables including color, race, age, creed, gender, religion, wealth, national origin, or location

Poverty will not exist, and every woman and man will earn as least as much as it costs them to live unless they are progressing toward being self-sufficient and self-reliant. No adult will be under the care, custody, or control of another person, agency, or substance: all adult citizens will be self-sufficient and self-reliant as minimally indicated by their consumption being equal to or less than their production.

---

results and consequences. When these responses were sorted out, an Ideal Vision emerged. This Ideal Vision cut successfully across nations, cultures, religions, and races. Whenever you make a decision, simply review its elements (see it as a fabric and not a bunch of individual strands) and ask, "Will this take us closer or further away from Mega?" The Ideal Vision is described in Figure 1.2.

Did you find anything in the Ideal Vision that you would not want others to apply when dealing with you and yours? If, like us, you focus on the good things society can agree on, why should you not do the same in your life and work?

Mega thinking, planning, and doing are both practical and ethical. We all depend on each other, so why not make everyone Mega thinkers, planners, and doers?

To quote John F. Kennedy, "If not us, who, and if not now, when?"

But desire and motivation to do evaluation are only the first step. You must also have insight and knowledge about what to do and how to do it. Often, you must also know what not to do.

## AVOIDING EVALUATION TRAPS AND
## ERRORS BY FOLLOWING EVALUATION RULES

### There are Some Traps to be Avoided
### In doing Educational Evaluation

We will show you the major common traps in the book as we move along.

Widespread misunderstandings and biases can (but should not be allowed to) creep in from ourselves and from our stakeholders. Collecting useful and complete data should provide answers to the key questions above, but there are some very common and some not-so-common reasons why evaluations can (and often do) get off track. We have identified some of these. We cover these at the end of each section of the book. Evaluation traps are situations that exist in the environment surrounding an evaluation study that involve active forces that cause studies to lose focus, avoid essential information, or gather irrelevant data. Errors are mistakes in planning and executing that trace back to misguided ideas or lack of expertise on the part of the evaluator. For each trap and error, we have provided some rules of the road that will help.

Educational evaluation is far too important to weaken its contributions by defects in our thinking and methods. True, education is "messy" in terms of all of the things that are going on in schools and the system. But still, despite this, our challenge—professionally and personally—is to ask and answer the right questions without mucking up the procedure with errors that can be avoided.

## THE GROWTH OF EVALUATION PRACTICE

### Building an Approach Based on the Best Features
### of Accepted Practice

As you plan to do evaluation, you will no doubt encounter some of the vast—the authors would call it "rich"—array of models, methods, and schools of evaluation. We have developed the chapters of this book to help you pick and choose from that assortment when you plan your own evaluation. We have based our own approach to evaluation on practices that have stood the test of time, meet our criteria for common sense, and generally fit within the framework of the AEA principles. The field of evaluation includes much that is useful and much that is distracting, argumentative, and hard to put to practical use. We start with *Mega planning* and *needs assessment,* which provide a framework to set educational goals and to control and analyze solution sets to obtain beneficial educational results. To that core, we have added from the field. Some of the more influential themes include the following.

## Testing and Measurement

Evaluation practice today is a synthesis of several other disciplines that have nourished the growth of the field. The most important of these was the widespread use of testing and measurement to better utilize personnel resource during time of war. This firmly established the discipline as a taproot for conducting evaluation studies to match students to courses of study and help them make career choices. The use of statistical tools soon expanded to include simulation computer models in the discipline of operations research, which applied multidisciplinary approaches to problem solving. This field was also conceived in time of war. But its lasting approach has spread to quality control in organizational/industrial and educational settings.

Evaluators too can now pick from a host of well-developed analysis tools that were developed under the banner of "Operations Research." Parallel to these developments, the study of human behavior blossomed with the work of Thorndike and B. F. Skinner. The advent of general system theory and disciplined study of organizations and group behavior in organizations added more tools and concepts that have contributed to the thinking in the new field of evaluation. Each of the divisions of the social sciences has contributed to evaluation, so that now it is commonplace to see a range in evaluation activity that extends from experimental and measurement-oriented studies to case studies and anthropology. It was only a matter of time, however, before writers influenced by these roots began to identify themselves as evaluators. This began in earnest in the late 1960s and 70s.

## The Growth of Models

In the early direction and new language of evaluation, the emergence of a host of evaluation models in the 1970s tended to center around the scholarship of academics, each with some distinctive features but all trying to solve three core problems of evaluation. For every evaluation, the evaluator must solve or answer the following:

1. What should be evaluated? This includes both the target and the limits of the target for evaluation.

2. How do I put myself, the evaluator, in a position to be able to make meaningful value judgments about the merit or worth of the thing being evaluated?

3. Who am I working for?

The history of movements and models in evaluation as a field can be traced by the way various evaluators have approached these three questions. In general, the trend has been from narrow focus to broad focus to focus linked to society.

## Performance Objectives

Education under the influence of a combination of pragmatism and sensible behaviorism was primed and ready when the use of so-called performance objectives was introduced with the work of Tyler (1966) and Popham (1974) and made rational by the influence of the book *Preparing Instructional Objectives*, by Mager (1997).[1]

Evaluation in some early models was the examination of programs to see whether the students met objectives. The evaluators were teachers or material developers intent on showing the utility of educational texts and programs that caused students to reach educational objectives. The model was very school centric. This model was warmly accepted by educators looking for a firm way to anchor the curriculum. However, at its best, the objectives-oriented model of evaluation caused a rather narrow focus, which left some scholars looking for broader conceptions—a flaw in implementation rather than concept. For some, having performance objectives that were in the correct format and measurable did not also guarantee the objectives were addressing the right things. Many also realized that focusing only on objectives could cause the evaluator to miss important data on Process and environment. Educators realized that evaluation could play a role in the development of educational programs to adjust content and procedure along the way to the final Products, Outputs, and Outcomes.[2] This realization gave rise to a famous distinction when Scriven (1967) introduced the terms "formative" and "summative" evaluation.[3] Now, evaluators had a term for the type of evaluation activity used to guide developmental activity in educational programs and another term when evaluation was used to comment on overall final value: What did we accomplish, and was it worth accomplishing?

## The Scientific vs. Naturalistic Method

As the conceptual underpinnings of evaluation evolved, other distinctions emerged. Many scholars admiring the progress and precision of the so-called hard sciences conceived of evaluation as an opportunity to conduct research and confirm the utility of programs using experimental and quasi-experimental designs. This was in contrast to a growing number of evaluators who advocated a less disruptive naturalistic form of inquiry that depended heavily on the sensitive skill of the observer, who would through close personal observation grasp the important variables in a program. Still other evaluators saw the organization as the proper focus of evaluation. Plans and programs were consequences of the way personnel conducted the daily business of the organization. The flow of information, resources, and decision making were examined, with the primary task of evaluation to support the decision-making tasks in the organization. The best of these models provided coherent linkage of organizational results and purpose with the Process or program (means) used to reach the desired ends. The role of the evaluator was to spot inefficiency or dysfunction and to develop data that would support the decisions that guided the enterprise. Curriculum planners and school administrators embraced this model.

## The Emergence of Key Evaluation Leaders

Evidence that evaluators were actively searching for answers to the questions posed by the emerging field can be found in the diversity of models described in the works of Worthen and Sanders (1973), Glass and Ellet (1980), and Stufflebeam and Webster (1980), who provided surveys of the field. House (1977) realized making a value claim is a form of argument, and he worked out a system of evaluation logic that took account of the audience for evaluation. Wolf (1979) took this idea a step further in framing evaluation as a form of argument similar to that of the legal system. Guba (1978) contrasted experimental and naturalistic approaches, showing that each had differing advantages.

The experimental approach to evaluation demonstrated a particular relation that was then valued, where the naturalistic approach gathered multiple-relationship data during the course of an evaluation. Some evaluators honed their skills in observation and their ideas about evaluation through years of practice. Stake and his colleagues at the Center for Instructional Research and Curriculum Evaluation at the University of Illinois have refined the case study method into what they refer to as "responsive evaluation." Here, evaluation teams take an in-depth look over an extended period of time and test their observations by getting multiple frames of reference and the use of "meta-evaluation" discussions. Stake (1974) emphasized the role of audience and the in-depth personal observation available through the case study method.

## The Department of Defense

Work for and by the Department of Defense added to the ideas of the early evaluators. Each service developed systematic models for the creation and delivery of instruction. Typical is the Joint Services Model created for the U.S. Army by Florida State, with Branson leading the team (see Branson, Rayner, & Cox, 1975). All of these models stressed the importance of evaluation. These models worked best when coupled with a disciplined investigation of requirements, which the military termed "front-end analysis." The concept, however, is better illustrated in Kaufman's work on needs assessment (e.g., Kaufman 1992a, 1995, 1998, 2000; Kaufman & English, 1979).

Evaluation model building gave rise to evaluation theory building. Platt (1982) proposed a general theory that tied key components of the evaluation process to the sources of value in the community, using a framework that outlined 14 key steps. Not all evaluation efforts contain all 14 steps, but Platt argued that many evaluations are incomplete or fail to reach a resolved state when key steps are omitted.

Much later, the issue of theory reemerged in the evaluation literature, not so much as theory about evaluation, but as use of theory related to the thing being evaluated, so as to bring order and criteria to the evaluation—the so-called theory-driven versus black-box debates.

### The Proliferation of Movements

As the evaluation field grew larger and as more evaluators filled its ranks, evaluation practice reflected a wide panorama of professional and academic interests. Special interest groups formed so that each special interest in education was also reflected in evaluation. Topical movements with names like Naturalism, Formalism, Individualism, Constructivism, Feminism, and many others became active in writing. A lively array of debates between adherents of differing points of view filled the pages of academic journals. In some circles, evaluation took on the mantle of an art form. Terms like *evaluation portraits* and *word pictures* were used in conjunction with lengthy descriptive narratives. The best of these took on the look and feel of a work of literature in which the insight and merit are as much a function of the writing as the original subject. The work took on value in the same manner that a work of art can show insight into great themes and the human condition. In contrast to this direction in evaluation, many evaluators wanted to address more down-to-earth concerns. Program evaluators (especially where funding was provided by the federal or state government) wanted to answer the mandates of contracts and guidelines. For a brief time, evaluators were common within the ranks of the federal government. That period of promise soon gave way to mounting pressure to reduce the size of government. But a few lasting effects made their way into federal law. The Government Performance and Results Act (GPRA) (1993), followed by the budget law, attempted to shift the focus of evaluation from Inputs and Processes to results and consequences.

### Classification Systems

The range of issues and approaches to evaluation was now broad enough to stimulate attempts to classify evaluation and to provide some means of talking about studies to point out what they did and did not accomplish. A very popular schema was devised by Kirkpatrick (1994). Kaufman and others have expanded on Kirkpatrick's attractive model and extended it to have a Level V: *Societal impact and consequences,* which is a fundamental dimension of this book (for example, Watkins, Leigh, Foshay, & Kaufman, 1998).

## THE PREMISE OF OUR APPROACH

Our premise is that we believe it is possible to meld the best features from the field that have stood the test of time with a societal value-added (or outside-in) derivation of needs (gaps in results) as drivers based on an Ideal Vision for society. We start with societal needs and requirements and roll down inside the educational organization and operation to define what should be done, accomplished, and delivered. (Earlier, we noted that *Mega* was the term for societal value added and provided a definition, which is the Ideal Vision.) We believe that it is the core job of evaluation to provide results-based data for decision making based on the value or merit of the educational enterprise. Our first focus is on *results.*

Not just any results will do. We believe that the educational enterprise must have legitimacy in a wide societal context. We must not only report on how well our goals are accomplished within the educational agency but also determine that we are pursuing the right goals. The topics and tools presented in the alignment and direction part of the action plan equip the evaluator with the means and perspective to determine that the school system is meeting legitimate needs of society. We stress the importance of asking the right questions, and those questions include, "Do we add value to our communities and shared society?"

From the questions, we derive criteria that tell us where to look for answers. Our second phase is observation. This is where we gather data that will help use answer evaluation questions. The question set determines the methods (and not the other way around). We allow for a wide range of methodology models (models that rely on the central figure of the evaluator as observer, on a system view of information flow, on scientific method, on case studies, and on attainment of prespecified ends). The results phase of our action plan has a primary emphasis on educational Outputs and Outcomes and a secondary focus on the Process and environmental factors that produce them. Our action phase connects evaluation results data with the administration of programs and decisions. We believe that continuous improvement is both possible and mandatory. This integrated approach to evaluation is a step in the right direction to solving some of the pressing problems of education. Figure 1.3 illustrates the way we see things.

**Figure 1.3**   Matching Process Efficiency to Goal Validity: Getting the Right
Things Done

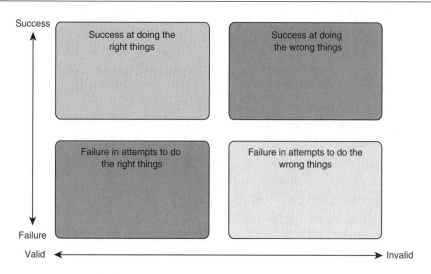

You can imagine four possible value and worth propositions for any educational program. You must ask yourself: *Will my evaluation efforts be able to detect each of these possibilities?* We suggest that any evaluation that misses one or more of these is incomplete.

As you consider the state of education today, in which many schools fail to prepare their students to enter society and in which there is a growing threat of physical violence, we hope that you agree that seeking an Ideal Vision is not only appropriate but also our moral and ethical duty. How we carry out this responsibility is the subject of this book. In dealing with fear of evaluation, we confront a major obstacle to improved educational evaluation.

If you agree, let's move on to the "Whats" and "Hows" of evaluating educational programs to improve our success with learners and in our shared world.

We intend that this book will help you in this adventure to design and carry out evaluations that can guide the educational enterprise to find what works and what doesn't.

## EVALUATION LOGIC

When evaluators set out to evaluate educational programs, the usual focus of the evaluation study is the nature of the program and the results of the program in terms of student learning. Does a reading program teach students to read? The desirability of learning to read is often taken for granted.

When a program seems to work, evaluators report the program as being effective, and perhaps even efficient, depending on resources consumed. This common approach to educational evaluation evaluated the means to an end and reported on the effectiveness in reaching the desired result. That is compatible with our approach, but we intend to take it one step further. We also caution that some evaluation studies focus on means apart from ends, and that is not what we recommend. We want to align everything we use, do, produce, and deliver in our schools and educational systems with value added to our shared society. To do less is questionable in terms of practical thinking and ethics.

Our approach has a wider scope because we also want the focus of evaluation to check to see whether the ends satisfy, or meet, valid needs. In the context of education, instructional programs are solutions that are carried out with a mix of stakeholders, resource providers, institutions, and individual teachers. That is why we include a discussion of needs assessment and Organizational Elements Model in a book on evaluation. We have integrated the evaluation of programs and societal needs in our four-phase approach. Evaluation of a program in that setting should flow from four primary sets of questions (a set for each phase of our action plan).

The next step is to determine what information is required to answer each evaluation question and how the information can be obtained, which leads to what to observe.

Observation requirements determine method, and not the other way around. Observations are recorded as data. Some observations can be made more precise by measurement. Some measurements can be further refined using statistics. Descriptive statistics reduces data to a clear picture. Inferential statistics reveals relationships that might not be apparent on the surface of the measurement data. We emphasize that this migration from question to data to statistic is driven from the top down. We caution that picking a statistic and limiting your evaluation inquiry to a single data set that fits the assumptions of the statistical routine can lead to some very striking errors and omissions in your study.

So, when doing educational evaluation, let us both *do it right* as well as *do what is right*. Our learners and stakeholders depend on it.

Let's start *Practical Evaluation for Educators*.

## NOTES

1.   These were earlier called "behavioral objectives," but practice refocused these on performance (Mager, 1997).

2. We will note later that there are three aligned levels of results, something that is almost always missed in conventional planning and evaluation. These three levels are societal, organizational, and individual contributions and accomplishments.

3. Scriven also provided evaluators with the term *goal-free evaluation,* where people ask—without reference to existing goals and objectives—"What really happened here?" in order to reveal unexpected results and consequences. This is a very powerful approach, since it frees the evaluators from being limited to preexisting purposes and intents.

# Part I

# Alignment and Direction

**Figure I**    A Phased Action Plan for Evaluation

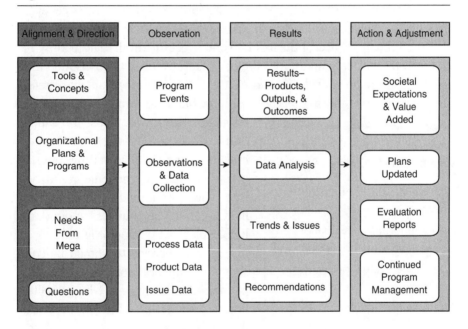

The fundamental purpose of evaluation is the determination of worth or merit of what an educational agency uses, does, and delivers. On this point, practitioners generally agree. However, the methods, the context, and the scope of evaluation activity surrounding this one point of agreement are wide-ranging indeed. We attempt to provide a perspective that will enable educators to conduct meaningful and useful evaluation to improve the educational enterprise—measurably improve it. To this end, this section is devoted to fundamental concepts of evaluation in an

---

**Prime Questions for Alignment and Direction Section**

What is the boundary of the evaluation study?

What valid needs support the enterprise of education in this system?

What are the goals and objectives to be realized?

Are the goals and objectives aligned with valid needs?

---

educational context that is derived from and serves the needs of society. We think it is possible to build an Ideal Vision for the school system in harmony with society. The "Alignment and Direction" chapters provide tools to establish the legitimacy of programs by linking them to valid societal needs.

When all is said and done and the totality of evaluation practice is considered, there are three large camps that characterize the field of evaluation. The first of these sees evaluation as the means to assess the results of programs designed to reach certain ends. The second sees evaluation as a means of discovery to find out what is good and bad in some social, organizational, or institutional setting. The third sees evaluation as a mechanism for advancing a social, religious, or idealistic agenda.

In this book, we accept the first two and reject the third. In accepting the first two, we consider important economic criteria, adding a proscription that the first conception of evaluation forms the core that is most valuable, useful, and practical for school settings because it is what steers future decisions relating to curriculum, methods, and allocation of resources. The second conception is also valuable in school settings but has great potential to consume resources. But when used in concert with the first, it can advance understanding and help explain why something took place in context. Therefore it should be considered a support tool to provide supplemental information when specific criteria are reached in the conduct of the first. We have developed "rules of the road" to help you sort out planning and conducting evaluation. These rules are pointed out in each of the narrative "scenario" evaluation examples at the end of each section. We realize that evaluation practitioners do not like to be sorted into camps, but you will be able to decide for yourself where the evaluators you encounter should (or could) be placed. You can tell them apart by the questions they ask (or do not ask). Therefore it is appropriate that we begin our chapter on fundamental concepts with *asking and answering the right questions.*

---

**Secondary Questions for Alignment and Direction Section**

Who are the stakeholders in this system?

Who will form the evaluation team and receive the report?

What is the evaluation team composition?

What is the schedule?

What resources are at the disposal of the evaluation team?

What is the specific list of issue questions to guide observation?

---

# Fundamental Principles and Tools of Evaluation

## 2

Evaluation seeks the answer to the wide-ranging question: *What worked, and what didn't?* Evaluation also asks, at the same time: *What value is this, and what does it contribute?* Successful evaluation hinges on how you frame the questions in the context of results-oriented programs that serve a societal as well as an educational purpose.

The results and consequences of evaluation are not arbitrary. It is important not only to see whether you get the results you hope for but also to ensure that what you hope for is reflected in the means selected and that the ultimate value was added by an educational program, project, or activity to learners, the educational system, and our shared society. All of these are important, just not one or two.

Hold on tight to your customary ideas about evaluation and even education. We are counting on your openness to new concepts. As part of our approach about evaluation, we might, at first, be "swimming upstream" in talking about a practical and sensible approach in a field that is often burdened with too much jargon and hidden agendas.

We are going to cover a lot of things in this chapter that set the stage for understanding what evaluation is and should be, in order for you to find out what worked, what didn't work, what to change, and what to keep. Some of the terms and concepts might seem new. It is not because we want to sound smart and knowledgeable, but because there are some important concepts and tools involved in sensible and sensitive evaluation. To do without these would be like going to sea without a compass.

> Professional evaluation should be clear, understandable, comprehensive, useful, and guided by a few basic principles.

Our approach is action—and results—oriented and presented as four distinct phases for conducting evaluation. In this first phase, we find the appropriate direction for our evaluation. It follows from the following premise.

Educational evaluation is the determination of what works and what doesn't. It also seeks to determine whether the results obtained, their merit, is based on the valid needs of society that can be accomplished through educating its members so as to contribute to our common well-being, our individual and collective survival, self-sufficiency, and quality of life.

Societal and educational needs—gaps in results—are met through organizational efforts focused on value-added Outcomes.[1] The primary focus of educational evaluation is to determine that the goals and objectives of programs are valid, as well as effective and efficient, in producing desired results.

In planning legitimate educational programs, one should start by first identifying societal *needs* (not wants) and moving into the educational operation to derive educational objectives, then further, to objectives of educational programs and to learner performance objectives. Thus evaluators should look at the alignment between educational programs, organizational objectives, and societal needs.[2] All must be clearly aligned—and linked.

This presents a two-part challenge for evaluators. To make sure that programs are the "right" programs, they must take a top-down approach, using needs assessment to make sure that the programs are in fact solutions to real problems facing the school and society. This form of evaluation establishes the legitimacy of a program. On the other hand, evaluators are also faced with the challenge of finding out whether solutions are effective. The curriculum is not only the right curriculum at the right time, but students learn from the methods and materials that are introduced by the program. This form of evaluation looks at results and checks the string of events that led to the results. If the results are good, the program is judged to be effective. If the results are not, then the evaluator looks for things to change or modify. These two parts of the evaluation picture make up the central message of this book.

These ideas are essential threads that must be woven into the fabric of every educational evaluation (see Figure 2.1).

In the chapters that follow, we will provide you with tools that will help you establish needs—measurable gaps in results—or check to see that others have done a valid and useful assessment of needs.

This might seem, at first, odd or different from what is usually said and done in evaluation: That is, to simply take goals and objectives at face value and move from there, rather than making sure the educational system is heading in a useful direction. We define words and concepts very rigorously, for evaluation should be used to measurably improve what we

**Figure 2.1**    The Two-Part Challenge of Evaluation

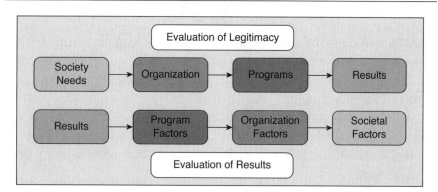

in education use, do, produce, and deliver. Fuzzy thinking and rushing prematurely into methods will not serve anyone well. Thus we ask for your thoughtfulness and patience as we create a new evaluation landscape. The journey will be worth your time and attention.

We will introduce you to the Organizational Elements Model (OEM) to provide you with a framework for examining the functional effectiveness and integration of organizations and their members who are charged with meeting the educational requirements (based on the identified needs of society). The model identifies and defines everything that any educational organization uses, does, produces, and delivers and the value these all add to learner success in school and in life.

We will talk about *goals* and their related *objectives, feasibility,* and *costs-consequences analysis.* These tools are critical for establishing the legitimacy of the educational enterprise and thus are the concern of an educational evaluation.

We will say many times in the coming chapters that it is not enough to evaluate the efficiency of the *means* we use (e.g., resources, policies, procedures, materials, techniques, and approaches). We must also evaluate in terms of the *ends* we want to—and must—reach, and ensure that they are worthwhile and contribute to our shared society.

The tools discussed here help us make sure we are headed in the right direction with an evaluation framework that ensures such an alignment. This approach "unloads" much of the possible influence of politics, "isms," and biases that often drive people. By using this approach, we tend to shift the conversation from *means* to *ends,* consequences, and useful payoffs for all stakeholders.

We do all of this by following a set of principles. Let's look at these as we start out, so we can define and determine what worked and what didn't in our educational journey.

## PRINCIPLE 1: EVALUATION—GOOD EVALUATION—IS BASED ON ASKING THE RIGHT QUESTIONS

In the Introduction (Chapter 1), we gave you advanced notice that evaluation was based on asking and answering the "right" questions. The right evaluation questions to be asked and answered depend on the view and scope of your investigation.

We make a fundamental assertion in this book that the scope of all evaluations must be wide enough to question the legitimacy of the educational enterprise as well as the effectiveness of its programs and learning opportunities.

Part of the evaluation criteria that you will use to "referee" the system should follow from an examination of how well stakeholders (and the educational system) have addressed the needs of society. Let us start by examining some typical sets of questions that relate to this point of view.

### Question Strings

*Societal String*

What is the role of the school in our community? What are the results we seek? Are the results of benefit to society? What should be taught at the school? How should it be taught? What are the conditions under which it will be taught? What resources will be invested in the school?

*A Process String*

How will this curriculum be implemented? What is the schedule for classes? What textbooks will be used? What are the limits of our power to discipline? What tests will be used? How will results be measured? What is the grading structure? What is my class load? What is the dress code?

*A Decision String*

Which curriculum materials will we buy or develop? What is the least-cost method that meets our objectives and criteria? How can we reduce class size? How long should the school be in session each year? What should teachers earn in their first year? What new programs should be implemented? What should each process add to our ability to meet needs?

*A System String*

What is the ultimate purpose of our educational system? What are the boundaries of this school system? Are all subsystems working for the greater system? What is the flow of Inputs, Processes, and results? What is the communication flow? What is the resource flow? Are there points of failure in the system? What is the critical path to reach each objective? Do all objectives add up to a coherent system goal and objective?

Different points of view produce different sets of questions. Each school board member, administrator, and teacher has a point of view. As an evaluator, you also have a point of view and a set of questions to ask that are related to how you conduct your evaluation study. You must also be aware of the unconscious or conscious questions that are asked by all stakeholders. What they ask or do not ask will be expressed in the performance that you are going to evaluate. One of your tasks as an evaluator is to ensure that all stakeholders—all of the educational partners—are seeking to answer the same set of questions about what worked and what didn't. If education is to improve, it must find out what is bringing about value and what might be improved.

While we are talking about some fundamental basics about educational evaluation, it is vital that evaluation is used only for fixing and improving and never for blaming. Never.

There are some subtle differences in these four examples of question sets as compared to most conventional approaches:

1. The first set implies a duty to society, a requirement to add value to our learners and to our shared society.

2. The second set is concerned with getting on with the job without considering alternatives.

3. The third set does imply consideration of alternatives, with cost as a possible factor in reaching decisions.

4. The last set asks how things fit together to make a functional system.

Related sets of questions hang in the background for every situation that you will encounter when doing educational evaluation. It is your job to tease out the strand of the question structure that is represented by the existing situation and stakeholder expectations and stakeholder requirements. If after you have completed your investigation you can identify a gap between intended results and existing results, these gaps will be the basis for the recommendations you make.

## Developing Questions to Guide an Evaluation

As an evaluator, you will have a prime set of questions, upon which this book is organized.

You must include questions that:

- Identify the legitimacy of the enterprise. How well are needs being met, or did they take the time to determine valid needs?
- Measure how effective and efficient the solutions are (methods, means, activities, programs, projects, activities). Are we getting the results we intended these solutions to deliver?
- Determine how the evaluation study should be implemented. What are the methods, resources, and schedule?
- How do I analyze the results data and report findings and recommendations that are credible and useful?

From these prime questions, a more specific set is directed at a specific evaluation target. For example:

- Does the school board show evidence of effective planning to meet the needs of society?
- At the organizational level, is the school system effective?
- Does it get useful results efficiently?
- What objectives in our educational mission did we achieve?
- What objectives in our educational mission did we miss or ignore?
- How do learners perform? Do their achievements carry into the job market? Do their achievements carry into their becoming good neighbors and good family members?
- Did our educational system and efforts add value to our communities and shared society?
- What did learners learn and master related to each educational program?
- Was what the learners mastered worth mastering?
- Are methods, techniques, and tools effective? Efficient? Appropriate?
- What should we keep, change, or stop?
- What value did we add for all internal and external stakeholders?
- What results do we have to justify our continued programs, projects, and activities?
- What are the recommendations for this school system? What should we do next?

The locus of decision making and the driving force in education is found at the organizational level. In our society, we have devised a system of education entrusted to carry out an important mission for society.

It is important that evaluators understand the role and functional behavior of organizations. As we will see shortly, another tool for asking and answering the right questions is the Organizational Elements Model (OEM). This framework identifies what each organization can use, do, produce, and deliver as well as the consequences for external clients and society. The alignment among the *organizational elements* is essential for educational success and thus is a prime area of focus for evaluation.

The inclusion of *external society* in evaluation has been called "Mega planning" because it adds a vital element to conventional evaluation (Kaufman & Unger, 2003).[3] By asking and answering these vital educational evaluation questions, we can prove our worth . . . to ourselves, our funders, and our stakeholders.

## PRINCIPLE 2: EVALUATION OF PROCESS (MEANS) IS A FUNCTION OF OBTAINED RESULTS (ENDS)

Evaluation compares results (and consequences) with intentions. Useful evaluations focus on *ends* and not just on *means*. Evaluation results provide data and information for making useful decisions relative to the merit and worth of what the educational system has used, done, produced, and delivered: *valuation.*

There are abundant guides to teacher evaluation and school system evaluation, often with self-contained criteria like class size, credentials, preferred methodologies, and similar variables. These have a place, but they are not in and of themselves sufficient unless it can be shown that these criteria lead to desired educational results. Linking what we use, do, produce, and deliver to our shared society is imperative, and this holistic framework is missing from most conventional evaluation and planning.

Evaluation can (and should) compare results with intentions for individuals (such as learners, teachers, and administrators) and the educational organization itself (such as a school, school system, or university); evaluations best have a primary focus on *ends, not just means* and resources.

### Identifying and Linking Ends and Means

If there is an area that really gets consistently blurred in education and indeed in life, it is from confusing *what* and *how*, and confusing *ends* and *means*. *Ends* and *means* are related but different. Just as you and your cousin are related, you are also different.

*Ends:* results, accomplishments, consequences

*Means:* the ways, methods, and resources that might be used to accomplish *ends*

**Figure 2.2**     A Basic Job Aid for Ensuring Objectives Focus on Ends
and Not Means

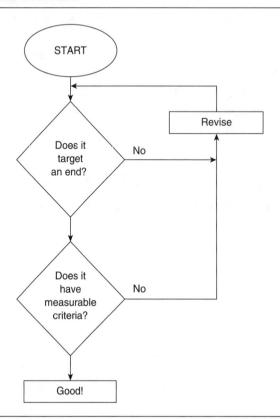

The most sensible way to select any *means* is on the basis of the *ends* to be accomplished. As basic as that sounds, most educators mix *means* into their objectives and thus blur this distinction. Objectives (performance, learning, or any type of objective) should NEVER have the *means* and/or resources stated in them, since by doing so, you would be selecting the solutions before having clearly identified the problem. This can be dangerous, to say the least. Educators (and evaluators of educators and their work) must learn to differentiate between *ends* and *means*, and to link them. Figure 2.2 is a basic job aid for preparing measurable objectives.

*Note:* Just for the record, almost all words in the English language that end in "ing" refer to process, or means.

To show the differences between *ends* and *means*, see Table 2.1a. There are some examples, and for each item on the list, put a mark in the appropriate column depending on whether it is primarily an *end* (results, consequence, or payoff) or a *means* (resources, methods, how-to-do-its, interventions, Processes, approaches, methods). Then, in Table 2.1b, check your answers with ours.

**Table 2.1a**   Means-Ends Quick Check

|  | End | Means |
|---|---|---|
| Learning problem solving |  |  |
| Looking for a job |  |  |
| Having positive self-esteem |  |  |
| Joining a class action lawsuit |  |  |
| Downsizing class size |  |  |
| Moving to school in Seattle |  |  |
| College graduate |  |  |
| Survival |  |  |
| Banning short skirts in school |  |  |
| Reengineering curriculum |  |  |
| Assessing needs |  |  |
| Training teachers |  |  |
| Continuous improvement |  |  |
| Team building |  |  |
| Loving |  |  |

**Table 2.1b**   Means-Ends Quick Check Answers

|  | *End* | *Means* |
|---|---|---|
| Learning problem solving |  | X |
| Looking for a job |  | X |
| Positive self-esteem | X |  |
| Joining a class action lawsuit |  | X |
| Downsizing class size |  | X |
| Moving to Seattle |  | X |
| College graduate | X |  |
| Survival | X |  |
| Banning tree cutting |  | X |
| Reengineering |  | X |
| Assessing needs |  | X |
| Training |  | X |
| Continuous improvement |  | X |
| Team building |  | X |
| Loving |  | X |

## PRINCIPLE 3: GOALS AND OBJECTIVES OF EDUCATION SYSTEMS SHOULD BE BASED ON VALID NEEDS

Where do valid and useful objectives come from? From a proper *needs* (not "wants") *assessment.* Again, we are going to deviate from the conventional wisdom about *needs* and *needs assessments;* our definition of *need* is based on gaps in results.

Not to be difficult, but to provide you with the best information and tools possible, here are some of the basics:

- *Needs* are gaps in results (between "what should be" and "what is"), not gaps in resources, or methods.
- *Needs* are collected at three levels of results and consequences (societal, organizational, and individual).[4]
- *Needs* are prioritized by determining the costs to meet the needs—closing the gaps in results compared with the costs of ignoring them.

By using *need* as a gap in results and collecting real and objective data, we can demonstrate the costs of meeting the *needs* (usually, when we report this alone, we get cut) as compared with the costs of ignoring the *needs* (the basis for shifting the responsibility to the decision makers if they decide not to meet the needs).

While we are on the topic of objectives, please note that we use the terms *objectives* and *performance indicators* in the same way. An objective states where we are headed and how to tell when we have arrived. The same is true of a performance indicator: Both supply the criteria for measuring accomplishment (though a particular objective could have more than one performance indicator).

> *Note:* The *What Should Be* items are the objectives. The *What Should Be* indicators provide the basis for reasonable and objective evaluation: One has only to plot the differences between the achieved results and the *What Should Be* to determine the extent to which the gaps have been closed.

Rich and robust sources for objectives come from a well-designed *needs assessment.* Remember, a *needs assessment* identifies the gaps between current and required results and prioritizes these gaps—*needs*—on the basis of the costs of meeting the needs as compared

> Needs ≠ Wants ≠ Demands

with the costs of ignoring them. This unique definition is very powerful. Consider these basic points about *needs assessments.*

NEEDS are gaps between current results and desired results at three levels (Mega, Macro, and Micro).

NEEDS ASSESSMENT is the identification and prioritization of NEEDS for selection, elimination, or reduction.

What are the implications for using *need* only as a noun (not as a verb or in a verb sense)? The answer is that you open the way to look at the widest possible range of ways to meet the *need;* you look at gaps in results and consequences, not at gaps in methods and resources.

When you use the word *need* as a verb, you are creating a self-contained specification of means to be used, and that limits other possibilities. For example, if you state, "Our school system 'needs' more teachers," that is a less-than-complete statement of the true *need*—gaps in results—behind that solution. The true *need* will be met by linking to useful means and resources, such as effective teaching and learning, to obtain desired results (results that will help students enter and be successful in society). The verb usage of *need* cuts off all consideration of other possible ways to obtain the desired results, and it assumes that the methods, solutions, or programs we rush into will meet the "need" and will close the gaps in results.

Other methods for teaching using student teams, teacher aids, computers, volunteers, change in study methods, parent help, and the like, are all no longer in play—no longer in play until we justify their use to meet the *needs,* to close the gaps in results.

Using *need* as a noun opens the way for documented investigation into solutions and cost-benefit analysis (which considers the effectiveness and efficiency of each means-related option) before a choice is made.

Why would we want to choose a solution unless it is on the basis of meeting needs and closing gaps in results? One "trick of the trade" to ensure that we choose the best means and resources is to first identify *needs* as gaps in results and then select how we will close those gaps.

*Note:* If you use this "need-as-a-noun" framework, you have your evaluation plan built in (as well as the justification for never having a proposal turned down).

So, what are *needs?* Here is, again, the basic definition. Because this is such a critical concept, note once again that *needs* are gaps in results, not gaps in resources or Processes. This is really important, and much more than semantics. (See Figure 2.3.)

## PRINCIPLE 4: THE VALID NEEDS OF SOCIETY ARE DERIVED USING A TOP-DOWN APPROACH—ROLLING DOWN FROM SOCIETAL AND COMMUNITY VALUE ADDED TO THE RESULTS AND METHODS USED WITHIN THE EDUCATIONAL ENTERPRISE

We live in a complex society that is multicultural, diverse in many ways, and full of competing interests. How do we sort this out, and what is the

**Figure 2.3**   Means-Ends Gap as Needs Between Current Results
and Desired Results

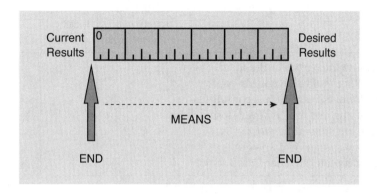

impact on the school systems? The answer is to identify the common good in terms of results and to carefully deal with competing issues, using some disciplined process to arrive at justifiable goals and objectives that relate to a better society and productive contributing citizens.

In the Introduction, we introduced the concept of the Ideal Vision. This is not meant to be an oversimplification of the complex interests in society; it is, rather, a recognition that at the basic level, we have many common desires and interests that should be driving us at the societal level, at the organizational level, and at the individual level. We provide a framework to analyze this set of relationships in the OEM, which recognizes the Inputs from the whole of society to be used as drivers for the organization: to determine where we are headed and why we want to get there.

We use the term *Mega* to represent this approach and societal value-added focus. The organizational level, *Macro,* is the educational system. The school organization is the proper focus for meeting educational needs. It is vital that the educational needs and objectives will achieve societal value added: *Mega-level* results and consequences.

The OEM provides a framework for aligning educational *means* and *ends,* results accomplished, and evaluation. If we are going to evaluate— compare our results with our intentions—then it is vital to make sure that what we are evaluating and measuring are the right things to work with. We can do this if we think and act in order to deliver societal value added. No sense in trying to achieve something that is not useful in the first place, or even wrong. (Remember the ancient school habit of not letting any children write with their left hands?)

Table 2.2 shows the steps in completing a *Mega-level needs assessment.*

**Table 2.2**     Mega-Level Needs Assessment Steps

|  | Person or Group Responsible | Date Assigned | Date Completed |
| --- | --- | --- | --- |
| Determine the part(s) of the Ideal Vision—societal value added—your educational organization is committed to delivering and moving ever closer toward, including indicators of its impact on the survival and quality of life of its external clients and society. |  |  |  |
| Determine your organization's current status with regard to its impact on external clients' and society's survival and quality of life. |  |  |  |
| Place Mega-level gaps in results (i.e., needs) between your Ideal Vision and the current status, in a priority order, based on the cost to ignore vs. the cost to successfully address the problem. |  |  |  |
| Write an Ideal-Vision-linked Mission Objective that includes a specific subobjective for each gap you decide to address (e.g., what you will have accomplished 5 or more years from now). |  |  |  |
| Break down your Mission Objective to functional building-block objectives . . . into functions. |  |  |  |
| Present your Macro-level needs to your clients for concurrence. |  |  |  |
| List alternative methods and means for addressing your Mega-level need(s) and identify the advantages and disadvantages of each. |  |  |  |

## PRINCIPLE 5: THE EDUCATIONAL ORGANIZATION IS RESPONSIBLE FOR RIGOROUS PLANNING TO CONVERT IDENTIFIED NEEDS INTO PROGRAMS THAT ACHIEVE USEFUL RESULTS

Society builds organizations to meet *needs.* The school organization may be able to cope with the challenge of teaching and learning in today's educational climate, or they may not be coping. The OEM presents a framework for understanding organizational relationships and how these are aligned to meet the *needs* of our shared communities and society, our children, our college students, and education in the professions.

A useful framework exists that identifies what every organization can use, do, produce, and deliver and link those to external results and consequences: the OEM. It provides a basic template or guide so that we identify and link all of the important

> The Organizational Elements Model (OEM)
>
> Linking Objectives to Organizational Success and Societal Value Added

aspects of education. After all, if we are going to evaluate, we must make certain that we are evaluating the correct things. On to this framework!

## Understanding the Organizational Elements Model (OEM)

The OEM (Kaufman, 1992b, 1998, 2000; Kaufman, Oakley-Browne, Watkins, & Leigh, 2003; Kaufman, Watkins, & Leigh, 2001) provides a practical yet dynamic framework for aligning everything an organization uses, does, produces, and delivers related to adding measurable value to our communities and shared society. It is a framework that provides a clear understanding of useful data that may be collected and used to measurably improve education.

The OEM also provides the basis for useful and practical evaluation, using the tool of needs assessment and the overarching concept of strategic planning to set the stage for planning, management, and evaluation. That sounds like a tall order, but the OEM can be basic and practical. And it has been used in literally hundreds of successful organizations. (See Table 2.3.)

The OEM defines and links what any organization uses, does, produces, and delivers with external client and societal value added. For each "element," there is an associated level of planning. Successful planning links and relates all of the "organizational elements," for each organization has external clients for which they must add value—measurable value.

## Evaluation Planning Using the OEM Approach

Planning to meet *needs* should flow from "Mega" down to organizational objectives and individual performance objectives. The consideration of what to do and how to do it and at what cost takes place inside the organization as we use performance data to decide what to use, do, produce, and deliver. The OEM can help us find the correct directions for what we do and deliver and the payoffs for our stakeholders.

**Table 2.3** Organizational Elements Model (OEM) Examples by Element and Level

| Name of the Organizational Element | Name of the Level of Planning and Primary Focus | Brief Description | Educational Examples |
|---|---|---|---|
| Outcomes | Mega (Societal) | Results and their consequences for external clients and society | Neighborhood, city, state, nation, our shared world |
| Outputs | Macro (Organizational) | The results an organization can or does deliver outside of itself | Graduates, completers, people granted certificates |
| Products | Micro (Individuals and Small Groups) | The building-block results that are produced within the organization | Course passed, competency certified |
| Processes | Process (Means, Activities, Programs) | The ways, means, activities, procedures, and methods used internally | Teaching, learning, evaluating, developing, curriculum, course |
| Inputs | Input (Resources, Organizational Ingredients) | The human, physical, and financial resources an organization can or does use | Teachers, validated course content, money, time, buildings, equipment |

**Figure 2.4**    Interactions of Means, Ends, and Resources:
A Continuing Process

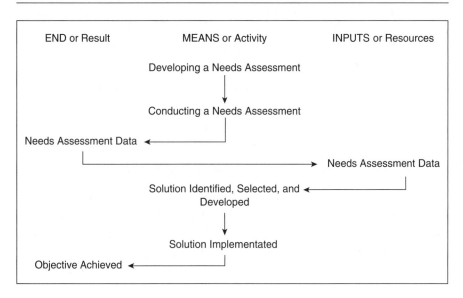

Planning that starts at the Mega-level (results that add value to society) is called "Mega (strategic) planning." It follows that evaluation that links to the Mega-level might be called "Mega evaluation," in that it relates everything that is used (Inputs) with the *means* and Processes/activities/projects/curriculum/teaching/learning of education to all three levels of results and consequences. While we are at it, please don't interpret or use the OEM in a linear or lockstep manner. The *organizational elements* are, in application, dynamic, and the accomplishment of one can be the Input to another.

Often, *means* and *ends* have dynamic relationships within an organization, as seen in Figure 2.4.

## Mega Planning Is Proactive

Many approaches to organizational improvement wait for problems to happen and then scramble to respond. Of course, as in true love, the course of organizational success hardly ever runs smoothly.

In fact, conventional wisdom has it that education and educators never change . . . or they get accused of changing without substantial reason to do so. Planning and then evaluating using the OEM provides the basis for proving that what we do and deliver adds value to all stakeholders: learners, teachers, administrators, parents, community members, and politicians.

But there is a temptation to react to problems and never take the time to plan. When we don't plan in advance, surprises spring up. By planning, fewer crises arise and success is defined in advance—before problems spring up—and then systematically achieved. When we start planning at the Mega- (or societal) level, we best ensure that there is *linkage* among what we educators use, do, produce, and deliver, and consider the impact of all of this for tomorrow's children and our shared world.

### Getting Commitment to Align Everything an Educational Organization Uses, Does, Produces, and Delivers to External Societal Value Added (Mega)

Sometimes, otherwise conscientious educational partners do not quickly grasp the importance of including and aligning all of the organizational elements. Table 2.4 shows a participative exercise on finding and agreeing on direction. Make sure that everyone—all educational partners—are included and sign (or initial) their answers to each question.

If anyone objects to any question for any reason ("Don't know what it means," "Not our job," or the like), simply ask them to select the "no" option. Usually, by the time they get to the middle of these questions, they realize that what is being suggested—aligning everything with Mega —is both essential and practical.

### PRINCIPLE 6: OUR AIM IN EDUCATION SHOULD BE THE BEST THAT SOCIETY CAN ATTAIN: TO ADD MEASURABLE VALUE FOR ALL STAKEHOLDERS, WITH EVALUATION STANDARDS LINKED TO AN IDEAL VISION

We want to make our point very clear, for real and useful evaluation hinges on linking what we use, do, produce, and deliver to adding value to society. If you opt to use a Mega approach, your success will be best ensured. Starting at Mega gives everyone a common "North Star" toward which we all can steer as well as make our appropriate unique contributions: alignment. Why should you care about Mega, alignment, measurability, and objectives? Simple. Our lives and our children's future depend on us doing so. Really.

*Think and Act Mega:* Our Children and Their Children Depend on it. Parents Worldwide do it Almost Instinctively

Figure 2.5 is the Ideal Vision that was derived from asking people all over our globe to define, in measurable terms, the kind of world they want

**Table 2.4**    Commitment Questions

| Questions All Educational Organizations Must Ask and Answer | Do You Commit: | |
|---|---|---|
| | Yes | No |
| Do you commit to deliver educational contributions that add value for your external clients AND society? (MEGA/Outcomes) | | |
| Do you commit to deliver educational contributions that have the quality required by your external partners? (MACRO/Outputs) | | |
| Do you commit to produce internal results that have the quality required by your internal partners? (MICRO/Products) | | |
| Do you commit to have efficient internal products, programs, projects, and activities? (PROCESSES) | | |
| Do you commit to create and ensure the quality and appropriateness of the human, capital, and physical resources available? (INPUTS) | | |
| Do you commit to deliver:<br><br>a. Products, activities, methods, and procedures that have positive value and worth? | | |
| b. The results and accomplishments defined by our objectives? | | |
| (EVALUATION/CONTINUOUS IMPROVEMENT) | | |

their children and grandchildren to live. Note that these people did not talk about *means* (credentials of teachers, class size, budgets, or benefits), but about *ends* and consequences:

*So, what if I don't want to select a Mega focus? Am I "doomed"?* Well, not exactly doomed, but why would you want not to do something you expect of

**Figure 2.5**   An Ideal Vision

### BASIC IDEAL VISION: The world we want to help create for tomorrow's child

There will be no losses of life nor elimination or reduction of levels of well-being, survival, self-sufficiency, or quality of life, from any source including (but not limited to):

> ➢ war and/or riot
> ➢ unintended human-caused changes to the environment including permanent destruction of the environment and/or rendering it non-renewable
> ➢ murder, rape, or crimes of violence, robbery, or destruction to property
> ➢ substance abuse
> ➢ disease
> ➢ starvation and/or malnutrition
> ➢ destructive behavior (including child, partner, spouse, self, elder, others)
> ➢ accidents, including transportation, home, and business/workplace
> ➢ discrimination based on irrelevant variables including color, race, age, creed, gender, religion, wealth, national origin, or location

Poverty will not exist, and every woman and man will earn at least as much as it costs them to live unless they are progressing toward being self-sufficient and self-reliant. No adult will be under the care, custody, or control of another person, agency, or substance: all adult citizens will be self-sufficient and self-reliant as minimally indicated by their consumption being equal to or less than their production.

---

everyone else? Don't you depend on your supermarket, car repair, auto manufacturer, airline, and other drivers to "act Mega"? Why, then, would you choose not to do something you expect of all others? Please think about it. Acting Mega is the most practical and safest thing you can do. And, in addition, it is ethical and professional.

> *Note:* Mega is related to an Ideal Vision. An Ideal Vision—the Mega-level of planning and results—is based on asking people from around the globe: "What kind of world (in measurable results terms) do you want to help create for tomorrow's child?"

The interesting aspect about this Ideal Vision (Mega-level) is that it is the same for all organizations, public and private. The unique contributions of any educational organization come from selecting what elements of the Ideal Vision they commit to deliver and move ever closer toward. That selection is the organization's Mission Objective.

An agreement table for involving all stakeholders in adopting a focus on Mega is at the end of this chapter.

So. *What does all of this have to do with educational evaluation?*

Plenty. Evaluation, if we are to collect and use valid data, we should target all three levels of organizational results (and levels of educational planning): Outcomes (Mega), Outputs (Macro), and Products (Micro).

Let's look at some examples.

*Outcomes/Mega-Level Results.* Possible objective: Every learner successfully completing our educational system will be self-sufficient and self-reliant members of their communities as indicated by (1) zero arrests and convictions, (2) not being on government transfer payments, and (3) not under the care, custody, or control of another person, agency, or substance.

*Discussion.* This is a minimal objective at the Mega-level of planning. The indicators for the Outcomes of our educational system provide hard-data criteria for measuring our success or shortfalls. It does not include indicators of good citizenship, quality of life, and adhering to our social contract.

*Outputs/Macro-Level.* Possible objectives: All learners in our education system will graduate or complete within 1 year of the average for all learners in our system and be declared competent in all required academic and social areas by valid and reliable indicators certified by the school board. In addition, they will secure and keep a job of their first, second, or third occupational choice or go to an accredited institution of higher learning without any deficiencies noted for their acceptance.

*Discussion.* This sample objective speaks measurably to what is required to graduate and complete the educational requirements. There are many useful skills not noted directly in this, and these might be added to a more complete objective at the Macro-level.

Note that achieving results at the Output/Macro-level does not ensure that Mega results and consequences will follow. For example, one could have been certified to complete our school system as a filling station attendant only to find that all of the employers use only self-pump facilities.

*Products/Micro-Level.* One hundred percent of all learners will demonstrate complete competence in numerical and computational skills of addition, subtraction, multiplication, and division as certified by the credentialed mathematics curriculum supervisor of each school.

*Discussion.* This is just one set of building-block skills required of both a successful learner as well as a competent citizen. There are many more of these Product/Micro-level essential competencies required for success in school and in life.

Note that just meeting this objective will not necessarily result in graduation or completion or being a self-sufficient and contributing member of society.

Table 2.5 shows some more examples of the educational applicability of the OEM. *These examples have an organizational reference; personal elements may vary.*

**Table 2.5**    Linking Objectives to Educational Success: Aligning

| | |
|---|---|
| Mega/Outcomes | • Everyone is self-sufficient and self-reliant<br>• Eliminated chronic illness due to air pollution<br>• Eliminated disabling fatalities<br>• Positive quality of life<br>• No welfare recipients<br>• Zero disabling crime<br>• Student's success over time as citizens (5 years and beyond) |
| Macro/Outputs | • Graduates<br>• Completers<br>• Grades delivered<br>• Dropouts<br>• Certified licensees |
| Micro/Products | • Courses completed<br>• Competent students in subject area<br>• Library books obtained<br>• Skill acquired<br>• Learner accomplishments<br>• Competency test passed<br>• Budget balanced<br>• Completed school improvement plan<br>• Competent students passed to next grade |
| Process | • School development<br>• In-service training<br>• Operating lunch room<br>• Curriculum development<br>• Lesson plan development<br>• Balancing classroom budget<br>• School improvement planning<br>• Assessing needs |
| Input | • Money          • Regulations<br>• People          • History<br>• Equipment     • Culture<br>• Facilities       • Problems<br>• Goals            • Existing materials<br>• Time             • Learner entry SKAAs[a]<br>• Resources     • Current staff and their SKAAs<br>• Values          • Characteristics of current and<br>• Laws               and incoming students |

SOURCE: a. SKAA: Skills, Knowledge, Abilities, Attitudes. Based on Kaufman, 2000.

Evaluation—good evaluation—is the best friend of the competent and caring educator, and thus the best friend of the learner and our shared world. Why would we want to evaluate objectives that are not useful? Why would we want to evaluate performance that did not lead to success in later education and life?

The job aid shown in Figure 2.6 may help you sort out your approach to evaluation.

**Figure 2.6**    Job Aid for Deciding on What to Do for Evaluation and Continuous Improvement

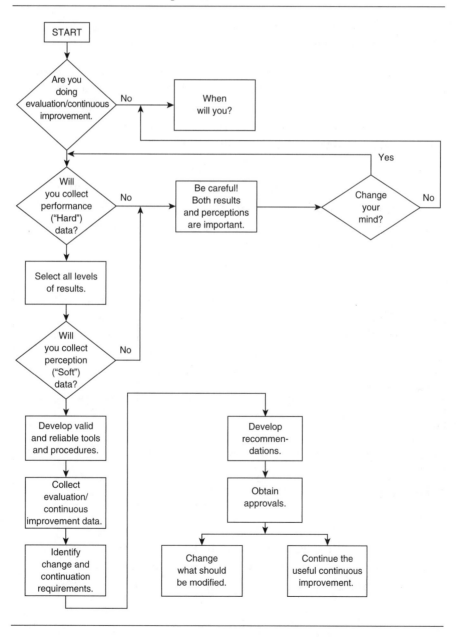

## PRINCIPLE 7: A SET OF EVALUATION QUESTIONS DRIVES THE EVALUATION STUDY

Just as the school system should strive to be in alignment with the Ideal Vision, the evaluation team should plan to identify the points in programs where success in this endeavor has been delivered or not occurred. The school will develop curriculum objectives. The evaluation team will develop evaluation questions related to each objective and the activities which lead to results in learning. The educational system as an organization will address the following types of questions.

### Organizational Questions

All educational organizations (and all others as well) must ask and answer a set of questions that take the following form. At issue in the evaluation study is, first, has the school system addressed each level? Second, has an adequate answer been advanced in educational programs, which are focused to yield valid goals and objectives?

1. Which of the questions do you think your organization and any of your internal and external clients can afford to NOT address formally? This means without identifying and dealing with each in measurable performance terms.

| Level of Planning and Type of Results | Can Afford to Not Address Formally and Rigorously | Must Address Formally and Rigorously |
|---|---|---|
| MEGA/OUTCOMES | | |
| MACRO/OUTPUTS | | |
| MICRO/PRODUCTS | | |
| PROCESSES | | |
| INPUTS | | |
| CONTINUOUS IMPROVEMENT | | |

2. Which of the questions do you believe your organization *and* any of its internal and external clients currently do and do not formally and completely address in measurable performance terms?

| Level of Planning and Type of Results | Do Not Address Formally and Rigorously | Do Address Formally and Rigorously |
|---|---|---|
| MEGA/OUTCOMES | | |
| MACRO/OUTPUTS | | |
| MICRO/PRODUCTS | | |
| PROCESSES | | |
| INPUTS | | |
| CONTINUOUS IMPROVEMENT | | |

3. What are the risks for starting at the Mega-level? What are the risks for NOT starting at the Mega-level?

4. In what ways are you adding value to your organization? To your external clients? To our society/community? What could you be doing and contributing?

## Organizational Questions Lead to Evaluation Questions

The evaluation team must formulate a set of study objectives based on evaluation questions. It is this set of questions that determines the activities that will be observed and the methods that will be used to observe and to gather and record data. We will keep repeating this logic in each chapter.

The validity of goals and objectives rests on the school system's linkage to Mega-level planning. The effectiveness of the curriculum based on valid goals depends on effective programs, which are the by-products of organization. The school, home, and classroom environment and the instructional tactics employed produce either positive or negative results.

The evaluation team will monitor the course of action with an eye on the goals and results. The criteria for evaluation will be based on the desired results and all that is known about effective organization, instructional strategy, and the alignment of the levels expressed in the OEM.

The next chapter is devoted to the idea and importance of alignment of all of the *organizational elements* and the related criteria for each level of results and contributions for evaluation. The set of evaluation questions you develop as a result of this wide view will be comprehensive and allow you to deal with both expected and unexpected results.

## NOTES

1.   Notice that here and elsewhere, we are using words in a very precise and rigorous manner. This rigor is vital for you to be able to define and deliver evaluation that is sensible, sensitive, and useful. Here, *Outcome* is the label for results at the societal level. We will use it consistently this way.

2.   This is another word that is critical in how we use it and define it. In this book we define *need* as a gap in results. We will justify this later.

3.   We provide complete citations in the "References" section at the end of the book.

4.   More on these three levels of results later. Thanks for your patience.

# Building Aligned    **3**
# Evaluation Criteria

---

T he concepts and tools of evaluation must be put to use in the context of social drivers using a top-down, needs-based approach. The resulting practical advantage is role clarification of the educational process and resulting educational Outcomes. The ideal societal state—an Ideal Vision—determines the criteria for identifying and selecting valid needs. Valid needs are the basis for the evaluation criteria for educational goals and objectives, and goals and objectives determine the evaluation criteria for results. Evaluation is integrated when these sets of criteria are complementary; the result at one educational level delivers useful results to the other levels. The system-based overview presented here provides the remaining levels of evaluation criteria. A fully integrated educational system will be able to maintain a balanced functional relationship between resources, the needs of stakeholders, and the educational process solutions that lead to valid results. In this way, desired educational Products, Outputs, and Outcomes will serve the community at large. The Mega top-down, needs-assessment-based approach to evaluation is one way to convert these ideas into action.

Education is a *system* when all of the parts work independently and together to achieve a worthy result: success for learners in school and in life. It is vital that we relate the parts of the educational system to the whole, with every component of the educational system working to the same end. We call this concept *alignment,* and understanding alignment is a major key to successful evaluation and education. Alignment and Integration work together to produce desired results.

So far, you have been introduced to a set of principles, concepts, and tools of evaluation. In this chapter, we provide more detail on the Organizational Elements Model (OEM) in the context of a functional educational system.

Society in general and the ultimate stakeholders in particular (students and their communities) form the top/broadest level of the educational system. To effectively evaluate its contributions and efforts, we must include and integrate society and communities into the OEM framework; this puts all elements of the educational system into the context of societal value added. Doing so also identifies the internal results and *means* required to get there.

The OEM is a framework that relates:

- What we use (Inputs)
- What we do (Processes)
- What we produce (Products)
- What we can deliver from our educational agencies (Outputs)
- What impacts we have for society and communities (Outcomes)

Try as we might, we cannot reasonably separate these elements out and treat them independently. They all have to work as integral parts of a whole educational system: independently and together to achieve useful Outcomes. We have to ensure that the linkages among these elements are in place, and we also must evaluate to certify that everything we use (Inputs), do (Processes), produce (Products), and deliver externally (Outputs) have positive value for society and community.

Thus not only should we evaluate each educational piece, or element, individually, but the linkages and alignment as well. This alignment is more often assumed than formally planned and evaluated. For example, most educational evaluation programs focus on a simple educational component, such as a class, a special program, or an educational method. This is not enough. Just as evaluating your blood pressure is not enough by itself but just one of a variety of health "vital signs," so too are all of the parts of an educational enterprise pieces of the puzzle that are not be confused with the entire puzzle.

Education is complex. We have the individual differences of learners, educators, parents, and community members, and these all have to interact constructively with everything we use and do. Just evaluating one piece of the puzzle is not only deceiving, but it is also risky. Good decisions about improving education, on purpose, must be holistic, and the evaluation data used may be holistic as well.

Unfortunately, most conventional educational evaluation just looks at a piece or two and never relates to the whole. Why? Several reasons are possible:

- We don't know how to plan for, or measure, alignment.
- We don't recognize that it is important.
- We don't think we are responsible or accountable.
- We don't care.

No matter what the argument for looking at only the parts of an educational system, it is not valid. We have to look at the total system and all of its components to ensure that the whole is made up of the contributions of its parts.

We have to use a *system approach* and not just the more conventional *systems approach*. Let's take a closer look at some of these relations, for even though it now sounds subtle, it is vital.

## SYSTEM VS. SYSTEMS APPROACHES

No, this is not more jargon . . . there is a real and important difference for us to consider in evaluation. May we take you on a very short journey that shows why we have to make some distinctions in ensuring that our evaluations are worthy and useful? To better understand the "What" and "How" of terminology, the following is a modification of an earlier work published in an April 2000 article in *Performance Improvement,* by Kaufman and Watkins.

We are increasingly responsible for results, consequences, and payoffs of our educational actions and inactions. We no longer have the luxury of leaving the big questions and issues to parents, legislators, politicians, educational leaders, supervisors, and board members.

The new era we face is defining and achieving useful results for all stakeholders, including both internal and external partners. And we must prove the value we add in terms of empirical data about what we deliver, what it accomplished, and what value it added for all stakeholders (not just the value it added to our team, our school, or our organization but to the entire educational system of internal and external partners).

We can no longer get away with "feel good" discussions of how we increased efficiency or effectiveness of processes that may or may not add value to all of our clients, our client's clients, and the society. When we are also serious about evaluation, we have to measure indicators—of our performance, accomplishments, and payoffs for the parts of the system as well as the whole system. We have to determine not only whether we got results at each of the three levels of results (Products, Outputs, and Outcomes) but also to see whether they worked together and aligned in terms of results and contributions.

For example, U.S. governmental agencies are increasingly becoming required to prove the value they add to citizens. Likewise, organizations worldwide are increasingly including societal value added as an integral ingredient of their organizational purpose (Kaufman, Oakley-Browne, Watkins, & Leigh, 2003; Kaufman, Watkins, & Leigh, 2001; Kaufman, Watkins, Triner, & Stith, 1998). Unfortunately, when we do talk about organizational results, we too often stop short of societal and external client value added.

Some traps in language can be costly. Instead of doing all of the internal and external linkages (using the OEM as a framework), we glibly refer to class size, test results, client satisfaction, or funding levels, and in so doing, we miss the emerging paradigm (Kaufman 1992b, 1998, 2000; Popcorn, 1991) that organizations—all organizations—are but *means* to societal *ends*. Currently, our focus is usually far too narrow. We tend to talk only about "systems"—the pieces and parts of any educational system—and not an overall and encompassing "system": the payoffs for all of our external stakeholders. When we talk about "systems," we misguidedly call all results "Outcomes," and we start our planning as if the only benefactor of our efforts were the organization itself (Kaufman, 1992b, 1998, 2000; Kaufman, et al., 2001; Kaufman et al., 2003). We narrow our focus and limit our value added in both words and deeds. Learners do not stop after each test they pass or after each course they complete. They don't stop at each grade level or stop at graduation. Learners—all learners—leave schools and become part of our social reality, and everything they do and experience in our schools are building blocks toward that external survival, self-sufficiency, and quality of life.

Our language, terms we use (and abuse), often robs us of adding value. Most of our performance improvement and evaluation approaches and methods, including the language we use in describing our profession, commonly leave questions concerning value added unanswered. We tend to talk about *means* (e.g., online education programs, Electronic Performance Support Systems [EPSS], CD-ROMs, computer-assisted learning, learning objects, learner-controlled instruction) and not *ends* (e.g., reduction in poverty, client value, learner competence, quality). Our language seems almost to encourage a number of confusions that "allow" for lack of precision and consequences.

The educational evaluator as well as the performance professional of the future must know how to improve performance as well as how to prove through credible evaluation data that there are useful results to both the educational clients and to society. From a societal perspective, value added includes the survival, health, and well-being of all partners. Planning for and achieving results at the societal level, value added for tomorrow's child, is termed *Mega planning* or *strategic thinking* (Kaufman, 1992b, 1998, 2000; Kaufman et al., 2001; Kaufman et al., 2003). It is this system or supersystem (society) that best begins our planning and serves as the basis for our evaluation and continuous improvement.

To be successful in planning for and demonstrating value added, we must use words with rigor and precision. Language that is crisp, to the

**Table 3.1**    System and Subsystems

| Checkpoints | Y/N |
|---|---|
| 1. Identified purpose of evaluation | |
| 2. Identified stakeholders | |
| 3. Determined the time and resources required for the evaluation | |
| 4. Identified intended societal impact and related evaluation questions | |
| 5. Identified intended organizational Outputs and related questions | |
| 6. Identified intended internal Products and related questions | |
| 7. Identified selected solutions intended to meet results at all organizational levels | |
| 8. Identified measurable indicators for results at all organizational levels | |
| 9. Identified measurable indicators for selected solutions (processes and inputs) | |
| 10. Identified data sources | |
| 11. Identified data collection methods | |
| 12. Determined timelines for data collection, analysis, interpretation, and reporting. | |

point, and focused on results (including societal payoffs) is essential for professional success. And then we must match our promises with deeds and payoffs that measurably add value, the value that we evaluate and report.

*System, Systems, Systematic, and Systemic:* related but not the same. To set the framework, let's define these basic terms, relate them, and then use them to put other vocabulary in context.

*Systems Approach:* Begins with the parts of a system—subsystems—that make up the "system."

When someone says they are using a "systems approach," they are really focusing on one or more subsystems—unfortunately, focusing on the parts and not the whole. When planning and doing at this level, they can only assume that the payoffs and consequences will add up to something useful to society and external clients, and this is usually a very big assumption.

*System Approach:* Begins with the sum total of parts working independently and together to achieve a useful set of results at the societal level, adding value for all internal and external partners.

*Systematic Approach:* An approach that does things in an orderly, predictable, and controlled manner. It is a reproducible process. Doing things, however, in a systematic manner does not ensure the achievement of useful results.

*Systemic Approach:* An approach that affects everything in the system. The definitions of "the system" are usually left up to the practitioner and may or not include external clients and society. It does not necessarily mean that when something is systemic, it is also useful.

Interestingly, these above terms are often used interchangeably. Yet they are not the same. Notice that when the words are used interchangeably and/or start at the systems level and not the system level, it will mean that we might not add value to external clients and society. When we plan and deliver our evaluation data, we must be clear about what it is we have evaluated and why the resulting data are useful for the decision on how to continuously improve our educational enterprise.

Semantic quibbling? We suggest just the opposite. If we talk about a "systems" approach and don't realize that we are focusing on splinters and not on the whole, we usually degrade what we use, do, produce, and deliver in terms of adding value inside and outside of the organization. When we take a "systems" approach, we risk losing a primary focus on societal survival, self-sufficiency, and quality of life. We risk staying narrow.

Aligning what we use, do, produce, and deliver with external value added is the key to useful evaluation. OK. We have spent a lot of time on the concepts. Thanks for thinking about these terms and distinctions. While doing this, we noted that all three levels of results must be aligned in both planning and evaluating. What we planned and delivered should be evaluated. In planning, we get the alignment among the three levels of results by rolling down from Mega to Macro to Micro (see Figure 3.1).

When we evaluate, we compare our new results with our intended results at the Mega-, Macro-, and Micro-levels. Another way of showing this alignment and linkages is shown in the following diagram.

**Mega/Outcomes**

$\updownarrow$

**Macro/Outputs**

$\updownarrow$

**Micro/Products**

**Figure 3.1**  System Alignment by Mega-, Macro-, and Micro-Level

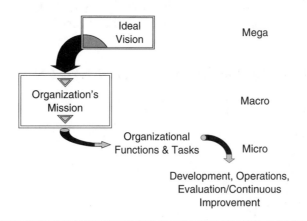

NOTE: Rolling down from outside (Mega) to inside the educational organization, moving from top down to ensure that the alignment of everything the educational organization uses, does, produces, and delivers adds value to our shared society (Kaufman, 2000).

For each, we compare our actual results with our intentions: evaluate.

If we want to further determine whether our means (curriculum, processes, activities, programs) and resources (teachers, equipment, facilities, funding) contributed to our desired results, we further the "alignment chain," as shown in the next diagram.

Now that we have identified the linkages, our task is to evaluate the extent to which we achieved results at each level, and then see whether there was a contribution from one level to the others.

## CONCEPTUAL GUIDE FOR EVALUATING ALIGNMENT

Step 1. Identify intended results for:

Mega

Macro

Micro

Step 2. Identify current results for:

Mega

Macro

Micro

Step 3. Identify the extent to which the desired results for each area of Micro have been achieved, and list the gaps between the intended and current results.

Step 4. Identify the extent to which the desired results for each area of Macro have been achieved, and list the gaps between the intended and current results.

Step 5. Identify the extent to which the desired results for each area of Mega have been achieved, and list the gaps between the intended and current results.

Step 6. Determine what methods, solutions, tactics, and resources have been effective/ineffective and thus should be kept, changed, or modified in order to reach or maintain desired results.

## SCOPING HOW EVALUATION IS DONE IN YOUR ORGANIZATION

Evaluation—good and complete evaluation—depends on us scoping the complete landscape of our educational world. We have to look at both the pieces and the whole.

Here are some variables for you to consider in looking at your organization and evaluation. Go over the list and compare these questions with how evaluation is done in your educational organization. Then check those that should characterize your organization. You will recognize some of these items from the self-assessment included earlier in this book. This is a more thorough list, which should help you identify strengths and weakness in evaluation within your organization.

## How the Organization "Sees" Evaluation

1. Concerned about results for individual performance accomplishment.

2. Concerned about results for small groups/teams.

3. Concerned about results for a department.

4. Concerned about results for the organization.

5. Skip formal evaluation because of time restraints.

6. Skip formal evaluation because of lack of evaluation abilities.

7. Skip formal evaluation because of not knowing what to do with the evaluation data.

8. Management is focused on results.

9. Staff is focused on results.

10. Our culture is results focused.

11. Evaluation is seen as comparing results with intentions.

12. Evaluation is seen as comparing results with intentions and deciding what to stop, what to continue, what to modify.

13. Evaluation functions are included in planning.

14. Evaluation results are shared with all internal partners.

## How the Organization Goes About Evaluation

1. Collects "hard" performance data for jobs and tasks.

2. Collects "hard" performance data for units within the organization.

3. Collects "hard" performance data for the organization.

4. Collects "hard" performance data for impact on external clients (i.e., results for clients and clients' clients).

5. Collects "hard" performance data for impact on society or community.

6. Collects "soft" (perception) performance-related data for jobs and tasks.

7. Collects "soft" (perception) performance-related data for units within the organization.

8. Collects "soft" (perception) performance-related data for the organization.

9. Collects "soft" (perception) performance-related data for impact on external clients (i.e., results for clients and clients' clients).

10. Collects "soft" (perception) performance-related data for impact on society or community.

11. Uses both "hard" and "soft" data for assessing needs.

12. Involves internal partners (staff) in setting objectives.

13. Involves external partners (clients and society) in setting objectives.

14. Formally evaluates results external to the organization (i.e., results for clients and clients' clients).

15. Formally evaluates results within the organization.

16. Formally evaluates results for work units.

17. Formally evaluates results for individuals and small groups.

18. Informally evaluates results external to the organization (i.e., results for clients and clients' clients).

19. Informally evaluates results within the organization.

20. Informally evaluates results for work units.

21. Informally evaluates results for individuals and small groups.

22. Prepares measurable objectives that state both what result is to be accomplished and how the accomplishment will be measured.

## The Bases for Evaluation Criteria

1. Plan on the basis of *ends.*

2. Plan on the basis of consequences of results for external clients.

3. Plan on the basis of consequences of results for society and community.

4. Plan only on the basis of individual performance.

5. Plan only on the basis of resources.

6. Plan only on the basis of activities, programs, and projects.

7. Plan only on the basis of desired individual results.

8. Plan on the basis of small-group results.

9. Plan on the basis of departmental or section results.

10. Plan on the basis of organizational results.

11. Plan on the basis of results for external clients.

12. Plan on the basis of results for society and community.

13. Plan to link resources to activities, programs, and projects.

14. Plan to link resources to results that add value for clients and clients' clients.

15. Choose *means* and resources (e.g., training, restructuring, layoffs) without first identifying results to be achieved.

16. Define and use *needs assessment* for identifying gaps in results for impact on external clients and society.

17. Define and use *needs assessment* for identifying gaps in results for impact on the organization itself (such as a business plan).

18. Define *needs assessment* for identifying gaps in results for impact on individual operations or tasks.

19. Rank order *needs* on the basis of the costs to meet the *needs* as compared to the costs of ignoring them.

20. Link organizational results to external consequences (i.e., results for clients and clients' clients).

21. Use data from a *needs assessment* to set objectives.

## Using Evaluation Data

1. Use evaluation data for improvement.

2. Use evaluation data for punishing.

3. Compare accomplishments to objectives established at the beginning of the project.

4. Compare accomplishments to the payoffs for those accomplishments for the organization.

5. Compare accomplishments to the payoffs for those accomplishments for individual projects.

6. Compare accomplishments to the payoffs for those accomplishments for political consequences.

7. Determine, while doing a program, project, or activity, what is working and what is not based on "hard" data.

8. Determine, while doing a program, project, or activity, what is working and what is not based on "soft" data.

9. Determine, while doing a program, project, or activity, what is working and what is not based on both "hard" and "soft" data.

We have provided some basic examples of objectives at the three educational levels of contribution: Outcomes/Mega, Outputs/Macro, and Products/Micro. Each objective can and should be evaluated: the actual results compared to the objective itself. When we do this performance-based evaluation, we can find out—based on data and actual performance—what worked and what did not.

Evaluation at the Product/Micro-level is necessary but not sufficient to ensure educational success. Of course, most of our evaluation efforts will be at this level: After all, this is where we spend most of our professional time and efforts. We use myriad assessment vehicles for evaluation at the Product/Micro level, including:

- Standardized and validated tests
- Teacher-constructed tests
- Performance assessments (such as portfolios, learning products, etc.)
- Observations by independent observers
- Observations by supervisors and/or administrators
- Results of statewide or national assessments
- Reviews of key documents (e.g., formal reports, statistics, policies, etc.)

No matter what the source of testing and evaluation, it is our professional responsibility to ensure that the criteria or both valid and reliable.

*Validity is* the extent to which something, such as an assessment instrument, measures what it says it is measuring. *Reliability* is the extent to which something, such as an assessment instrument, measures something and consistently obtains the same results.

Any useful instrument or assessment vehicle should be both valid and reliable. If it is not, what real sense can we ever make of the results of its application? Care enough about learners and education to ensure validity and reliability. Usefulness of objectives and criteria comes from assessing needs—gaps in results—at the Mega-, Macro-, and Micro-levels.

## Keying Evaluation to Decision Making

So, how do we make sure that our evaluation *processes* and procedures will drive both our data collection as well as the resulting decision making? That is not as difficult as it might at first sound. Here are the key questions for you to ask and answer as you develop your evaluation objectives and related *processes:*

• Are all of our objectives measurable on an *interval* or *ratio scale* (see Chapter 4)? If not, do so, or be very specific that the rigor and precision normally desired are missing and thus there are possible threats to the validity of what is done and delivered.

• Are all of the objectives, taken together, an accurate representation of the skills, knowledge, attitudes, and abilities required for demonstrated competence in the areas being evaluated?

• Are the objectives culturally fair? Do they capture the required performance that is understandable in the culture and values of the learners involved? While it is at first simpler to brush everyone with the same stroke, be sensitive to the fact that education today has a rich and diverse set of learners, parents, and educators. Thus it is vital that what is required for performance and the rationale for those performances are understood and useful in our rich environment.

• Are you sure that the objectives at all levels are linked correctly? Will the performances elicited and measured at the Product/Micro-level add value at the Outputs/Macro-level? And will results at the Outputs/Macro-level add value at the Outcomes/Mega-level? If not, you might be teaching and transferring skills, knowledge, and attitudes that are not useful in today's or tomorrow's world.

• Are the methods, tools, and techniques employed (and thus being evaluated as "drivers" of performance on the objectives) based on scientific research? Fortunately, credible research is being done on the methods of teaching and learning. Unhappily for some, there are reasons to reconsider many of the "old paradigms" and wisdom of the past.

• Have you differentiated between *means* (activities, resources, methods) and *ends?* Evaluation should relate to *ends*, results, and consequences. *Means* are useful only to the extent to which they deliver useful *ends*. For example, objectives should NEVER include what resources, methods, or activities will be used.

• Are all decisions using evaluation data from valid and reliable *means?* If not, watch out!

### Key Considerations in Writing Measurable Objectives

Objectives tell you where you are headed and how to tell when you have arrived. There are several reasons for writing rigorous objectives:

- They describe a desired future and give clear direction.
- They improve performance by providing performance targets (that can be used for evaluation and continuous improvement).
- They describe desired results in measurable terms.
- They are a communication tool; they provide a vehicle for developing shared meaning about where the group, educational organization, and community wants to go.
- They provide a justifiable foundation for allocating financial resources.
- They motivate people.
- They provide a foundation basis for measuring success or failure.
- They clarify expectations on what results are expected of a specific role in an educational organization.
- They provide an opportunity for positive reinforcement if they are achieved, and provide solid criteria for continuous improvement.
- They are the first step in effective planning for results.
- They define accountability and responsibility in measurable terms.
- They give individuals or team control over their lives.
- They convert stated and implicit values into action and measurable results: They allow Mega, Macro, and Micro to "come alive."
- They are the foundation basis for performance review and appraisal and performance improvement.

Perhaps the clearest statement of objectives came from Robert Mager (1997), when he identified the basic characteristics of measurable objectives:

- *Behavior/Result:* where we are (or were) headed
- *Responsible Party:* who/what is responsible for demonstrating (not doing) such a result

- *Measurable Criteria:* how to tell when we have arrived (in clear rigorous terms)
- *Conditions:* identifies the conditions under which the performance will be observed

## CONSTRUCTING A SPECIFIC SET
## OF EVALUATION STUDY QUESTIONS

We hope you are beginning to see how alignment sets the stage for you to ask the right questions, derive evaluation criteria, and plan to observe the situation to gain information and collect it as data.

The next section of our book will talk about observation, but before that, we introduce a translation of our ideas in the form of a concrete example. Scenario 1, "Supporting Anita," will show how one school official copes with evaluation, complete with problems pitfalls and some advice on avoiding traps and errors by following some simple rules.

---

**Evaluation Management Plan:**

The plan should include a statement of purpose, a schedule, description of the team and resources available, needs assessment findings, the evaluation approach based on evaluation questions. The main product of this phase is the detailed set of evaluation questions and approaches to answering them.

---

**Detailed set of questions:**

This will set the stage for the observation phase, where inquiry methods will gather data required to answer each question. Note that additional questions can be added to the list at any point in the study to accommodate unforeseen events.

# Scenario 1

## *Supporting Anita*

---

Anita Jackson was a good district superintendent. She had risen from being a new teacher in the Southside elementary school to become the head of education for Cobb County Schools. She had "paid her dues" and worked as a mother, while at the same time earning her doctorate in educational administration.

To be sure, this was not the easiest education job in the United States, but she was smart, compassionate, and tough when required. She did what was appropriate. She involved parents, community members, politicians, and learners. She was charged with lifting the district's success in all schools, and she thought she had made good progress. Very good progress, she thought.

But as she opened this morning's newspaper, the editorial caught her eye. (She took the time to stay informed whether or not the news was good, and she worked hard to build bridges with all constituents: learners, teachers, administrators, parents, employers, and community members.) The editorial read:

Is it time for a change in educational leadership in Cobb County?

Cobb County is a proud county. We are diverse in our residents and we share a deep concern for our children's futures regardless of economic condition: from the rich to poorest families. Statewide test results are disappointing this year. Again. We have some schools on the Southside of town where kids are not performing. The County Council passed financial aids packages, and the Rotary and Kiwanis Clubs donated equipment and organized school volunteers. We have had town hall meetings called by Dr. Jackson, and we did strategic planning. Still, the scores have not met State standards.

We suggest that the time for waiting and hoping for better schools for our kids seems to have passed. When do we see results? At long last? How patient should we be with a beloved school leader who has not delivered a district where our schools—all schools—meet state standards?

We suggest the time is now to think about changing our leadership. We should thank Dr. Jackson for her efforts and good intentions, and move on.

What do you think? Please contact the editor of this newspaper with your thoughts.

The editorial did not make superintendent Jackson's day. She had worked long and hard and knew in her heart that she was moving in the right direction. It was not the time to talk about her moving on. She knew she was doing the right things and that given time and more resources, she could get the job done. But she pondered how to survive this seeming attack. Could she buy more time and retain her dignity? She had to find ways to prove that Cobb County Schools were on the right track. She considered her situation:

• Before taking over as superintendent, 7 out of 10 of the schools in her district had received failing grades on the state's rating system. In the 2 years of her tenure, the slide to the bottom had slowed down, and now only 3 schools had received the failing grade. She also knew that the midrange scores of most of her schools were a less-than-desirable end state.

• Anita took stock of the resources she had at her disposal. Her district was on the edge of an urban area that had lost a lot of solid manufacturing jobs, and the small family farms on the other side of town were gradually being bought out by large corporations. A swelling population of workers had moved into town to take advantage of inexpensive housing and nearby farm labor jobs.

• Her program to turn the school district around had several lines of attack. She took the radical step of changing the school day to add more time for supervised study and mentoring. She negotiated a contract with core teachers that kept them employed the entire year and provided for an 8-hour day. This was in return for a modest increase in pay. That pay increase came at the expense of adding more teachers. Her core teachers each taught four 50-minute classes each day and spent the other 4 hours preparing and coaching. A special feature of the school day was a period where each teacher was available to answerer questions about assignments and in some cases tutor at-risk students. Anita had built up a core of volunteers who helped with study halls and cafeteria duty, which was no longer an additional duty for teachers. She emphasized the basics of reading and math in the elementary schools and kept the sports program in the high school. She knew that many of her high school students were there only to play on the traditionally strong football team.

• Anita also knew that a small private prep school that had opened in the next town had drawn many of the college-hopeful students away from her middle school and high school. These schools had a competitive advantage in that there were many state policies and procedures that they did not have to follow.

• Anita required her teachers to test often to build up test-taking skills. She took the extra step of requiring teachers to do some diagnostic testing and provide extra help for students who fall behind.

• She knew that one of her biggest problems was student turnover from the mobile population of farm workers. She knew that so far, school discipline was reasonably good, but it was getting harder to motivate students who saw no future except low-paying jobs in the service industry.

Anita hired a consultant to conduct an evaluation to find out what was working and what was not. The consultant agreed to work for 1 week, for a fixed fee, to look at the conduct and content of instruction in the school and also to interview school board members and concerned parents. The consultant interviewed each school board member and 10 parents who were active in the Parent Teacher Association.

The consultant visited several schools to observe class in session. He would slip into a classroom while the teacher was presenting a lesson. If the teacher stopped to recognize his presence, he would say, "Don't mind me, pretend I am not here." Most of the teachers were a bit nervous about having a stranger enter the room unannounced. Some of the students began to make up rumors that the stranger was a narcotics officer, a police officer looking for someone. In the teachers lounge, the conversation began to include speculation that the stranger was a private investigator who was working for the school board to identify poor teachers. One teacher came to Anita to complain that the presence of the stranger was disruptive to the class.

The consultant prepared a written report and made an oral presentation to Anita. His findings stated that instructors appeared to be competent to teach, that better discipline in the hallways and in study halls was required, and that one particular school board member and one parent were particularly upset with "conditions" in the school. They were unhappy with dress code violations and the activity of the students on varsity teams toward some nonathletic students, and they wanted to see more money go to the school orchestra. The consultant did not do any testing or review any test procedures for any of the classes.

## What Can We Say About This Evaluation?

- The evaluator did provide some useful information to Anita.
- The evaluator's presence contributed to fear and anxiety on the part of some students and teachers.
- The focus of the evaluation was limited to *processes* and methods of doing things, and not considering results and consequences.
- The findings were not substantiated by other observations.
- Anita was not presented any alternative courses of action that would lead to a decision that would change the status quo.
- Anita did, however, have a better idea of where the newspaper concern originated. Coupled with the lead provided by the evaluator and some independent investigation of her own, she identified several concerned parties.

Anita was somewhat disappointed in the evaluation study conducted by the consultant. Although she did get some useful information, she felt she did not yet have a course of action that would improve the situation. She decided to ask the help of one of the professors at the university where she did her graduate work. He suggested that she approach the school board and the community and start with actual needs, not just gaps in *processes*, procedures, and activities, but *needs* as gaps in results. She had been trying to sort out school issues and the desires of strident voices here and there without a grounded idea of what really mattered.

*Scenario Teaching Point:* So far, the scenario represents a typical approach to school solutions and to evaluation. The main focus has been on Process: how the system did things. The emphasis is on *means* rather than *ends*. Let's see what happens when Anita changes her approach.

The school board was responsive to Anita's suggestion to conduct *needs assessment* and to base educational planning on *needs*. While not familiar with the type of *needs assessment* Anita was suggesting, they did like the idea of looking at gaps in results, not just gaps in procedures and resources.

Anita stressed that the goal of this effort would be to identify *needs*—gaps in results—and then align organizational efforts and resources to meet those *needs*. She also promised the school board that she would provide evaluation data that would confirm that they were getting the results that would meet the *needs*.

Anita knew that doing a good job with the evaluation was going to be important if any of the new planning was going to take root and stay on track. She formed her evaluation team with that thought in mind.

> *Scenario Teaching Point:*
> To see examples of *needs assessment* being carried out, see the references cited as well as references for organizational alignment. This scenario is about doing evaluation once a proper *needs assessment* has been completed.

## PUTTING CHANGE IN MOTION

Anita knew she had to do something, something tangible. She wanted to "turn around" the previous attacks; so knowing that change was important, she swung into action on the basis of what she thought was important. Something would be done—and now.

### New Educational Goals

The county seemed to rally around the new, open process of deciding the goals of education based on the needs of the community and a vision of a better life ahead. It became clear that the community did not want to lose that sense of small-town unity. They did not want the school system to turn into a fractionated system, with college-bound students in one system and migrant workers in another. They wanted all students to master the skills required to enter society and have no student prevented from getting ahead simply due to an arbitrary classification based on the part of town they came from or what their parents did for a living. And they wanted to be active participants in defining their shared future. Their formally stated list of goals included the following:

- Every student will graduate from high school.
- Every school in the district will achieve an "A" rating from the state.
- Graduating students will be qualified for entry-level jobs or to enter military service or to enter collage.
- The school system will be drug free, gang free, and pregnancy free.
- Teachers will love their jobs.

- Students will be motivated.
- The schools rating, based on standardized national testing, will rank in the upper third of the nation's schools.
- Every learner will become a self-sufficient and self-reliant member of the community.

## The New Curriculum

The community and the school board agreed, based on the agreed-upon goals, that instead of cutting things out, more art and music as well as a full line of sports activities should be preserved. The core curriculum would consist of Mathematics, English, General Science, Biology, Chemistry, Personal Health, American History, Spanish, and French. Many of these changes were based on the requirements for learners to be successful in school as well as in later life.

There would also be several types of industrial arts class and home economics, and three new subjects were added: computer science, a combination reading/literature/library course, and a course that was simply called "Tutorial."

## How Did They Make It Work?
## The New Approach to Teaching and Learning

Anita realized that some of the innovations that she had already put into place would fit into the new set of requirements, but she still had to cope with the normal range of resource problems that all public school systems face today. Nonetheless, she had the community aroused and ready to help. They felt a new sense of empowerment, and Anita wanted to keep that momentum. She came up with a few more innovative ideas:

- There would be "tracks" for the college-bound and job market bound students, but the old way of separating the children early and branding themselves as "smarties" (or "nerds") and "dummies" was scrapped. Now, all children were required to take the basic core.
- Students who progressed rapidly were required to tutor students who were having difficulty. This was done in the tutorial session, which was the last period of the school day, and the tutoring was done with the help of the entire faculty, who were required to be at this class.
- Volunteers from the community, who were qualified based on years in the workplace, were asked to mentor students.
- To teach the large-class selection, Anita was able to hire some part-time teachers from the private school, who came over 1 day a week for their special subjects.

- To get into the college track, students had to earn their way by completing the core and participating in the tutorial program.
- All students were required to play one sport. Varsity players would tutor the less gifted athletes (sometimes the same students who were tutoring the athletes in algebra or biology).
- Homework assignments were changed. Students were not assigned homework to take home; instead, they were given practice exercises and assignments to be completed in supervised study hall. Each student was, however, required to visit the town library and write a paper each term. Every student had to do this, no exceptions.
- A strict dress code was adopted.

Change was going to happen.

## Anita's Evaluation Team

Anita knew that the managing the new curriculum and the new approach to teaching would be a full-time job. She also knew that she was going to have to prove to some skeptical state officials that the new approach was working and producing the results intended. Evaluation would be a key concern for her, for the state officials, and for all of the stakeholders who now had their hope restored. Anita asked for help from a friend whom she had met at one of the state workshops for school administrators. Dr. Mackenzie, head of the Center for Curriculum Development and Evaluation at State University, agreed to help with the evaluation effort. He suggested that the school district could contract with the Center to provide two of his graduate students to supplement Anita's team. She and Dr. Roger Mackenzie put together the following team:

- The team leader was John Quick, the mathematics teacher. John also had some project management experience and had earned his Professional Project Manager Certification by taking classes on weekends and evenings. John would manage the evaluation, keep things on schedule, and assist with data analysis.
- Anita wanted one of the teachers on the team to get an insider's view of the implementation of the program, so Shirley Lopez, the Spanish teacher, was added to the team as a participant observer coordinator.
- The English teacher, Myrna Grey, was added to help with report writing.
- Anita's deputy, Fred Bliss, was added to keep track of resources.
- The two graduate students, William DuPont and Judith Andrews, would be outside observers and do most of the interviews and data collection in general.

- Dr. Mackenzie would meet regularly with the group to lead weekly meetings, where trends and issues of the developing study would be discussed. Roger would assist John in making data collection assignments.
- Anita rounded out the team with the school computer/audiovisual specialist, who would document events using audio and video recording.

### The Set of Evaluation Questions

Anita provided a set of prime questions to the group to get planning started, and then she let John lead the team in the creation of an evaluation management plan. Here are the primary and secondary lead questions that Anita gave the team.

### The Evaluation Management Plan

*Prime Questions of Alignment and Direction*

Do the results we seek stem from valid *needs* (gaps in results and consequences, not gaps in resources or methods)?

Are the mechanisms, organizations, resources, and programs designed to produce desired result effective with goals and objectives based on valid *needs*?

*Secondary Questions*

Who are the stakeholders? What are the limits of this inquiry in time and resources and range of issues considered? What solutions are in place to meet valid needs? Are the solutions effective? Are the solutions efficient? What is the effect over time? What intervening variables affect Products, Outputs, and Outcomes?

How do we recognize, record, or measure Outputs and Outcomes?

John Quick wasted no time outlining an evaluation management plan to organize the study and schedule evaluation events. Each event was designed to gather information that would later serve as data for the analysis. The information to be obtained was the information that would answer the questions of the study. Here is the outline for the management plan that John used to guide the group:

- Statement of the purpose of the study
- The scope of work for the evaluation effort
- The detailed evaluation question set
- The information targets relating to each question
- The observation methods to be used and controls
- Testing schedule
- Task assignments (work breakdown structure)
- Overall project schedule
- Analysis and reduction of data
- Reports and recommendations

## REFLECTING ON THE SCENARIO

We want you to think about the story of Anita and her use of evaluation in conjunction with the new approach in her school district. Is she off to a good start? What could yet go wrong? Remember the first example of the short evaluation that left Anita without a clear course of action. That sort of evaluation is very typical. How about community values? It sounds great to say you are for community values, but what does that really mean? Do community values lead us to a better place? Do they separate us into groups? Do these groups cooperate? Do they lead to learners being successful both in school and in later life? There are a lot of pitfalls and traps yet ahead on the path to the Ideal Vision. We talk about some of these next, along with some rules that will help you stay on the right track.

> *Scenario Teaching Point:* Some of the items on the evaluation management plan outline will be covered in the coming chapters. It is important that the full scope of topics of the management plan be listed together.

### Lessons Learned and Helpful Guidance

Based on this scenario, and others to follow in this book, we provide some lessons learned, guidance from the chapters that proceed these, and helpful hints for your future as you find out what worked and what did not, and pursue sensible, sensitive, and useful evaluation.

## TRAPS, ERRORS, AND RULES OF THE ROAD IN THE ALIGNMENT AND DIRECTION EVALUATION PHASE

Why do some educators shy away from evaluation? Why are some evaluations controversial? Why do some evaluation efforts, no matter do how well intended, attract criticism? Attract fear? Part of the answer to these questions is that a lot of educators have been burned by evaluations gone bad. There is a pattern to bad evaluation, and we have identified a number of traps that cause otherwise well-meaning evaluators to introduce error and confound the evaluation process.

### The Values Trap

How did we get wrapped up in words, and what do they really mean? In this book, we make lots of distinctions, which sound picky at first: needs versus wants versus desires; Outcomes/Outputs/Products; means versus ends; and now value versus values. We want to shift from *Alice in Wonderland*, where it was said, "Words mean anything I want them to mean, no more and no less." Using the same words to mean different things is certain to cause confusion. And confusion is what we have in education in general and educational evaluation in particular. This book is designed to cut away a lot of the confusion and replace it with clarity. So, let's talk about a frequent confusion between *value* (merit or worth of something) versus *values* (what options in life we choose knowingly or almost reflexively).

If evaluation is about the assessment of results, many readers will have also encountered the phrase: "Determine the value of the results." We want to make an important distinction here. For us, the results should be based on the culmination of careful planning and execution of educational programs that were designed to achieve desired and justified results.

If the results are as expected, the "value" of the desired *end* was determined back in the planning stage, based on *needs assessment,* with top-down alignment to societal good. The *process* and results of evaluation in this case is a confirmation that agreed-upon goals and objectives were achieved (or not achieved). But what if the expected results were not achieved? In this case, it is the task of evaluation and evaluators to provide data that will aid decision makers in the redesigning or appropriate revisions of the program, to get the intended results and identify variables that conflict with or support the educational enterprise as a whole.

### The Values Error

Enter the distinction and confusion between value and values. We in education hear a lot about *values.* These almost always refer to the choices we make in our lives and organizations: birth control versus right to life; democracy versus Marxism; premarital sex versus chastity, and the like. *Value,* on the other hand, has to do with what something is worth to us (or to our organization or society). When we find a result and impact of an educational effort or program from our evaluation, we know what we intended and what resulted. The value was identified in the needs assessment process, in which we made decisions on the basis of the "cost to meet the *need*" compared with the "cost to ignore the *need.*" At that decision point, we chose among interventions, implemented what we chose, and then determined whether we got the results we set out to achieve. The value of the result was determined by the needs assessment and the educational partners who decided the priorities for meeting *needs.* It is not complex: What did we want to achieve based on the payoffs for success and the penalties for failures?

Values are something else. They are about the choices we make in life. We often act on our values without knowing we have options. Values are often unchallenged personal choices we make without benefit of looking at alternative results and payoffs from the "values-driven" choices. *Value* is about ends; *values* are about means.

It is this choice of the evaluator, given the results compared with the expected results, that sometimes leads to the "values trap." Often, the results obtained do not match with political factions within and outside of the educational system; they wanted something else. There can be pressure put on evaluators to substantiate another set of values rather than make recommendations on the basis of actual documented needs and results. The pressure becomes focused on wants and processes (favorite ways of thinking and doing) and not on objective results and return on investment. When evaluators become enmeshed in the process of determining the values for the school system, they risk making "the error of local value." Evaluators who abandon the role of objective observer to become advocates with agendas to put forward must not hide that advocacy in their role of the evaluator. Evaluators can facilitate active discussion through the process of needs assessment, but they are not free to insert private agendas and opinions into the findings. (Note this is not the same as reporting that certain groups have agendas and opinions.) There is a line between private values—choices among options—and publicly accepted objectives based on partnership-determined needs. In commenting on findings, evaluators must ground their statements in the *needs* derived by objective performance data that flow from the public process of planning and the ethical professional standards. In short, evaluators must not have a "values ax to grind." "Just the facts, Ma'am."

*Error of Local Value*

Evaluation is concerned with making an unambiguous statement about what is good and what is bad and what is useful—not what to save and what to throw out. It is important, however, to remember that what we take as good at one level of a system is derived from the next level up, and sooner or later, we arrive at societal level of good. Morality and ethics (philosophers talk of "normative" as dealing with value, but this is not to be confused with the statistical notion of normality) cannot be divorced from the everyday workings of education. However, sometimes we get so wrapped up in local issues that we define what is good based on a closed system that in the extreme can be devoid of ethics and acceptable morality. Cults and gangs try to "educate" members and shield them from the larger societal view. That is the error of local value. If we are not adding value to our shared society, we might be subtracting it.[1]

**The Process-Product Trap**

For us, evaluation is concerned with results, but we do not intend to separate *means* and *ends* or *Process* and *Product;* these must be distinguished and then linked. *Ends* relate to purpose setting during planning, but they are also the result of means upon execution. *Ends* are a function of means, but *means* in the short run are often taken as milestones. This sets the stage for a very common evaluation trap that is found in organizations that reward initiatives without accountability for results. Textbooks that emphasize *processes*, activity, and procedural skills without an initial concern with results will mislead us: They will encourage us to select solutions before we know the problems and the results we should achieve.

### The Means-Ends Error

The *means-ends error* occurs when we focus on means without considering where they lead or what results they should deliver. Here, we must make an important distinction. We do look at means during an evaluation, but we gather data to see what is going on in case the means do not produce the desired ends. We do not construct elaborate criteria for judging means that are arbitrary. This is the *means-ends* error. This is an easy one to commit because we do have an enormous body of knowledge on how we should do things in education. What we are saying is that not all of that knowledge is based on results, and results-derived criteria make a better grounding for judging the educational process.

Every *process* leads to some kind of result. The point is to have the right result. When you get the wrong result, you must adjust the *processes*, activities, and methods to make a correction or find a different set of ways to do things. In very large industrial operations, quality-control mechanisms can spot a growing process-procedure problem and halt production before enormous quantities of out-of-tolerance goods are produced. In education, we have a more difficult problem. The history of educational philosophy is replete with efforts to describe the ideal educational methods and the ideal educational Outcome: societal impact. A frequent problem with these excursions into philosophy of education is that they blur *ends* and *means* and confuse levels of results. They don't usually differentiate or align learner accomplishments, school accomplishments, and societal value added.

Many controversies center on the differing ways that Process and Outcome have been described and how they are related. We do not solve these issues here.

What we do attempt is to point out how effective evaluation and the proper use of *needs assessment* as well as precise definition of terms and concepts (we usually flag these by putting the terms in italics) can keep efforts from the trap of unending heated debate—and disappointing results.

*Needs assessment* forces you to define and justify the results you want to deliver in a layered context that includes individual, organizational, and societal assessment and then identification and agreement on the desired state of affairs. If you have this going on in an evaluation, you will be less distracted by side agendas.

Having a clear idea of desired Products, Outputs, and Outcomes provides the criteria for assessing your results. It also provides a better way of assessing the methods, means, program, project, and activity mechanisms—the *processes*—of educational programs that are expected to deliver the desired educational results and contributions: Products, Outputs, and Outcomes. In our evaluation model, we emphasize the results criterion as the primary way to determine functional from dysfunctional *process* activity. This does not mean, however, that evaluation is limited to waiting for final results. We sometimes want to track our progress to make sure we are on track to meeting our overall objectives. We therefore endorse the idea of *formative evaluation.*

Every *process* is composed of finer, smaller process steps that feed into later steps. When this is charted in flow models, an opportunity is created to observe each step to see whether the suboperation remains true to the overall purpose of the effort. When the suboperation becomes an *end* to itself (system analysts call this "suboptimization"), evaluators can identify the problem before the overall system is put at risk. There may be a difference in scale and resources, but never underestimate the value of direct observation by an experienced teacher. In fact, this is so important that we have made it one of our "rules of the road" for evaluation: Plan for direct observation in all parts of the evaluation.

## RULES OF THE ROAD FOR ALIGNMENT AND DIRECTION

*Rule 1.* Time and resources must be devoted to evaluation.

*Rule 2.* You must know *what* to evaluate, *how* to evaluate, and *when* to evaluate.

*Rule 3.* Develop *evaluation criteria* based on the suggestion that program goals and objectives should be based on valid *needs*.

*Scenario Teaching Point:* Use a checklist to form your list of evaluation questions:

1. Is the educational enterprise aligned to meet *needs* of both the learners and the community?

2. Does the Ideal Vision guide planning?

3. Have *needs* been identified?

4. Has the school organized to meet *needs*?

5. Have solutions been selected from alternatives?

6. Do the solutions get desired results?

7. If not, why not?

8. Are there any environmental factors working for or against the existing solution set?

*Rule 4.* Evaluation data should be based on the effectiveness of education and educational programs in terms of what was learned.

*Rule 5.* The delivery method, instructional tactics and methods, curriculum content, learning tools, classroom environment, and instructor skill knowledge and attitude all combine to contribute to effective instruction leading to student learning, performance, and learner competence. Therefore evaluation must take into account the interaction of all of these, and all of these must be evaluated. We seek to find out what worked, what didn't, what should be changed, and what should be continued.

*Rule 6.* Judge Process—means, methods, programs, projects, activities, interventions—by the Products they deliver. Evaluators should ask and report as to whether the results meet the *needs.*

*Rule 7.* Gather data on Process to get a calibration of what went on, but suspend judgment on methods, tools, and techniques until the results are determined and found worthy.

*Rule 8.* For each *end* (educational objective) a cost-effective means by considering alternatives should have been selected. Evaluators should ask whether this was done.

*Rule 9.* When planning an evaluation, ask the right questions, but remain open to unforeseen issues. Plan for direct observation and direct performance data to cover all parts of the program.

*Rule 10.* The point of education is to provide learners to be effective citizens and productive in the workplace. Therefore evaluation should always follow students in life and keep the societal viewpoint in terms of the value that was added to our shared world.

*Evaluation Management Plan:* The plan should include a statement of purpose, a schedule, description of the team and resources available, *needs assessment* findings, and the evaluation approach based on evaluation questions. The main product of this phase is the detailed set of evaluation questions and approaches to answering them.

*Detailed Set of Questions:* This will set the stage for the observation phase, where inquiry methods will gather data required to answer each question. Note that additional questions can be added to the list at any point in the study to accommodate unforeseen events.

## PLANNING CHECKLIST EXAMPLE

Make a plan that includes all 10 of the rules above and includes issues from the checklist to end up with specific study objectives and questions for your evaluation study. (See Table 1.A).

**Table I**     A Planning Checklist Example

| Checkpoints | Y/N |
|---|---|
| 1. Identified purpose of evaluation | |
| 2. Identified stakeholders | |
| 3. Determined the time and resources required for the evaluation | |
| 4. Identified intended societal impact and related evaluation questions | |
| 5. Identified intended organizational Outputs and related questions | |
| 6. Identified intended internal Products and related questions | |
| 7. Identified selected solutions intended to meet results at all organizational levels | |
| 8. Identified measurable indicators for results at all organizational levels | |
| 9. Identified measurable indicators for selected solutions (processes and inputs) | |
| 10. Identified data sources | |
| 11. Identified data collection methods | |
| 12. Determined timelines for data collection, analysis, interpretation, and reporting. | |

## NOTES

1. A proposition first suggested by Professor Emeritus Dale Brethower (Western Michigan University).

# Part II

# Observation

**Figure II**    A Phased Action Plan for Evaluation

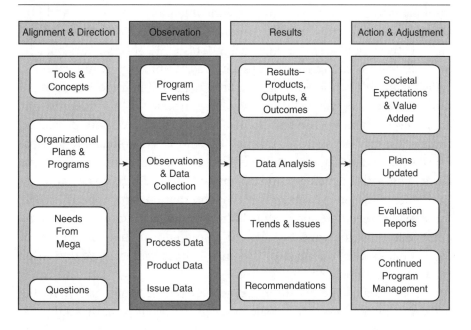

I n this section, we cover ideas that in other texts are addressed as "methodology." We strongly believe that methodology should be the servant of data-gathering requirements, not the other way around. When a methodology is selected too soon, it can become a limiting factor; it is selecting a solution before we know the problem.

Information collection methods are selected to obtain the data that you must have to make sense of the situation—to find out what worked and what did not—and report findings in terms of results and the consequences of those results. Educational effectiveness depends on the Products of the learning process (and subsequent Outputs and Outcomes) to add value to all stakeholders—all stakeholders in the school and in our communities.

We recommend a balanced and sensible mix of direct observation by evaluators and, when useful, collection and use of perceptions concerning what worked and what did not. Decision guides for determining that mix will be addressed. But it is most important to recognize that the data collection process extends throughout the educational world, inward from societal and community and outward from performance results to related process factors, implementation factors, and environmental factors. This is complex, but it is definitely not a random, scattergun approach. Both the restraints and the productivity of the inquiry are determined by the questions asked.

The art and science of observation are often taken for granted when thinking about evaluation but are fundamentally important and the bedrock of useful evaluation. To conduct useful evaluation, we have combined both art and science, often using tools and concepts developed in other disciplines, such as law and psychology. We have instrumentation to collect data on phenomena that are both too small and too large for the human eye to see unaided. We have different kinds of instruments that record events, and we use tests to measure learning. We have developed testing that predicts success and classifies and sorts persons into groups. The testing and measurement community has devised conceptual criteria for dealing with the validity and reliability of tests. Both science and law have rules of evidence to make sure that observations are properly used as the basis for reaching conclusions. There is much to admire in modern observation methodology, but there is also a danger that routine use of certain data collection methods becomes a superficial exercise to answer the wrong questions.

There is logic to observation, just as there is logic to evaluation. In this book, we have expressed that logic in the *phased action plan.* By asking the right questions, you provide a focus for observation and useful methods for mining useful performance data. By basing those questions on an Ideal Vision—the kind of world we want to create for tomorrow's child—that is, an outside-in approach, we ensure there is an alignment between what we use, do, produce, and deliver within our schools with societal value added. If we are not adding value to our shared society, what are we doing?

It is this orientation and alignment that will allow evaluation to develop information for useful decision making: making decisions that measurably improve the results of education within our schools and the contribution to our shared society.

## PRIME QUESTIONS OF OBSERVATION PHASE

- What data are required to answer the evaluation question set?
- What data collection methods will yield the information that will, in turn, yield the answers?
- How will observations be recorded as data?
- Will testing and measurement be used to make data more precise?
- How do we ensure both validity and usefulness of our evaluation questions and the data we get?

## SECONDARY QUESTIONS

- What will be observed?
- Who will be responsible for observations?
- What is the observation schedule?
- How is bias controlled?
- What resources are provided to the evaluation team?
- How often will the evaluation team coordinate or report to sponsors?
- How do we ensure agreement on what we ask and the answers we get?

# Identifying What Data Must Be Collected

# 4

The heart of your evaluation plan will be the steps you take to gather information required to answer the questions that guide the inquiry: finding out what worked, what did not, and why. You now take a closer look at the *educational system* that is the basis for implementing programs and obtaining results in student learning and performance. You must now decide what data to gather and where to look for it. With the organization as the unit of analysis, the Organizational Elements Model (OEM) can provide a framework for answering the right questions based on the right data. The data you collect must match the questions you want answered.

Isn't it frustrating to be judged based upon incomplete or irrelevant data? Haven't we all experienced being called to account for something where others had the wrong information? Getting it right is important to us all. Yet we often end up making judgments in that very fashion—based on wrong or incomplete data—particularly when we try to force connections between unsuitable data and the decisions we must make. We run into this trap when we look at existing data for answers simply because the data are there. Convenience is not the same as being correct. When we make this error, what we are doing is essentially limiting our range of sight to what is immediately in front of us, and the decisions that we make will be based on this limited range of sight. It is important to get and use the entire picture. You would want the same for yourself, and others are owed the big picture as well. Get the data, the whole set of data, and the right data.

## WHAT COUNTS AS DATA?

For purposes of evaluation, *data* can be any documented record of performance, of ends. It may be of something that took place during the period under study or took place at some other time but is relevant to the evaluation.

Data are what you want to collect in order to answer the evaluation questions you have agreed to answer. Data could include graduation rates, retention rates, instructors' notes, observers' records, incident reports, test scores, questionnaire results, school room temperature readings, tape recordings of learners in school, opinion polls of parents and teachers, test item analysis results of tests used in a program, and the like. These all meet the definition of data (i.e., these all could take place in the flow of events under study, or they are relevant to the study by some chain of logic or rationale).

By the way, do not confuse the term *data* (information that has been recorded and is useful for making decisions) with the *source* of information (things and events that must be observed). Some data will exist in documents and files already and some will have to be created from the observations in the evaluation study.

However, all data may not carry the same weight in reaching conclusions, and some data may be misleading due to bias of one kind or another. All data are about performance, but not all data are useful. One of your challenges is to make sure you get the right data about the right things.

Let's take a look at more things to consider about data.

## What Are the Characteristics of Data Used for Evaluation?

Sound decisions are made on the basis of data that are relevant (related to important questions we want to answer), reliable (consistent, measurable, and trustworthy), and valid (true indications of the results we want to measure). These data should come from measurable indicators of the results we want to accomplish.

Unfortunately, this is not always as easy as it sounds. In a typical educational evaluation investigation of any kind, there are bits and pieces of information flowing in all directions. We are awash in data, but the challenge is to pick the useful data from all of the data that exist. How do we separate the reliable, trustworthy, and valid information from the rumor, innuendo, misperceptions, and lies? When detective Joe Friday said, "Just give me the facts ma'am," he was requesting that only the relevant and verifiable information be provided. No fillers, no deceptions, no extraneous distracters. But often, the people we interview will not know what is relevant and what is not, and their recollections of events can be biased or just plain wrong. Our purpose in an evaluation is to gather relevant data that will stand up to scrutiny and that will answer our evaluation questions accurately and justifiably.

We will cover some of the tests for useful data, but first let us introduce our own—and important—definitions for the commonly misused terms: *hard data* and *soft data*. This simply means that we can divide our data sources into two kinds, and both are important if we are to do sensible, sensitive, and useful evaluation: if we are to find out what worked and what didn't in our educational enterprise.

*Hard Data*

While some people might think of *hard data* as just putting a number to something, we make the distinction that hard data are independently verifiable through multiple external sources; they are externally verifiable. Just having numbers does not make data hard. Have you ever encountered the phrase, "Figures don't lie, but liars do figure"? Hard data must consist of independently verifiable facts. Hard data consist of measurement data that quantify relevant information.

Evaluation—good evaluation—has some cautions, and the use of hard data is no exception. If you are going to perform statistical operations of numerical data, you must consider the scale of measurement used. If you gather nominal data and use a statistical routine that assumes *interval or ratio scales* (further discussed later in this chapter as well as in Chapter 6), it will lead to errors in interpretation. We commonly try to make evaluation measurements using interval or ratio scale terms, because statistical treatment is possible, and it allows the verifiable measurable results to be appropriately interpreted. Again, there will more details on this to help you later in this chapter and in Chapter 6.

*Soft Data*

Feelings, perceptions, and opinions are *soft data*. Soft data are important but cannot be independently verified and should not be the only source of evidence. Soft data are private.

Soft data can be supported by hard data to make evidence more robust. One example could be the anecdotal information that is collected from interviews, focus groups, and interviews. Soft data can be very useful when used as a way to get clues. The clues can be followed up with investigation that may uncover important facts. If we take care not to interpret opinions outside of the context in which they are relevant, the information can be valuable. For example, we may want to know what students think about the class they just completed. Their likes and dislikes may be useful for thinking about motivational issues, but we must take care not to confuse opinions about liking a class with the actual effectiveness of the method and whether or not they mastered content and became competent in that area. In this situation, opinions are only pointers that may help us form a hypothesis about the treatment that will be proved or disproved using additional investigation and hard data. The soft data about liking the class might give some cues to teachers about how to better present learning opportunities.

A valuable use of soft data is that they can support hard data. Soft data often reveal areas for further inquiry, which leads to sources for hard data yet to be collected. This cycle of investigation-discovery-further investigation-discovery can be a powerful one, as long as the focus on relevant, reliable, and valid data is maintained and as long as the focus remains on asking and answering the right evaluation questions. Do not fall in the trap of seeking data for their own sake, or because they are simply accessible, if they will not add significant value to your evaluation.

### Fact and Fiction

When are data considered to be true "facts," and when are they not true, or fictitious? What are facts anyway? Facts are statements about things that can be verified as true or false. This can lead to some distinctions normally the domain of lawyers, but it is also an important point for evaluators. If John Smith says something in an interview that turns out to be a lie, it is nevertheless a fact that John Smith made the statement. This in itself constitutes data and may—or may not—turn out to impact your overall findings. This may sound like splitting hairs, but it is at the very heart of converting soft data into hard data before acting on those data for making decisions about change and adjustments to programs. That is why data are subject to the following tests:

- The data must be verifiable by independent sources.
- The data must be free of hidden opinions and biases.
- The data collection chain of events must be unbroken as it moves to answer the basic evaluation questions.
- The data source must be reliable, trustworthy, and identified (not necessarily tracked to an individual by name, but supported by citing the source, e.g. student survey, teacher interview, and the like).
- Data consisting of opinions must be identified as opinions, as soft data.
- Data must be timely and up to date.
- Data must be relevant; they must relate to the evaluation questions.

Let's look at some more important evaluation considerations.

## Qualitative and Quantitative

Two related and essential terms, which refer to both data and the techniques used to collect them, are *qualitative* and *quantitative*. The *qualitative technique* requires careful and detailed observation and description, expressed through narrative rather than figures (McMillan, 1992). Qualitative techniques have been developed and improved by sociologists, who often use observation to understand what is happening. Early sociological work included standing on street corners and observing gangs, and talking with homemakers about the cuts of meat they bought and used.

Appropriate ways to collect qualitative data include observations, interviews, surveys, reviewing existing documents, and case studies. *Quantitative techniques* are used to establish facts objectively, to predict, and to show causal relationships. They are based on what people think, feel, and do.

For instance, Likert scale surveys, in which respondents are asked to select a response ranging from "strongly disagree" to "strongly agree" or ranging from "never" to "always," often have numbers associated with each response option. These numbers are then used to make computations, such as estimating the average response. Yet these numbers are merely symbols of a qualitative category; they do not represent real figures. Even if the right descriptive statistic is used to summarize the data, such as the median score (see Chapter 6), we must not forget that when we are dealing with opinions, there is an ever-present possibility that the person expressing the opinion may make statements that contain error. For example, if asked whether you like chocolate, your opinion can be taken as a good indicator of your like of a specific food item, but what if you were asked about a matter that is subject to independent verification? If you were asked to judge the weight of the man who was seen running from the bank, your opinion would likely contain some error. As a general rule, we ask for opinions on matters where the opinion is given about a topic that is relevant to the evaluation and where the information gained is about the person's likes and dislikes.

The distinction between qualitative and quantitative does not have to be black and white, either/or for the evaluator. If you start an evaluation with qualitative observation, that may help clarify unforeseen issues that develop in any study. More important, with a little work, qualitative information can be augmented with quantitative information. Qualitative opinions can be gathered and counted. Just think of the importance of polling in election years where the quantitative statistics often are the basis for campaign decisions. (This is something not altogether unfamiliar to elected school board leaders.) Opinions and soft data can guide us in making useful decisions, but we should always realize that it is best if we can get agreement between the soft data and the hard data.

## THE RELATIONSHIP BETWEEN
## DATA AND METHOD OF DATA COLLECTION

The data you collect are a function of the methods you select. A problem can arise, however, if evaluators limit the data they collect by employing an overly narrow set of observation methods based on the way it has always been done and/or personal preference.

A central point of this book is that the methodology of data collection is selected to generate the information required to answer your evaluation questions and not the other way around. You will not have unlimited resources at your disposal. You do not want to end up gathering too much irrelevant data and too little meaningful data because you have run out of time and money. What data should you try to gather?

You cannot gather all possible data generated in a school setting. Nor should you. Fortunately, you should target only the data that will provide answers to the evaluation questions. If you follow our advice on the basic question set, you will reduce the chance of missing relevant data or collecting data that will not help make better decisions and get better results. The most important thing is that data collection tools and methods support the collection of the required data and the required data will be relevant to answering the evaluation question set. It is an error to pick the tools first and then be limited by the data that the tools will generate. Some evaluators, like Mohr (1992), limit the focus of their studies to the impact analysis of just one result per program. In his words, Mohr does not consider the worthwhileness of the program in order to concentrate on the logical relationship between the program and the selected result. What is for some the gain of precision in describing relationships is for others the avoidance of the central issue. Our emphasis, for example, argues that the prime criterion for evaluation is the worthwhileness of the program as the program meets valid needs. This is a case where the desire for precision (and avoidance of political considerations) has narrowed the methodology and the focus of the evaluation study. Other evaluators, like Stake (2004), cast a wider net and have adopted methodologies that allow for the inclusion of controversy, politics, and fairness to multiple stakeholders and side effects. Pick your methods on the basis of what will best answer your evaluation questions, not on

> **Observation Methods**
>
> *Person Centered:* Direct observation–participation, nonparticipation, interviewing, focus groups, town meetings.
>
> *Instrument Centered:* Testing, questionnaires, surveys.
>
> *Treatment Centered:* Experiments, simulations, task forces.
>
> *Document Centered:* Records review, literature review.

convenience or the way other people do evaluation. It is your evaluation, your educational system, and your recommendations that are vital.

There are two ways to classify data collection, by method and by source. Let's start with method.

## Data Collection Methods

### Direct Primary-Source Data

Data that are observed directly from the source, as in a firsthand account of a witness or test scores gathered directly after the test was taken, are desirable because the distortion and error created by translation or transmission are reduced. One consideration is to record the data and keep track of them, with no gaps between the original observation and the use of the data later on for analysis and conclusion. The legal system imposes "rules of evidence" to ensure that testimony and other evidence are authentic and unchanged as they are presented at trial. Evaluators have a similar duty to preserve the integrity of the data. Primary-source data can include notes from direct observation, test scores from tests taken by the population in question and during the evaluation study period, and measurements that are current and relevant.

> **Observation Sources**
>
> *Primary-Source Data* are gathered as events unfold, by the evaluation staff, from participants, or from firsthand observers.
>
> Evaluators try to maintain a direct chain of custody between observed events and recorded information.
>
> Observation cross-checks control error.
>
> *Secondary-Source Data* are obtained from secondhand accounts. The events reported on may not be current.
>
> Data from indicators can be useful by having a demonstrated relationship with the phenomena in question.

### Secondary-Source Data

Secondary-source data are not observed directly. One common type of indirect data is the use of *indicators.* The temperature this morning at the local airport gives us an idea of what the temperature is in the city, and it is not precisely the same as measuring at city hall, but it is close enough for us to figure out how warm it is where we are.

Indicators are observable phenomena that are linked to something that is not directly observed. Indicators can provide information that will answer an evaluation question without forcing us to collect more specific data.

Indicators may be used to deal with constructs like "self-sufficiency" or a "healthy school environment" or "good quality of life." The evaluator must take pains to show that the use of indicators in any evaluation study bears a reliable and valid relationship with the thing being indicated. This is not unlike the requirement for test items to be reliable and valid measures of the construct or quality being measured in the test.

### Measurement Data

Measurement data result when evaluators intend to add precision to any of the observation methods by using one of the four measurement scales. It is important to recognize that all forms of data resulting from all forms of observation are potentially subject to measurement.

### Measurement Error

The precision that measurement adds to the data-gathering and data usefulness process can, if we are not mindful, be offset by measurement error. Undetected measurement error can lead to erroneous conclusions and biased findings. We have listed several references in the "References" section of this book that cover the subject of measurement error, especially in test construction and interpretation. We would like to point out that rigorous measurement can (and should) be applied to all observation methods. This means that the possibility of measurement error can be present in each method:

- Direct observation of classroom behavior where observers tabulate student behavior in reaction to lessons presented is subject to human error due to fatigue.
- Collection of data using the wrong scale and then manipulating the data by statistical routines can produce error.
- Tests may have errors in relation to construct validity.
- Using a sample size that is too small can confound certain statistics.

### Scales of Measurement

One of they key things to consider in collecting data is the appropriate level of measurement. There are four levels of measurement: *nominal, ordinal, interval,* and *ratio,* each with its own utility and precision. Table 4.1 illustrates the unique characteristics of each scale, along with some examples.

Nominal and ordinal data are usually associated with qualitative data, while internal and ratio data are referred to as quantitative data. While all these levels are valid for their own purposes, nominal and ordinal

**Table 4.1**   Scales of Measurement and Their Characteristics

| Scale | Characteristics | Examples |
|---|---|---|
| Nominal | • Used for labeling or describing<br>• Categories are mutually exclusive<br>• No value or order is placed on categories | • Gender<br>• Ethnicity<br>• Educational level<br>• Job classification |
| Ordinal | • More precise than nominal<br>• Used for ranking<br>• No assumptions of measurable and equal distance between the categories (i.e., ordinal data can measure the order, but not the degree of separation between the categories) | • Likert scales ranging from "strongly disagree" to "strongly agree"<br>• Arranging response options from "most preferred" to "least preferred"<br>• Arranging response options from "most important" to "least important" (e.g., 1, 2, 3, 4, 5, etc., or A, B, C, D, E, F, etc.)<br>• Arranging response options from high to low |
| Interval | • Can also be used to rank order.<br>• Distance between the categories is known—the degree of separation, or distance, between two consecutive points is the same no matter where in the scale (e.g., the distance between 2 and 3 is the same as between 17 and 18)<br>• No absolute 0 point (i.e., a value of 0 does not imply the absolute absence of something) | • Test scores<br>• Temperature in Celsius or Fahrenheit |
| Ratio | • Includes characteristics of the previous level<br>• In addition, has an absolute 0 point | • Money<br>• Distance<br>• Weight<br>• Temperature in Kelvin |

scale measurements are not as rigorous as we would like for practical and useful educational evaluation. The more consistently we can measure something on an interval or ratio scale, the more confidence we may have in those data.

**Table 4.2**    Question-to-Observation Matrix

| | | |
|---|---|---|
| Question: Did the school board establish the reading curriculum based on a needs assessment? | Data Required: paper trail evidence and testimony of key personnel. | Collection Method: review documents and interview key personnel. |
| Question: What skills are required on the part of teachers who will use the new reading program? | Data required: skills and knowledge required to implement as specified by the program designer. | Collection Methods: review program material and interview program designers, observe teachers as they implement the program. |
| Question: Did the reading program achieve learning objectives? | Data Required: scores on standardized reading test. | Collection Method: administer the test and record scores. |
| Question: Is the new reading program cost-effective? | Data Required: all program costs and results. | Collection Method: review cost records and student scores. This can be compared to past program data. |
| Question: Are there any harmful side effects of the new program? | Data Required: student feedback, teacher feedback, parents' feedback, and observations of the program in use. | Collection Methods: interviews, direct observation, and questionnaires. |

*Matching Evaluation Questions to Inquiry Method*

Using the tools of *needs assessment*—identifying and prioritizing gaps in results—and the OEM, you have examined the specific situation for the school system, the goals, objectives, and the programs set in place to achieve the goals and objectives. From this point on, you can focus on gathering data that will answer each question that relates to the results obtained and the organizational factors that produced them. We suggest that you build a question-to-observation matrix (see Table 4.2) to help you organize and manage the evaluation process. Any study that you design will no doubt include more questions than the example, but the principle of matching the question to the method is shown.

## Data Sources

Another important issue to consider before collecting data is determining where you will find the data. Data can be found from a variety of financial, social, political, and technological sources. Data can be found in school records, teacher records, standardized and teacher-constructed tests, and incidents in classes and school grounds. Today, our access to data is unprecedented. The Internet and advances in telecommunications and other technologies allow us to link to reports, documents, databases, experts, and other sources as never before possible. Educational accountability[1] has given rise to mountains of data, mountains of data that are not always useful.

For example, social indicators such as those related to quality of life (average income levels, divorce rates, crime levels, and the like) can often be found in chamber of commerce archives, census reports, police records, and community quality-of-life reports, many of which are available electronically. Others, such as those related to the environment (pollution, corporate toxic waste, etc.), could also be obtained from the Environmental Protection Agency (EPA), as well as from studies published in scientific journals. A number of other government agencies and research institutions, nationally and internationally, also publish a series of official studies and reports that could prove to be valuable sources of data.

In many cases, you can find the data that you are looking for in your own organization. Existing records about past and current performance may already be available, but collected by different parties in your organization and for different reasons. Be sure to thoroughly search for these potential sources, as it could save valuable time, money, and other resources.

Other sources may include people: students, administrators, teachers, vendors, experts on a given issue, test scores, reported behavior or health incidents, and the like.

*Confidentiality:* One of the potential issues in getting access to data is confidentiality. If you are denied access altogether, there may be a way around this. If it is not important to collect individually identifying data, then aggregate data (e.g., averages, totals, etc.) should do the trick and present little to no obstacle to gather.

### Defining Required Data From Performance Objectives

One of our first and prime sources for deriving useful evaluation questions is our list of performance objectives. These performance objectives should have been the product of a *needs assessment* process, in which each of the needs identified and selected for reduction were clearly stated as performance objectives. Recall that based on the OEM, these needs represent

**Figure 4.1**    Process Flow for Required Data Definition,
Assuring Flow and Linkage

| | Needs Assessment | | | | Evaluation |
|---|---|---|---|---|---|
| OEM Level | What Should Be → | What Is → | Gap → | Objectives → | Evaluation Questions → |
| Mega | | | | | |
| Macro | | | | | |
| Micro | | | | | |
| Processes | | | | | |
| Input | | | | | |

| | Evaluation | | | |
|---|---|---|---|---|
| OEM Level | Evaluation Questions → | Indicator(s)/ Required Data → | Data Source → | Data Collection Tools/Procedures → |
| Mega | | | | |
| Macro | | | | |
| Micro | | | | |
| Processes | | | | |
| Input | | | | |

gaps at three levels of organizational results, and quasi-needs represent gaps in Processes and Inputs. The overall Process flow would look like that shown on Figure 4.1.

For instance, if our desired state is a 100% successful completion rate for a given educational program by the end of Year X, and during the *needs assessment* we found the current state to be at 85%, then that gap, 85/100, would become the basis for our performance objectives as such:

*By the end of Year X, the ABC Program will increase successful completion rate by 15%, as indicated by the Annual Program Report prepared by the Office for Performance Records.*

Thus the evaluation questions we ask should be driven primarily by the objectives we set out to achieve. The evaluation question for the objective above would look something like this:

*Did the ABC Program increase successful completion rate by 15% at the end of Year X?*

So, our tables above may start to be populated as in Figure 4.2.

**Figure 4.2**    Example of Process Flow for Required Data Definition

| | Needs Assessment | | | | Evaluation |
| --- | --- | --- | --- | --- | --- |
| OEM Level | What Should Be ⟶ | What Is ⟶ | Gap ⟶ | Objectives ⟶ | Evaluation Questions ⟶ |
| Mega | | | | | |
| Macro | 100% completion rate | 85% | 15% | By the end of Year X, the ABC Program will increase successful completion rate by 15%, as indicated by the Annual Program Report prepared by the Office for Performance Records. | Did the ABC Program increase successful completion rate by 15% at the end of Year X? |
| Micro | | | | | |
| Processes | | | | | |
| Input | | | | | |

| | Evaluation | | | |
| --- | --- | --- | --- | --- |
| OEM Level | Evaluation Questions ⟶ | Indicator(s)/ Required Data ⟶ | Data Source ⟶ | Data Collection Tools/ Procedures ⟶ |
| Mega | | | | |
| Macro | Did the ABC Program increase successful completion rate by 15% at the end of Year X? | Completion records | Academic Records, Office Database | Review of extant data |
| Micro | | | | |
| Processes | | | | |
| Input | | | | |

As we have discussed before, all organizations are after results. Furthermore, results should be identified and aligned at all levels of the organization. If properly planned and conducted, the *needs assessment*, as proposed by the OEM, should have provided the evaluation framework— that is, created a list of objectives for each identified need at each level of result, along with the supporting Processes and Inputs required to deliver those results. Results, however (particularly when stated as general goals), cannot always be directly measured and may require the careful identification of metrics that indicate whether or not such results have been measured. Once again, those metrics already should have been identified during the needs assessment.

## Using the OEM to Develop Measurable Indicators

Indicators can form an important part of your data collection because they are observable and measurable phenomenon that tell you something about the programs being evaluated. Indicators must, however, bear a constant relationship to the thing being indicated. They must be reliable and valid, just as tests must be reliable and valid. Using indicators that are developed by disciplined *needs assessment* and that are derived using the structure of the OEM will tend to meet those criteria. Here is an example of a set of indicators developed from a vocational rehabilitation program. Table 4.3 illustrates this process from an earlier stage and in a more detailed fashion. This table was actually derived during a *needs assessment* phase and thus became the basic data collection framework for both the *needs assessment* itself and the evaluation phase down the road. This example is taken from an education-related area: the Florida Division of Blind Services that are intended, like conventional education, to provide people with the skills, knowledge, attitudes, and abilities to be self-sufficient and self-reliant.

The first step in this project was to identify all required results at every organizational level, and then the Processes and Inputs required for the attainment of such results. To that end, a review of the procedures manual, policies and regulations, and discussions by the stakeholders was conducted. A top-down approach was taken by identifying the most comprehensive results, or Outcomes: societal self-sufficiency,[2] self-reliance,[3] and quality of life of current and possible clients (see Table 4.3).

Table 4.4 is a higher-education illustration of strategic—Mega-level— linkage. The Sonora Institute of Technology (Instituto Tecnico de Sonora, or ITSON, a Mexican university) has been using the OEM model as its framework for planning, assessment, and evaluation since 1993. The city of Cuidad Obregon, home to ITSON, thanks in large measure to this

*(Text continues on p. 102)*

**Table 4.3**    Vocational Rehabilitation Program

| OEM Level | Result | Some Indicators |
|---|---|---|
| MEGA[a] (Societal) LEVEL RESULTS | Self-Sufficiency Self-Reliance Quality of Life (QOL) | • Government transfer payments<br>• Private disability payment<br>• Worker's compensation<br>• Insurance compensation<br>• Institutionalization where the participants are $C \leq P$[b] (e.g., sheltered workshops, mental hospitals, drug abuse treatment centers, etc.) |
| | Continued Employment at $C < P$ level | • Income (itemized benefits + expenses) over time<br>• Employment catchment area cost of living or higher<br>• Annual earnings rate > general population |
| MACRO (Organizational) LEVEL RESULTS | Successful Competitive Employment | • Employed a minimum of 90 days full-time or part-time Integrated work setting (based on Integrated Plan of Employment objectives)<br>• Benefits for Visually Impaired = those for non-VI (benefits = health, vision, dental, life, disability, other)<br>• Job skills, knowledge, attitudes, and abilities (SKAAs) requirement and client SKAAs matched<br>• Employee satisfaction with employment at 5 or higher on 7-point Likert scale survey<br>• Employer satisfaction with employee at 5 or higher on 7-point Likert scale survey |
| | Successful Self-Employment or Integration into Homemaker Role, Bureau of Business Enterprise, or Homemaker | • Setting certified as fulfilling requirements of IPE by rehabilitation counselor<br>• Client satisfaction with situation at 5 or higher on 7-point Likert scale survey |
| MICRO (Team/ Individual) LEVEL RESULTS | Attainment of Individual Plan for Employment (IPE) Objectives | • SKAAs attained<br>• Activities of Daily Living training completed[c]<br>• Vocational training completed |

*(Continued)*

**Table 4.3** (Continued)

| OEM Level | Result | Some Indicators |
|---|---|---|
| | | <ul><li>Postsecondary education completed</li><li>On-the-job integrated training completed<ul><li>– Social preparation for integration setting completed</li><li>– Socialization completed</li><li>– Socialization training completed</li></ul></li><li>Recreational training completed</li><li>Management of medical treatments</li><li>Job placement obtained</li></ul> |
| | **Central Processes Involved** | |
| PROCESS LEVEL | Developing IPEs | <ul><li>Listing all options and steps for individual to complete IPE</li><li>Determining client strengths, priorities, concerns, abilities, capabilities, career interests</li><li>Determining client currently used SKAAs</li><li>Facilitating client informed choice of services, service providers, and vocational goal</li><li>Determining all physical/mental restorative measures</li><li>Approving plan</li></ul> |
| | Implementing IPEs | <ul><li>Delivering services as outlined on IPE</li><li>Scheduling and carrying out Progress Reviews (annually at minimum)</li><li>Amending plan as required</li></ul> |
| | Determining Eligibility (These are the processes involved. If completed to criterion levels, they become Products.) | **Determining Ineligible Criteria That Might Be Used**<ul><li>No bilateral eye pathology as certified by MD[d]</li><li>Individual has no impediment to employment</li><li>Individual does not require VR services</li><li>Individual cannot benefit from VR[e] services because disability is too severe as evidenced by trial work experience and extended evaluation</li><li>Referring individual to appropriate agency</li></ul> |

| OEM Level | Result | Some Indicators |
|-----------|--------|-----------------|
| | | **Determining Eligible Criteria**<br><br>• Determining Bilateral VI[f]/ Determining Bilateral VI as primary disability/ Determining Bilateral VI as impediment to employment<br>• Determining individual to require VR services to obtain employment<br><br>**Not Determining Eligibility**<br><br>• Unable to locate<br>• Refused services for one<br>• Uncooperativeness<br>• Death<br>• Institutionalization<br>• Moving<br>• Referral to appropriate agency |
| | | **Key Resources Involved** |
| INPUTS LEVEL | | • Applicant histories<br>• Medical records<br>• Applicant work histories<br>• Educational histories<br>• SSA records<br>• Counselor observations<br>• Economic situation (including transfer payments)<br>• Individual and family information<br>• Client input<br>• Training reports<br>• Work reviews<br>• Trial work experiences<br>• Career/interest inventories<br>• Vocational assessment<br>• Labor market<br>• FDBS policies and procedures<br>• Funding for medical treatments<br>• Federal and state rules, regulations, and laws<br>• Referrals to FDBS<br>• Community resources<br>• Transportation |

*(Continued)*

**Table 4.3** (Continued)

| OEM Level | Result | Some Indicators |
|---|---|---|
| | | • Housing<br>• Community Rehabilitation Programs (CRP)<br>• DBS human resources<br>• Levels of federal and state funding |

a. This example builds on Mega, such as the level of graduates/completers/leavers who are self-sufficient and self-reliant. This Mega-level in the chart thus is not completed here.

b. "C" is Consumption, and "P" is Production. This equation reads, "Costs will be equal to or less than production." This is a basic indicator of economic viability.

c. This and others are Micro because they are only one possible result among many required for adding value at the Macro- and Mega-levels.

d. Medical Doctor.

e. Vocational Rehabilitation.

f. Visual Impairment.

university, is a rapidly developing town. ITSON has embraced its responsibility in improving the city by not only focusing on education but also on the economy, health, culture, and other community and society system elements that interact to deliver the vision of the institution. The indicators listed below are only a sample of the complete framework, and these are limited to the Mega, Macro, and Micro results in the academic area.

As we move toward the furthermost column on the right, you can see how the precision with which the organization defines the results to be pursued increases, and thus the precision or the efforts (including the strategically driven allocation of our very limited resources!) to achieve them, and furthermore, the precision with which the organization can measure whether or not it achieved them. It is this kind of rigor, articulation, and linkages that provide strategic alignment.

Since these indicators will become the basis for the data collection plan, making such linkages is at the core of our proposed approach to *needs assessment* and evaluation. Our view of reality (e.g., what is actually going on with our programs, internally and externally) will be framed by these indicators, and thus it is critical that we ensure they are in fact fair and complete indicators of the results we want to achieve. This requires the active engagement of the entire team (i.e., evaluators, administrators, instructors/teachers, support staff, program participants, and the whole education team). The more perspectives that serve as Input, the more accurate the picture we paint will likely be.

**Table 4.4**    ITSON Sample Indicators

| OEM Level | Result | Some Indicators |
|---|---|---|
|  | • Self-Sufficiency<br>• Self-Reliance<br>• Quality of Life (QOL)<br>• Continued Employment at C < P[a] level | • Optimal Employment (i.e., graduate working in the field for which he/she studied) within 6 months of graduation<br>• Earned Income trend over a 7-year period<br>• Employer Satisfaction Index<br>• Continued employment<br>  o Local<br>  o Out of town<br>  o Income Trend (slope)<br>• Subemployment<br><br>All further analyzed according to:<br>  o Gender<br>  o Age<br>  o Social/economic class<br>  o Father's occupation<br>  o Parents' education<br>  o Marital status<br>  o Single parent<br>  o Divorced<br>  o Disease, health |
| Macro | Graduation | • Graduation rate<br>• Number of dropouts (first-year deserters)<br>  o Number of dropouts who are making same or more than when they started<br>• Number of noncompleters (complete first 2 years)<br>  o Number of noncompleters who are making same or more than when they started<br>• Number of years for completion |
| Micro | Program Completion<br>Course Completion | • Completion rate per program<br>• Dropout rate per program<br>• Completion rate per course<br>• Dropout rate per course |

a. "C" is Consumption, and "P" is Production.

One thing worth noting here is that while we want as complete a list of indicators as possible, data may not be available for each and every one of them. This in itself is important information! It is very difficult to determine whether or not something is being achieved, done, or used if we have no data upon which to base such determinations. In turn, if we don't have data to make those determinations, how do we make sound decisions about what to keep, what to modify, or what to abandon? Thus this ideal list of indicators can also serve as Input for making decisions about what additional data should be tracked from that point forward, and how. Just tracking key data alone can be a powerful tool for improvement. If taken seriously, it can increase awareness, promote accountability, increase motivation, facilitate just-in-time feedback, and so on.

Our specific performance objectives, and thus evaluation questions from which they derive, will come from indicators. For example, did we increase the number of program participants whose income is equal or greater than the general population? Did we decrease the number of program participants requiring government transfer payments? Questions such as these flow directly from the objectives and their rigorous performance criteria.

In the context of an evaluation, it is also possible that not every single indicator requires a related evaluation question. If no gaps were found for a given indicator during the *needs assessment* process and thus no "solutions" implemented in response, then those indicators are not central to our evaluation efforts (though at times it may be important to consider what "unintended" effects a given solution may have had on other areas).[4]

Of course, there is still work to do in-between identifying the right indicators/data and actually collecting them. One must identify the data sources. It does us little good to identify which data we should be collecting if we don't also find out where to collect the data (if they are being collected at all, which is an important finding in and of itself!). The evaluation team members should together be able to provide excellent leads as to where these data might be found. The section on data sources later in this chapter will provide further information.

Last, additional evaluation questions may arise as a result of the preliminary findings of the evaluation. For example, if results reveal that a particular result is not being achieved, the obvious related question is, "Why not?" Thus specific follow-up questions that get at the causes for not reaching our targets will likely have to be derived and answered before the data findings are fully interpreted.

Several tasks must be completed before any data can actually be collected:

1. Make a data collection plan that identifies the data required to answer each of the evaluation questions (not to be confused with the overall evaluation plan, which is broader in scope and includes the data collection plan).

2. Identify the sources of the data and the type of data that you will collect.

3. Obtain and learn how to use any data collection tools/methods required to obtain desired data.

4. Prepare a data collection schedule. The issue of alignment will once again come into play: how to get all of the important questions and related data to tie together for a coherent whole. The type of data sought should play a central role in the selection of appropriate data collection vehicles.

## PUTTING IT ALL TOGETHER: THE DATA COLLECTION PLAN

Now that we have discussed the various issues to consider in collecting useful and relevant data, you should have a fairly good idea of how these pieces fit together into the data collection plan. However, in the event that there are still some doubts, the matrix in Figure 4.3 should serve as a job

**Figure 4.3**    Data Collection Organization Matrix

| Questions | Related Results | Level (i.e., Mega, Macro, Micro) | Required Data/ Measurable Indicators | Data Source | Data Collection Tools/ Procedures | Data Collected By (Date) | Primary Responsibility |
|---|---|---|---|---|---|---|---|
|  |  |  |  |  |  |  |  |
|  |  |  |  |  |  |  |  |

SOURCE: © From Guerra, I. (2003). Asking and Answering the Right Questions: Collecting Relevant and Useful Data. *Performance Improvement*, 42(10), 24–28.

aid for creating a data collection plan. With the exception of the sixth column, "Data Collection Tools and Procedures" (Chapter 5), the matrix summarizes and links all the key elements to consider in the general data collection plan, as discussed in this chapter. Certainly, each row will require its own detailed plan, depending on the where, how, and when of that given indicator/data.

## NOTES

1. Unfortunately, some have distorted "educational accountability" to "educational countability," and this has resulted in lots of data points without much coherent organization of those data for answering important planning and evaluation questions. For example, the number of program participants is not a key indicator of program effectiveness.

2. The principal indicator of *self-sufficiency* is an individual's consumption being less than or equal to their production ($C \leq P$).

3. *Self-reliance* refers to an individual being independent of the care, custody, or control of any other individual or organization.

4. Just because no needs—gaps in results—emerge does not mean that critical areas can be ignored. One important role for evaluation is to track progress and performance to ensure that no gaps—needs—emerge in vital areas.

# Collecting the Data 5

Y ou cannot find what you do not look for. And it pays to also be looking for useful things: to ask and answer the right questions. Observation can, but does not always, result in meaningful data collection. You must become aware of what to look for and the many ways of looking.

We share some formal and informal techniques, but the most important thing is that you develop a coherent approach that is efficient yet comprehensive and fruitful. Some kinds of data can be gathered by direct observation, and some kinds of data are produced by using tests and data collection procedures. The *efficiency* of evaluation depends on the resources and methods expended to get data. The *effectiveness* of evaluation depends on what you choose to obtain so that the evaluation questions will be answered with validity and confidence.

Once key evaluation questions have been identified, the evaluation team must gather data that will lead to reasonable and responsible answers. In this chapter, we describe the most common and useful approaches to data collection in more detail and include a discussion of the strong and weak points of each method. This will be organized in the following way:

- General description of the method
- Strong points and advantages
- Weak points and disadvantages
- Measurement considerations

This section will provide an overview of the options for data collection available to you and will discuss the advantages and disadvantages of each. This information will serve you well as you consider each option in the context of your own evaluation project. However, in addition to these inherent advantages and disadvantages, you should also consider factors such as the characteristics of your sample, time, cost and budget,

> The set of questions you ask determines the data required to answer them. The data required determine the method of observation. This chapter is about observation methods.

comprehensiveness, past experience with a given instrument, and feasibility, among others.

Also very worth noting is that successful data collection depends in great part on the support and/or sponsorship of key stakeholders. If all of the educational partners agree with the evaluation questions and what value there will be for improvement of the system if they are answered properly, then cooperation will greet you.

## OBSERVATION METHODOLOGY AND THE GOAL OF MEASUREMENT

Before we cover the methods for data collection, let us make the point one more time that all methods include some form of measurement. Measurement is the application of some form of scale to count something as a result of observation and data collection. The data can come from events that produce clear numbers, like instrument readings, or less precise things, like opinions, judgments, and impressions based on firsthand observation. Sometimes the terms *hard* and *soft* are used to distinguish between these two ideas of data. Our point is that both forms can yield measurement. But the application of measurement to data is not automatic or easy. You have to work at it, and while it is not an automatic feature of observation, it should be your goal in every evaluation. For example, in an evaluation where several opinions have been gathered, the things to measure may not at first be apparent. But with some analysis and understanding of the situation, you can begin to count the number of times a specific problem has been referred to by the people being interviewed. You can note the length of time they dwell on aspects of their story. At some point, you may even devise a checklist to assist you in recording quantifiable aspects of the interview. To make our point on measurement clear, we have devised some simple rules to help clear up confusion and provide clear guidance.

- Every observation can be reduced to measurement.
- Rigorous measurement makes comparison more precise and meaningful—the more rigorous and precise the measurement, the more confidence you can have in the measurement.
- Not all measurements make sense—*what* you are measuring is primary.
- Pay attention to measurement scales; select the right scale based on the nature of the data you collect.

### Process and Results Evaluation Data

There are two types of measurements that you will likely want: process and results. Data relating to results is the prime focus of an evaluation. Data gathered on the processes, or activity—how things are going—is a second focus of an evaluation.

Process evaluation may be done while any program or intervention is going on, but only to check and make sure that things are operating properly. Process evaluation data are also useful after results data are collected and available. Process data will support analysis and decision making in the event the results are not what was intended in order for us to meet the needs—gaps in results—identified during planning.

A third variety of data that is really "process" data may be gathered on factors and issues that intervene to support or detract from the program or project educational activities or venture. Indirect effects such as bad weather, sudden budget supplement or reduction, equipment breakdown, and other disruptions fall into this category. This environmental data will also be used in the analysis of the results and decision making to modify, keep, or discard the educational program that is being evaluated: What do we keep and what do we change?

## PERSON-CENTERED DIRECT-OBSERVATION METHODS

A popular organization text featured a management technique called "managing by walking around" (Peters & Waterman, 1982), in which the manager stays on top of the operation by getting out into the field, the shop floor, the cubicles, or the production lines to see directly what is taking place and to chat with workers. We suggest that "evaluation by walking around" be included in your inventory of methods.

Direct observation has a few variations. One variation is to participate in activities and get to know what is going on from the participant's point of view. Social scientists call this approach "participant observation." It has some good points and some possible drawbacks. Participants tend to identify with the personnel who can lead to insider information, but at the same time, the participant observer may be co-opted by the group, which can bias observations made in this way. Nonparticipant observation can also have some risk, because the mere presence of an outsider (especially an evaluator) can change the conditions in the observation setting. A stranger who slips into a classroom unannounced and just stands at the back of the room will no doubt make the teacher nervous and the students uneasy. Direct observation options are valuable and can be free of fear if a little common courtesy is afforded the persons under the looking glass. Start by arranging to make the visit ahead of time, and visit often to ease the tension and gain the trust of those involved. Be candid, open, and honest. Your credibility is at stake and so is the credibility of the data you collect.

## Classroom Observation

Classroom observation is a way of gathering data on day-to-day events in the teaching and learning environment. Traditional classroom observation does not involve active participation in classroom events. The observer can watch events unfold, take notes, and make passive recordings, but the observer does not ask questions, interrupt activities, or control events. It is helpful for the observer to list categories of what they are looking for, such as interactions, participation, tone of language, distractions, and other variables that might be important data relating to the evaluation questions.

Observation as a method for gathering data can be very broadly defined, as in Adler and Adler (1994), where they described observation as "gathering impressions of the surrounding world through all relevant human faculties" (p. 378). The practical extension of this definition is that it recognizes that in many cases, the evaluator can be an effective data collection vehicle that can take in the total environment and respond to any event contingency without prior mind-set or data collection instrument that can limit observation potential. The mind-set that is created by preset expectations can be problematic if it prevents us from detecting other aspects of the educational setting that contribute to or detract from student learning.

- *General description of the method:* An observer stands or sits quietly observing class activity without taking part. The observer may take notes.

- *Strong points and advantages:* The observer can encounter the unexpected, change observation schedule and focus, and get a firsthand account of events.

- *Weak points and disadvantages:* The presence of an observer can be disruptive or change the climate of the classroom; the observer must contend with his or her own bias.

- *Measurement considerations:* The observer can begin observations without imposing structure but can progress as issues develop to focus on specific themes and behavior that can be counted and incorporated into data sets that can be statistically manipulated. Tools exist to assist, that structure observations, and assist in data presentation (see below).

Scriven (1973) coined the term "goal-free evaluation" to prevent the sometimes narrow objectives becoming the only focus of evaluation. *Goal-free evaluation* is when one looks at what happened, both in terms of processes and results, without knowing about the existing goals and objectives. By doing so, the evaluator is not limited to what purposes were supposed to be accomplished, but looks objectively only at what happened. This type of evaluation can be very powerful, for it lets the evaluator know about the unexpected without being confined to the existing objectives. We, of course, want evaluators to look at objectives and the results, but at the same time, we do not want to be limited to preestablished objectives and intentions. Goal-free evaluation provides an after-the-intervention set of data that show things that did arise unexpectedly, especially where it is relevant to the reasons why objectives were obtained or not. We can learn useful things from both the data relative to existing objectives as well as from those free of the existing objectives.

During normal direct observation in the classroom, what is noticed provides the evaluator with firsthand knowledge of what is going on, and direct observation can be flexible and responsive to the situation. Unexpected events can be noted. Subsequent observation opportunities can be focused based on developing trends and issues. However, these advantages are counterbalanced by some limitations.

### To Be or Not to Be Obtrusive

Observations can either be "obtrusive," when individuals being observed are aware they are being observed, or "unobtrusive," when individuals being observed are not aware they are being observed. The key is to have a well-defined purpose for observation. Some classrooms may be equipped with observation rooms that have one-way mirrors. After some time, students do get used to the possibility of being observed, and the effects become submerged in the classroom events. If observers take the time to inform teachers and students and observe often, the intrusive nature of the observation visit is reduced over time. Try to make classroom observation a regular part of the school activities, and never let information learned from classroom observations become part of the gossip in the school setting.

### To Structure or Not to Structure Observation

After several observations visits, you may want to narrow the focus to look for specific behavior. You can use observation *rubrics,* such as a behavior checklist, which can aid the observer in recording and measuring specific predetermined behaviors. These can be designed to record whether the behaviors occurred at all (e.g., "yes" or "no"), as a rating scale, or frequency count, depending on what is appropriate for the behaviors being observed. While observations may be conducted without highly structured observation guides that specify beforehand what indicators to look for, the increase in precision and accuracy that results from a structured approach tends to make up for the limits in range that are imposed. This, of course, presupposes that the targeted information is justified by its relevance to an evaluation question.

### The Use of Observation Tools

Today, it is hard to escape the use of computers. We do not resist the use of this modern tool, as long as you use it wisely and realize that the use of a computer does not guarantee that your data will be more valid or more credible. The computer does only what you tell it to do, so it is no better than what you put into it. What the computer does offer is enormous efficiency that is hard to pass up. Observation programs are now available on CD that help you structure the recording of information and also provide for storage and reporting of the data, noting time, place, and other information that will be required for later analysis. (See Steel, 2004, *Teacher Evaluation Works* CD.)

### Controls on Classroom Observation

Two serious problems can arise from classroom observation. These are (1) the observations can be tainted by observer bias, and (2) the observer can incorrectly classify instances of classroom behavior that are called out on structured checklists.

The first problem is controlled by making sure that each evaluator is questioned by the team in order to eliminate any candidate observers who have obvious bias or bigotry, sexism, or racism. These types of bias have no place in an evaluation study. However, we all have many hidden, perhaps unconscious, biases that may color our observations. That bias can be controlled by using more than one observer and cross-checking findings, called "inter-rater reliability." Periodic discussions of observation findings can clarify emerging issues and weed out irrelevant data and bring issues into clear focus. There is always room for good objective thinking. Leading such discussion takes skill and patience. Not every evaluation leader, because of temperament and personality, can perform this function. So, we caution you to keep a healthy skepticism alive as you accept observation data into your study.

The second problem is controlled by carefully examining the checklist and limiting the categories of behavior to observable performance. For example, when observing a class that is attempting to foster such "constructs" as creativity and initiative to gifted students, observers may differ on what they think is creative behavior and who is more or less gifted. These labels or classifications are laden with what philosophers call "surplus meaning." Recorded instances using these constructs may prove to be unreliable across observers. On the other hand, it is relatively easy for observers to note with more consistency specific behaviors like frequency of raising a hand to answer a question, frequency of the use of different tools or props to arrive at a solution to a problem, different approaches to problem solving, and the like. Note however, that the operational definitions used— defining things in terms of what measures are used to create them—must be proven over time to add up to the construct in question.

## Participant Observation

Participant observation is a method of data gathering used in the field of sociology mainly for observation, discovery, and description. It is increasingly being used by evaluators to gain insight into groups and organizations in their natural settings. When program evaluators sense that something is going on inside a program that is not immediately apparent to the outsider, they may try this method to find out what is really going on.

- *General description of the method:* An observer who can function as a member of a group works alongside other members to perform tasks and engage in normal communication with group members. The observer then reports insights, problems, and event descriptions to the evaluation team.

- *Strong points and advantages:* The observer may find out important behind-the-scenes information and uncover practices that are hidden from outsiders. The observer may gain the trust of other members and learn their point of view.

- *Weak points and disadvantages:* The observer may be rejected by the group or co-opted by the group, loosing a sense of balance and objective reporting. The method takes a considerable investment in time and resources.

- *Measurement considerations:* The observer may find events and behavior that can be counted, and construct tables and matrices comparing productivity, resource utilization, and other interactions between members and members and outsiders.

*When to Use Participant Observation*

In one sense, teachers, students, and administrators are all participants in the schooling process. As they engage in teaching and learning aimed at achieving specific goals and objectives—learner performance and competence—they can all be interviewed to obtain information about performance, reactions to the curriculum, teaching methods, and the school environment in general.

Although information that is volunteered by the persons being interviewed is valuable, they are simply responding to questions, and it is the evaluator who provides purpose and structure to the questions asked. If the evaluator has a blind spot, something may be missed. A participant observer who is aware of his or her role can obtain data on events as they unfold. This will often include surprises and unforeseen circumstances that would not be included in the question set of an outsider.

Effective participant observation requires considerable skill. Although the observer remains open to events, some sense of what is important and what is trivial must govern the observation process. Not everyone can maintain that sense of awareness and yet blend convincingly into the group. The use of a participant observer should be reserved for those occasions when the evaluation team has a member who can fill the role successfully, meeting the criteria of group membership while maintaining the frame of mind of the disciplined observer.

### Acceptance by the Group

The participant observer will not be able to function effectively if he or she is not accepted by the coworkers, teachers, or students who comprise the group. The participant observer must be able to fit into the group. Age range, general background, skill, and knowledge must be compatible with the other members of the group.

### What are the Effects of Participation?

Will the participant observer change the behavior of the group? Suppose a group effort was failing to complete a task and the participant observer joined the group and provided leadership, insight, skill, and knowledge that the group did not have before his or her arrival. What can be said of the observations that will result from such a case? This certainly changes the "design" of the intervention and adds a dimension that cannot be replicated if the method is to be used elsewhere. Thus there has been a change in methods, and these might well be contrary to what was intended in terms of the teaching-learning process under evaluation. We discourage evaluators becoming part of the intervention.

The evaluation team leader must tease out the threads of cause and effect. This may often require the addition of more observers and a period of continued observation. A situational matrix may be useful (see Chapter 6).

Think of evaluation when there is an observer as a referee in a basketball game. When is it appropriate for the referee to mix into the game? The same is true of an observer doing an evaluation.

## Interview Methods

The interview methods allow analysts to gather information directly from all categories of clients and stakeholders. Interviewing requires a high degree of competence and commitment from the analyst. Interviews are suitable for *soft data* collection.

The protocol here also contains similar elements to those of focus groups: approval for the participants' willingness to cooperate, a brief overview of the evaluation project and purpose of the interview and the purpose of the evaluation, key questions/items to cover based on previously identified indicators, and general concluding remarks, once again thanking them for their participation.

Interviews also have some of the same advantages that focus groups have over questionnaires. They have a better participation rate and allow the interviewer to read facial expressions and body language, clarify responses, ask follow-up questions, and sense areas for further inquiry. One of the disadvantages, however, is that they are not nearly as efficient as questionnaires in reaching a large number of participants. The two methods can be successfully combined when appropriate. Interviews may be used as a follow-up to questionnaires when the latter reveal that further probing is required.

The protocol here also contains similar elements to those of focus groups:

- *General description of the method:* An interviewer asks a series of questions—either face-to-face or telephone—and records the answers.

- *Strong points and advantages:* They have a better participation rate than questionnaires. Interviewer can record nonverbal cues. In addition, they allow the interviewer to ask spontaneous follow-up questions as deemed appropriate. Useful in gathering detailed descriptions and anecdotal information. Respondent is not limited to predetermined answers.

- *Weak points and disadvantages:* It is inefficient— time and potentially other resources—for reaching a large number of participants. Data collected may be more time consuming to analyze. Unintended bias can be introduced by the interviewer as well as by the participants.

- *Measurement considerations:* A structured interview protocol can be derived, with each question representing a specific and required data point. Qualitative data analysis techniques can be used for coding and even counting responses.

appreciation for the participants' willingness to cooperate, a brief overview of the evaluation project and purpose of the interview and the evaluation; key questions/items to cover, based on previously identified indicators; and general concluding remarks, once again thanking them for their participation.

---

- *General description of the method:* A facilitator interacts face-to-face with a group of 6-12 people to get a variety of perspectives on a given issue.

- *Strong points and advantages:* They have a better participation rate than questionnaires. Interviewer can record nonverbal cues. In addition, they allow the interviewer to ask spontaneous follow-up questions as deemed appropriate. Useful in gathering detailed descriptions and anecdotal information. Respondent is not limited to predetermined answers. Its selectiveness can send participants a metamessage of importance.

- *Weak points and disadvantages:* Anonymity cannot be guaranteed. Not as efficient in reaching a large number of people, as say, a questionnaire. Data collected may be more time-consuming to analyze. Participants can manipulate the discussion.

- *Measurement considerations:* A structured focus group protocol can be derived, with each question representing a specific and required data point. Qualitative data analysis techniques can be used for coding and even counting responses.

---

## Focus Groups

Conducting focus groups is another powerful and popular way to collect data. The process basically consists of evaluator(s) interacting face-to-face with a group of anywhere from 6 to 12 people to collect more in-depth input on a given topic, and it can take place over a 2- to 4-hour period. Like questionnaires, focus groups tend to be used to collect qualitative data, and its key questions should be based on previously identified indicators. The purpose here is not necessarily to have everyone agree on the "right" response, but rather to learn from a variety of different perspectives on a given issue. Focus groups are particularly useful if detailed descriptions and explanations are required.

One of the advantages that this process has over questionnaires is the ability of the evaluator/facilitator to "read" the participants' facial expressions and body language, which in itself can be useful information, and, in turn, can help uncover underlying key issues. This can also lead to important spontaneous follow-up questions, which do not occur when using a questionnaire. In addition, there is interaction among the participants, which can further stimulate them to reflect on, clarify, and support their perspectives. When outside-of-the-protocol responses are provided, these should be reported as such, perhaps under a category "additional findings."

Another advantage of using focus groups is the potential metamessage it sends to participants with regard to the importance of the data collection effort and their input. Participating in a focus group appears to be a more selective process than being asked to participate in a mail-out or online questionnaire, and thus one's input can be perceived as being more valuable. The drawback in this situation, however, is that anonymity cannot be guaranteed on the same level as questionnaires. Still, measures can be taken to assure participants that their input will not be linked to any one individual when findings are reported. When making any privacy assertions, be absolutely certain that privacy will, in fact, be respected.

Another relative disadvantage over the questionnaire is that it is not as efficient in reaching a wide range of participants, both in terms of time, effort, and cost. This is particularly true when respondents are dispersed across a wide geographical area. Thus this should be a consideration when estimating its utility in a given data collection situation. However, if the target population is relatively small or manageable and is geographically centralized, the focus groups can be efficient and inexpensive.

*Process*

When planning focus groups, careful attention should be given to making each group homogeneous with regard to characteristics relevant to the type of data being sought. For instance, if the required data are the perceived value added by a given program and there are various stakeholders from whom this data should be collected (e.g., teachers, parents, administrators, etc.), any given focus group should consist of only one type of stakeholder. In this case, their role with regard to the program in question will likely have an impact on their perception.

*Does the Sample Represent the Population?*

This is still crucial for purposes of generalization. For instance, the sample of teachers selected to participate in the focus groups should be representative of the population of teachers, in the same way that the sample of parents should be representative of the population of parents. Make certain that your population is indeed a representative sample of the larger group that you want to tap.

Though focus group sessions can be informally structured, a protocol should still be developed in advance to give the facilitator some organizing framework for both conducting the process and arranging the data gathered. The basic elements of a protocol should include an introduction that thanks the participants for taking the time to be there and provides them with a brief background and purpose for conducting the focus group. The protocol should also include a basic overview of the agenda and process (e.g., participant introductions, dynamics of the discussion, breaks, etc.). With this basic context, the protocol should in addition include the key questions/items to cover during the focus groups. Last, it should contain general concluding remarks or points—including gratitude for their cooperation—with which the facilitator can close the session. This protocol should be used as a general guide for the facilitator, rather than a strict agenda read aloud to the participants.

When conducting the focus group, the facilitator should remain unbiased to any particular point of view while also creating a supportive environment in which participants feel comfortable sharing their ideas. The facilitator should listen carefully and talk mainly when it is required in order to keep the discussion going or when it is important to clarify and/or summarize an idea. Keeping a discussion going may mean more than asking additional questions when input is minimal; it also means bringing the participants back to the subject at hand when the conversation derails to irrelevant topics. Be careful not to interject oneself or one's biases into the discussion. And don't subtly shape it to move it in a direction you would like to see it move.

Participants' tone of voice, facial expressions, and body posture can be very revealing; for this reason, the facilitator should be very observant throughout and intuitively detect key emotions behind comments. These can reveal underlying issues that, although not initially planned to be discussed, can become important data.

It is also important that the facilitator recognize underlying themes. While qualitative data analyses techniques (see Chapter 4) can be used to detect patterns once the data have been collected, it is also useful to be cognizant of such themes during the focus group, as it allows the facilitator to ask important follow-up questions.

Directly after concluding the focus group process, it is critical that the facilitator review and further record the data collected. The data should be arranged according to the items and sequence included in the protocol. If unplanned but important issues arose, they should be arranged in relation to the items that triggered such issues. It is possible that the official information recorder is someone other than the facilitator. In this case, it is important that the two compare notes and reconcile any inconsistencies.

Just as it would be very difficult to generalize the findings of one questionnaire to an entire population, it is difficult to justifiably use the findings of one focus group to an entire population. If findings from additional—and comparable—focus groups are consistent, then generalizations may be more credible.

## Nominal Group Technique

Another group process for collecting data is the *nominal group technique,* though it is only a group process in name, since input is recorded on an individual basis. Unlike focus groups, the nominal group technique is used for consensus building, and as such, one of the advantages is that each individual has the opportunity to contribute. It is more structured than a focus group in that its main purpose is to identify and rank issues in order of importance for the participants.

The recommended group size is roughly the same as it is for focus groups, as are sampling issues and the elements of its protocol; however, the actual process differs. Here, the respondents are asked to take a few minutes to brainstorm or think carefully about the question posed, and then write down their responses. After giving them sufficient time, perhaps 10 minutes, the facilitator asks each participant to share their first responses. Each response is then recorded on flipchart paper. Once everyone in the group has provided a response, this process is repeated for a second or third time until all participant responses have been recorded.

The facilitator once again plays an important role, as he or she must make sure that the procedure is properly and objectively applied in order to generate reliable data. The facilitator may also ask for clarification of any of the

- *General description of the method:* A facilitator interacts face-to-face with a group of people, where each has at least one opportunity to provide their individual input on a specific issue. All input is categorized and ranked in order of importance.

- *Strong points and advantages:* They have a better participation rate than questionnaires. Interviewer can record nonverbal cues. In addition, they allow the interviewer to ask spontaneous follow-up questions as deemed appropriate. Useful in gathering detailed descriptions and anecdotal information. Respondent is not limited to predetermined answers. Its selectiveness can send participants a metamessage of importance.

- *Weak points and disadvantages:* Anonymity cannot be guaranteed. Not as efficient as a questionnaire in reaching a large number of people.

- *Measurement considerations:* One may want to tally the number of similar responses provided, as well as the rankings. Table 5.1 provides a framework for such tallying.

responses before proceeding to request participants to rank order their ideas. During this period, duplications may be omitted, and each idea is then assigned a number or letter to uniquely identify it. The facilitator then instructs participants to choose up to 10 or 12 responses that they consider of most importance, and then rank them according to their relative

**Table 5.1**    Example of Ranking and Record Keeping in Using a Nominal Group Technique

| Response | Participant 1 | Participant 2 | Participant 3 | Order of importance |
|----------|---------------|---------------|---------------|---------------------|
| A | ranked 1st | ranked 2nd | ranked 2nd | 5 = ranked 1st |
| B | ranked 3rd | ranked 1st | ranked 3rd | 7 = ranked 3rd |
| C | ranked 2nd | ranked 3rd | ranked 1st | 6 = ranked 2nd |
| D | ranked 4th | ranked 4th | ranked 4th | 12 = ranked 4th |

importance. Rankings are collected from all participants and then aggregated. Table 5.1 provides an illustration of such ranking and record keeping.

### Delphi Technique

Like the other group techniques, the purpose of the *Delphi technique* is to elicit information and judgments from participants to facilitate problem solving, planning, and decision making. Unlike the other group data collection processes, it does so without assembling the participants face-to-face. Rather, participant input is exchanged through other mediums such as regular mail, fax, or e-mail.

Participants usually consist of up to 40 to 60 (or perhaps even more) experts or individuals considered to have significant knowledge about the issue. The facilitator must then obtain the commitment of the group to participate in a few questionnaires, spread out over time.

The facilitator uses the input gathered from each of the questionnaires to develop the next. Respondents examine the degree to which their responses are similar or differ from those of the group, thereby simulating the type of pressure for agreement experienced in other face-to-face groups. Additional questionnaires may be sent out until consensus has been reached. The iterative nature of this process is one of the main things that sets it apart from the other techniques.

- *General description of the method:* Collect group data without convening groups. All data collection and common sharing is done virtually.
- *Strong points and advantages:* More rapid than face-to-face groups.
- *Weak points and disadvantages:* Anonymity cannot be guaranteed. It does miss the subtle effects of personal interaction, such as body language.
- *Measurement considerations:* Objectivity, objectivity, objectivity.

The Delphi technique requires the facilitator to organize requests for information and information received and to be responsible for communication with the participants. It also requires a reliable communication channel to link the facilitator with each of the participants. It is common to use regular mail for this purpose; however, faxes and e-mail can decrease the time required for this process. Even with the time other mediums can save the overall process, there is still significant work required by the facilitator.

## INSTRUMENT-CENTERED METHODS

Using tests and other data collection instruments, like questionnaires and surveys, is perhaps the most common approach to collecting data. When using an instrument to collect data, you are magnifying your ability to reach more information targets, but at the same time, you are limiting the response possibilities to some extent. Open-ended items on questionnaires can expose some information that was unforeseen in the design of the data collection instrument, but not to the same extent that an observer can do in person. Nevertheless, the efficiency of using instruments like tests makes them an attractive option. This is especially true when the tests are well made. The structure of the test can ensure that all items of importance are covered in which observers are subject to forgetfulness and inconsistency. Tests must, of course, be reliable and valid. Questionnaires must also be well structured and carefully worded to eliminate ambiguity of meaning for those responding to items and for later interpretation of the responses.

### Choosing the Right Instrument

More than likely, the evaluators will have identified a whole range of indicators, which may call for different kinds of data collection tools. The first thing to consider is the type of data each indicator represents and what type of data collection method would be the most appropriate for that type of data. Answering a given evaluation question may call for the collection of several indicators, and each of these indicators may represent a different type of data. For instance, if financial data must be collected, extant-data reviews would certainly be more appropriate than an attitudinal questionnaire. Another indicator may call for program participants' attitudes about their experiences, in which case one or more of the qualitative data collection tools may be appropriate (e.g., questionnaires, focus groups, etc.).

In addition, the source of the data or target population may also impact the type of tool to be used. For instance, evaluators may want to collect attitudinal data from community members, faculty and staff, and institutional leaders. Because the community members are much more numerous and dispersed across a relatively large geographic area, a questionnaire can be used to obtain their input. Faculty and staff are relatively easy to bring together in one location because they, for the most part, already work proximally to each other and are substantially less in number. Moreover, institutional leaders are much fewer in number, and arranging their schedules so that they can all meet at the same time in the same place could be quite a challenge; thus individual interviews would be the most appropriate way to collect input from them.

Target population characteristics such as culture, language, education, past experiences, and gender, among others, are also essential to consider. Whether written questionnaires, group techniques, interviews, or tests are used, one must understand the impact of these characteristics when deriving questions and methods to collect data from individuals. One question can mean different things to different people, based on a multitude of factors.

In some instances, those developing the data collection instruments can unconsciously overrely on their own experiences and sense of "What is." Such is the case with questions that include colloquialisms that although well-known for one group of people, are completely unfamiliar to others. The results from these questions are often misleading, as the interpretations of these questions can potentially be as numerous as the respondents. Similarly, one approach can be appropriate in a given culture but perhaps not others. For instance, in some cultures, it is considered rude to publicly disagree with the positions of others. In such cases, it may be difficult to use a standard group technique to elicit honest responses from a group.

Other important factors to consider when selecting data collection instruments are the relative costs, time, and expertise required to develop and/or obtain them. Once a range of suitable alternatives have been identified based on the type of data required and their sources, the ultimate selection should be based on the relative feasibility of each alternative. While a face-to-face interview might be the best choice in terms of the data the evaluator is after on a given project, the sheer number of those to be interviewed might put the time and money required beyond the scope of the project.

## Traditional Text-Based Testing

Perhaps the most widely used method of determining what someone has learned is the use of a paper-based test. Given the availability of technology-based mediums today, perhaps a more inclusive term is *text-based testing.*

In either case, an enormous amount of information is available to guide the construction and use of such tests. Provided the tests are well made (valid and reliable), they are a good choice to measure knowledge, and they are efficient and economical to administer. When tests are *standardized*, they yield information about the relative ranking of test takers in a general target population. When they are valid predictors, they can be used in screening and selection. However, most teacher-made, paper-based tests are not validated as predictive or standardized instruments and so have much less interpretive value related only to the direct content in the test. Paper tests can play a role in performance measurement of skills that involve physical action integrated with knowledge, but only to a limited degree. They cannot replace performance testing that involves actions and interactions of the test takers with physical tools or operator controls.

*Teacher-Made Tests*

Teacher-made tests are the most pervasive form of data collection used in education today. They vary in quality due to the informal method of development that sometimes includes a mixed bag of methods and types. In general, teachers want to measure the learning of the students related to the content of the lessons and teaching objectives that were used in the instructional phase of teaching. Rarely do teachers make testing exhaustive.

The issue of domain effects validity of a test, but domain is not the determining factor in the selection of criterion referenced or normative referenced use of the raw score.

It is the purpose of the test that influences the decision to use the raw score data in a normative or set criterion way.

When the purpose of a test is to certify that a student meets a set standard, the domain size of test items must be appropriate to that standard.

When the purpose of a test is to compare and rank students, the domain size of test items must be large enough to ensure reliability and validity of the test.

When the purpose of a test is to predict or screen, the reference population on which the test was normed or validated must be a sufficiently large sample from the population domain to ensure valid inference relative to the test-taking domain.

When the purpose of a test is diagnostic, the test item domain must include all possible indicators, faults, or errors related to the condition or problem being diagnosed.

That would be a good way to find out what the students know or do not recall from the instruction, but it is not very efficient. Therefore most teachers sample from the content and make the test content a subset of the delivered content. Typical errors can occur here: (1) The sample content is not representative; (2) the test contains new content not featured in the instruction; or (3) the test requires a level of integration of content and behavior to synthesize answers that was not part of the instructional sequence.

Two points must be made here. First, the teacher must take pains to ensure that the tests are not compromised, resulting in no ability to assume a relation between the test results (base on the sample) and the learning that took place. Second, for the most part, the teacher must avoid the three errors noted. There may be some situations in which the second and third errors are actually good tactics for advanced students, but other than that, tests that include these errors are generally regarded by the testing community, and especially by the students, as unfair.

Research data often warn us that teacher-constructed tests are notoriously unreliable and often not valid, which is not surprising given that test construction is rarely a part of teacher training.

### Criterion-Referenced Tests

A popular form of testing that has gained use in recent years is *criterion-referenced testing.* The main feature of this form of testing is that the test items are scored relative to a fixed standard, relative to known and precise performance standards.

Criterion-referenced tests tend to include more performance objectives, although knowledge-based tests can also be based on fixed standards. The key idea is that students are expected to obtain a desired level of performance—performance relative to the standards. If students must know the safety procedure for using a tool in shop class, the instructor wants them to use the entire procedure. Relative class ranking has no bearing if being the best in the group still results in cutting off a finger in the band saw.

The reliability and validity of criterion testing have been discussed by Berk (1980). In general, testing and reuse of the test over time can establish the reliability of the test. Validity of criterion testing rests in the relationship between skill and knowledge required to perform in some designated situation and the fidelity of the test situation to duplicate that skill and knowledge in a testing mode. In issuing drivers' licenses, states want to see a demonstration of minimum skills and knowledge related to safe operation of the vehicle on the public highways. Criterion-referenced tests are good for areas of performance that involve minimum performance for safety or demonstrated skill at some tasks (especially when human well-being is involved.)

The validity of a criterion-referenced test lies in the accomplishment of the testing aim. There are two important issues that relate to the aims of testing: domain coverage and the inference made from results. Consider two questions when approaching a testing situation. The first is: How comprehensive or inclusive should the content of the test be? And second: What do the test results mean? The first question is often considered to be an issue of domain, and the second deals with using the results in a practical way.

Suppose you are training a high school shop class to safely change the saw blade in a band saw. If there were seven steps and all were essential to doing the task correctly, you could make a test that had each student perform each step. In a criterion-referenced test, the standard could be that each step has to be completed correctly. Students who get all of the steps pass, and students who miss a step fail. In this example, the test items and the test objective have what Berk (1980) referred to as "item-objective congruence." Here, the domain is small (just seven items, one for each step), and the test is a virtual reproduction of the desired objective to correctly change a band saw blade. The instructor can have high confidence that students who pass the test can now change the band saw blade. But what about different models of band saws or blades of other tools, like arbor saws, jigsaws, and planers? This is where the issue of domain and transfer enters the picture. If the shop teacher wants to be sure that students can change all of the blades, the domain of test items can be enlarged. Now, the test would include all of the procedures and take longer to administer. The validation of tests that include all items in the domain hinges on the clarity of instructions, availability of required resources tools, and inclusiveness of required test items (issues that can also affect reliability of the test). Shop class may have a large but manageable total domain of items over the course of a class period.

What if our instructional objective implies a really large, perhaps infinite, domain? The mathematics professor wants students of advanced calculus to be able to solve every conceivable problem that will ever arise within the limits of analytical calculus. How will a test be constructed to meet this objective? What criterion standard could ever be used to declare that a student was competent in calculus?

The answer lies in the nature of the subject matter. Whereas the shop procedures were specific to the limited domain, the application of calculus involves a different level on Bloom's taxonomy. In calculus, the abstractions and generalizations of problem procedure enable students to cope with each new problem. It is the large but finite domain of rules, models, principles, language, notation, and complex procedures and generalizations that has to be mastered. The domain of potential problems is infinite, but the learning domain of rules, models, principles, language, notation, and procedures is not. True, it is much larger than the shop class example, but still manageable. Test construction here could include breaking the subject into small sections, but the accumulation of all of the subtests would eventually measure the entire domain. The teacher still can require a set standard and specify a fixed criterion related to the set of tests (a criterion-referenced approach), or the teacher can use the scores to compare students with each other (a normative-referenced approach). It is useful to consider the role of domain in this decision.

### Norm-Referenced Tests

Norm-referenced tests have a strong traditional history in education, which tends to make them acceptable and familiar to teachers even when used unwisely.

The essence of norm-referenced testing is that the standard or criteria involves a raw score and then a relative score, which is based on the curve of performance. Norm-referenced testing compares each learner with other learners rather than comparing their performance to a specific reference standard (as in criterion-referenced testing). Usually, a normal curve is assumed.

When the objective of the testing is to sort out stronger from weaker students (as measured by the test items), the normative test is a good choice. However, some cautions are due here. Effective teaching will tend to skew the normal curve to the positive end. Ineffective teaching is more likely to preserve the normal distribution of students. Some who knew the material before the instruction will score higher than others; some will score in the middle; and some will fall on the low end, having picked up little or no benefit from the instruction. The important point here is also where that median score lies based on the total content specified in the course objectives. A teacher can assign grades based on the position of the student on the curve no matter if the curve itself is at the low end, the middle, or the high end of the content continuum. Hence some grades may not be comparable from one test to another or from one teacher to another. Norm-referenced testing may not reveal quality of instructing, but it does sort out students relative to any given learning event regardless of how much learning took place in absolute terms. Some instructors actually do a combination of norm-referenced and criterion-referenced testing when they use a series of criterion-referenced subtests in which the score does relate to content learned. The subtest scores are then averaged, and the norm occurs when the instructor rank orders students by final average score. The inference that can be made from such a method depends on the inclusiveness of each subtest relative to the skill and knowledge pool that is associated with the course goals and objectives.

**Table 5.2**    Selecting Norm-Referenced and Criterion-Referenced Test Types

| | |
|---|---|
| The objective of testing is to make sure learners are able to perform a critical function in plant maintenance. | A criterion-referenced performance test will provide information relative to that critical function, relative to a specific performance standard. |
| The objective of the test is to determine how much a student has learned. | A criterion-referenced knowledge test will show how much a test taker has learned. |
| The objective of the testing is to rank order students for selection or placement. | A norm-referenced test will provide the relative standing required as compared to others who take the same test. The test must also have some predictive norms. |
| The objective of the test is to compare standing to a large population. | A standardized norm-referenced test will show where the test taker ranks in a national group. |
| The objective of the test is to grant certification in some skill, like driving. | A criterion-referenced test will determine whether the test taker has reached the minimum level of skill to safely drive a car. |
| The objective of the test is diagnostic. | A combination of normative- and criterion-testing features will provide information of weak areas of performance when the norm establishes strong and weak performance. This is usually by stratified category inside a broad area, like math, science, English, etc. |
| The objective of the test is to select the best candidate to go into space; the test can screen candidates with known predictive outcome. | A norm-referenced test will separate candidates, and determine whether the predictive value of test items has been validated using a reference population. Screening tests use features of criterion-referenced tests when a cutoff score becomes a criterion. |

*Selecting Norm-Referenced and Criterion-Referenced Test Types*

As you can probably gather (and we have mentioned before), it is important to identify the type of information you want before you administer a test. Otherwise, you may have test results data, but they may not be the right data for the type of decision you must make. All stakeholders, including decision makers, must clearly define the purpose of a test before selecting and administering it. Both criterion- and norm-referenced tests have areas in which they tend to be the best fit for the situation. Table 5.2 lists several testing situations and the rationale for selecting between the two approaches.

It should be noted that the same test questions in some cases can be used in both a normative- and criterion-test setting. It is the way the cumulative answers are used by the test giver that causes the procedure to be called norm referenced or criterion referenced. Robert Mager (1997) used an amusing example in his book *Measuring Instructional Results* to make this point. He lists a 10-step process for making coffee, in which each step is tested. If the student were to miss one item (e.g., putting the coffee in the filter), in norm-referenced scoring, that student would be given a score of 90%. However, if the criterion-referenced approach were used (with the standard being making a cup of coffee), the latter score would be "not yet complete."

> A distinction must be made between the use of raw scores in either a normative or criterion mode after the testing, and the use of norms in test construction. Tests with construct validity or predictive validity make use of reference populations to establish the relationship between the test items and the construct or desired behavior. Tests that claim to measure mathematical ability or mechanical aptitude or fitness to become a naval aviator all fit this category. The use of cutoff scores in conjunction with these tests is in a way a criterion-referenced procedure, but the cutoff score in order to be meaningful has to be validated by a reference population, which is a normative procedure.

Some additional confusion includes the use of testing in relation to assigning grades in educational settings. The time-honored use of the letter grades "A, B, C, D, F" has been used in conjunction with the normal curve, in which the standard deviations serve as rough dividing lines for assignment of the grades. This appears to be such an elegant solution to the problem of grading that many teachers (and some evaluators) insist that having a normal distribution of grades is desirable and even mandatory.

We point out that a normal curve is often found in nature when events or phenomena are measured. Any random assembly of students, for example, would tend to fall into a normal distribution on measures of height, weight, strength, and other physical attributes. In fact, if a teacher were to administer a final exam to students at the beginning of a course (where the students knew nothing of the content of the course) instead of the end, the results, although low, would most likely form a normal distribution. Getting a normal distribution is taken by some teachers as a sign of rigor (only an easy teacher would have all As).

But a normal distribution at the end of a program of instruction intended to impart learning could also be interpreted as a sign of ineffective teaching. The students who could learn on their own end up on the high end, and those who are completely lost end up on the low end. It is also worth pointing out that two teachers of the same subject could have identical-shaped grading curves, one class curve ranging from 50% to 100% of content learned and the other from 10% to 60%. Presumably, an "A" student in one class would have earned an "F" in the other. The problem exists with nonstandardized normative testing. Teachers without access to commercial standardized tests, however, can avoid the problem above by using the same criterion standard in both classes. Thus the assignment of grades becomes fairer between the two classes but is still not free of all problems associated with grading. The ranking of students does identify the best and the brightest, and part of the grading system is intended to reward the intellectually gifted or hardworking. Setting the standard in a criterion-referenced testing situation requires careful consideration of both rigor and fairness.

### Objective Tests

This term has come to represent a type of test that involves straightforward answers to the test questions, which are also clear and constructed to eliminate ambiguity in scoring a correct response. Multiple-choice tests are one type of objective test. These tests ask questions or make statements

- *General description of the method:* Documents are created using several types of formats to send or mail to respondents who answer each question or item. This can include telephone surveys where a voice message is the stimulus and a voice response is made by the target population.

- *Strong points and advantages:* The method is efficient for reaching a large population and relatively easy to process.

- *Weak points and disadvantages:* The method can gather information only about the questions asked, although some open-ended items can generate a wider response.

- *Measurement considerations:* The method is easily adapted to measurement procedures. Responses can be displayed using tables, pie charts, bar graphs, and other descriptive display. The method can also be adapted for use of inferential statistics.

and then provide a list of answers from which the students can select. When these tests are validated using large populations and used in situations like college entrance exams, they are useful and efficient, especially if they are in a form that can be read by an electronic scoring method. However, when constructed by teachers without demonstrated reliability and validity, they can be problematic for the following reasons. All of the test items have prompts built into the answer set. Some students with partial knowledge can select the correct answer. If the test was fill-in-the-blank, that same student may not have responded correctly. In situations where the course objectives require unprompted performance and recall ability, the multiple-choice test does not measure the full range of knowledge (or lack of knowledge) required in the objective. Objective tests can be very useful, but only if they are carefully prepared.

As with the other data collection tools, the first place to start is the data indicators the evaluator is after. In the case of tests, these indicators may be in the form of objectives, which are often interchangeably referred to as *performance objectives, learner objectives, behavioral objectives,* or other labels that all refer to the format for defining "Where are you headed" and "How you know when you have arrived."

### The Relation of Tests to Learning Objectives

Since these objectives are meant to indicate what learners should be able to do upon completion of a program or course, one of the first evaluation questions tends to be whether learners can in fact perform what is indicated in these objectives. Thus the test items should be parallel to the objectives. That is, the specific actions or behaviors specified in the objectives should be elicited during testing. This should be a major criterion in selecting the test format. For example, some common test formats of the objective test discussed above include the following:

- *True/False:* This is a test where the student has only two possible selections (true or false), and the point of the test is to construct questions that will test the student's ability to discriminate from the wording and his or her knowledge of the subject whether the answer is a true or false. Such tests can be improved through item analysis to remove poorly worded items that fail to discriminate those who know the material from those who are guessing.

- *Matching:* This is a test where the student is expected to match words or phrases with definitions or other phases that have a meaningful relation to the item. As in true/false, these tests can be improved using item analysis.

- *Multiple Choice:* This is a test where the student is required to select from a set of possible answers. The tests are usually a mixture of questions, with only one correct response; no correct response ("none of the above"); all correct responses ("all of the above"); or some combination. Again, this form of test can be improved using item analysis. It is possible that this form of test is overused and undervalidated. Contrary to popular practice, a multiple-choice format is not appropriate for measuring every type of skill or knowledge.

In fact, during instructional design, the objectives and testing instruments are often derived simultaneously. In many instances, formulating the specific test items helps us figure out exactly what we expect from learners and thus provides feedback for revising objectives if there is a discrepancy. Unfortunately, this process is not always followed, resulting in tests that do not accurately measure the predetermined objectives. As we will see later in this chapter, for a measurement instrument to be valid, it must in fact measure what it sets out to measure.

### The Role of Sampling

The interpretation of test results has meaning only in relation to the size of the domain of items that make up the test. But now, our instructor decides that testing the entire domain is too time-consuming and a shortcut is in order. A random sample of the items will be used to make a more efficient test. To preserve the strong inference that a result indicates coverage of the entire domain, the tests items must be kept a secret or the test will be compromised. The criterion-referenced testing movement has argued for clear and open objectives (and test items) and to limit the surprise factor associated with testing. Although the raw scores from a test that was a sample of the domain can still be used in both a criterion and normative way, the surprise feature is an issue of instructional approach that is discouraged by many in the criterion-referenced camp. There is one more test construction issue that uses norms in the test item development. That is when the purpose of the test is to measure constructs like intelligence or predict the future success or general aptitude for different types of work.

### Reliability and Validity of Tests

When interpreting test results, no matter how positive or negative the results may seem, we should rely on them only if we have established confidence in these results. This confidence can be established only if the test measures what it is supposed to measure (valid); and when it consistently yields the same results for a given individual (reliable).

*Validity.* There is no simple way of precisely determining validity, since a test can be valid for one purpose and audience and not for others. There are, however, a variety of ways of determining whether a test is sufficiently valid to be useful. One of the simplest is *content validity*. Content-related validity, which should begin with instrument construction and is based on the judgment of experts, involves the careful examination of the test content to determine whether it is representative of the behavior domain in question. Content validity requires both *item validity* (Do the test items measure the intended content area?) and *sampling validity* (How well does the test sample the total content area?). Still, while a test may look valid, it can still measure something different, such as test-taking ability, guessing, or insight. Thus content validity does not guarantee a good and valid test.

*Face validity* has been used to describe tests, and while this is not a rigorous approach, it can be useful in initial screening in test selection. It basically refers to the degree to which a test appears to measure what it claims to measure: On its face, does it seem to go with what it is supposed to deliver? Face validity is more likely to be used when the test is a high-fidelity copy of the performance desired in the instructional objective. Face validity is not a term used to describe the validity of screening tests and predictive tests. When we respond to people such as politicians, many of us rely on face validity: The person seems to know what he or she is talking about. Don't we all wish that would be true!

A more rigorous approach to determining validity is to compare the instrument with a predetermined criterion of validity. One type of criterion-related validity is *concurrent*. Concurrent criterion-related validity deals with measures that can be administered at the same time as the measure to be validated. For example, to establish this type of validity, a test designer may want to correlate the results of a new personality inventory test with the results of an already-established one, such as the Myers-Briggs test, the MMPI (Minnesota Multiphasic Personality Inventory), or other validated instrument. This correlation yields a numeric value known as a validity coefficient, which indicates the degree of validity of that new test.

The other type of criterion-referenced validity is *predictive validity*, which seeks to determine the degree to which a new test predicts a future behavior or how well a test taker will do in the future. This type of validity is critical for tests that will be used to classify or select individuals, such as the Scholastic Assessment Test (SAT), and the Graduate Record Examination (GRE). Predictive validity is determined by administering the test and later correlating the scores of the test to some other measure of success. This correlation yields a predictive validity coefficient.

*Construct validity* is the degree to which a test measures a hypothetical construct. A *construct* is a nonobservable trait that is derived to explain behavior. For instance, intelligence is a construct that was created to explain why some learners learn better than others. While we cannot observe intelligence directly, we can infer intelligence based on the observable indicators. Establishing this type of validity involves testing hypotheses deduced from theory. A number of independent studies are usually required to establish the validity of a construct measure.

*Reliability. Reliability* refers to the degree to which a test gives consistent results each time it is administered, provided it is done under the same circumstances. If a test is not reliable, it is useless, since we cannot place any confidence in the results. For a test to be valid, it must be reliable, though reliability is not sufficient to establish validity.

There are various ways of establishing reliability. The *test/retest method,* as the name implies, requires that the same test be given twice and that the correlation between the first and second set of scores be determined. One of the problems with this approach is that memory can sometimes play a role in the test results. While extending the period of time between test administrations can reduce this problem, if the interval is too long, the test takers may have changed on the trait being measured.

*Equivalent* or *alternate forms method* is another approach to establishing reliability, one that eliminates the memory problem associated with the test/retest approach. Here, two tests are identical in every way except for the actual items included. Both tests are administered to a group, again, under the same circumstances, and the test scores for each are then correlated.

If a test is derived to measure one specific concept, it is safe to assume that the items of that test are highly correlated with each other. *Split-half reliability* is an approach used to determine internal consistency reliability. It involves splitting a test into two equivalent halves, administering each part to one group and establishing the correlation between the two sets of scores. If the correlation is high, the test has a good split-half reliability.

Yet another approach to establishing internal consistency is the *Kuder-Richardson method,* where the extent to which items in one form of the test have as much in common with one another as they do to those of the other form. Thus these procedures are sometimes referred to as *item-total correlations.* Perhaps one of the most commonly known internal consistency coefficients is *Alpha.* It is similar to the Kuder-Richardson but can be used on multiple-choice tests rather than merely a yes/no or right/wrong format (e.g., attitudinal surveys that use Likert scales).

It is important to stress that internal consistency measures are appropriate only if a test contains similar items that measure only one concept. For instance, while they would be appropriate if a test measures math ability, it would be inappropriate if the test included one section for math ability, another for geometry, and so on.

## Questionnaires and Surveys

One of the most widely used—and perhaps misused—data collection tools is the questionnaire. Questionnaires are commonly used to collect soft data[1] (e.g. perceptions, attitudes etc.) but if designed accordingly may also be used to collect hard data (e.g., independently verifiable). Usually, questionnaires are used to gather data about the respondent's perception or "personal reality," as is the case in attitude surveys. Thus results should be interpreted and presented in that context.

As a general guideline for increasing the utility of questionnaires, questions posed in a questionnaire are geared toward informed opinion, such as those based on the target group's personal experience, knowledge, background, and vantage point for observation. Questionnaire designers are well-advised to stay away from posing questions that lead the respondent to speculate about the information being requested, nor should they use a questionnaire to confirm or shape a preexisting bias: "Just the facts, ma'am."

Perhaps no questionnaire can be regarded as perfect or ideal for soliciting all the information required, and in fact, most have inherent advantages, as well as flaws (Rea & Parker, 1997). However, there are factors, including professional experience and judgment, that may help ensure any advantages and reduce the effects of inherent flaws of questionnaires.

For just about every questionnaire advantage, one could perhaps find a disadvantage. In the context of a survey method, as an inherent advantage, questionnaires can be used to solicit information from a large number of people across a large geographic location, and relatively inexpensively. However, there is no opportunity for instant clarification or follow-up questions, as there is in focus groups or interviews, for instance.

Another advantage of using questionnaires in this context is that they can be completed by respondents at their own convenience and at their own pace. Though a deadline for completion should be given to respondents, they still have sufficient time to carefully reflect, elaborate, and if appropriate, verify their responses. Of course, the drawback here is that mail-out or online questionnaires can require significantly more time to administer than other methods. The sooner you can get a response, the more likely it will be done.

Perhaps one of the most important advantages is that of providing the possibility of anonymity.[2] Questionnaires can be administered in such a way that responses are not traced back to individual respondents. Explicitly communicating this to potential respondents tends to increase the chances for their cooperation on at least two levels: (1) completing the survey to begin with and (2) being more forthcoming and honest in their responses. However, even if guaranteed anonymity may increase response rate, the overall response rate for questionnaires is usually still lower than for other methods.

When responses are slow or thin, follow-ups, oversampling, respondent replacements, and nonrespondent studies can contribute toward a more representative random sample, which is critical for generalization of findings. Still, there will usually be some bias in the sample due to self-selection; some people, for their own reasons, might not respond to a questionnaire. But a representative sample is a "must."

There are a number of characteristics across which respondents and nonrespondents may differ and thus can impact the findings. You want to know where people agree and where they do not. This is another important issue to acknowledge with interpreting and presenting data collected through questionnaires.

So exactly what data are collected with questionnaires? How does one determine what questions to ask? The fundamental source of information for the items that will be included in your questionnaire instrument is the set of results, indicators, and related questions you want answered as a result of the evaluation (or a needs assessment process, if that's the context of the data collection). Let us now to turn our attention to questionnaire development.

### Basic Types of Questionnaire Questions

While some question crafters speak of the simplicity, intelligibility, and clarity of questionnaire items, experimental researchers speak of task difficulty and respondent burden. Either way, what we are talking about here is that many questionnaires are difficult to understand and answer (Converse & Presser, 1986). Keep in mind who the authors of questionnaires usually are—educated people with an in-depth understanding of the topic at hand—and thus the questions or items are often directed at individuals with similar characteristics. The importance of simplicity in language and tasks of a questionnaire cannot be overstated. But don't oversimplify to the point that the important variables and nuances are eliminated.

### Open- and Closed-Ended Questions

*Open-ended questions* require the respondent to provide a response in their own words, in approximately a few sentences. For example:

What results have you experienced as a result of having your child participate in this after-school program?

_____

_____

*Closed-ended questions* provide the respondent with a list of answers to choose from. Examples of closed-ended questions are multiple choice and category scales.

Below is an example of a multiple-choice item:

What results have you experienced as a result of having your child participate in this after-school program?

A. Higher academic achievement

B. Decreased behavioral problems (reported fights in school, conflicts at home, etc.)

C. Improved social interaction

D. Increased participation in school activities

E. None of these.

*Category scales* may focus on frequency (e.g., from "always" to "never"), amount (from most to least), agreement ("completely agree" to "completely disagree"), and so on. To force a decision toward one side of the range or another, even-numbered scales (e.g., 4 point, 6 point) can be used.

The most frequently seen type of item in questionnaires is possibly the closed-ended response option. Closed-ended questions tend to increase the likelihood of getting a response, since they require less time and/or work on the part of the respondent. It certainly seems easier to choose an appropriate answer that is already provided rather than create a response. Another distinct advantage to this format is the relative simplicity with which one can make comparisons among responses, thereby facilitating the data analysis phase. Having predetermined categories of responses helps the respondents focus exclusively on the responses that are of particular interest to the evaluation team; by the same token, however, these may also exclude or limit other important responses not thought of by the questionnaire creators and therefore force respondents to choose responses that do not apply to them.

Open-ended questions are one way to avoid these potential drawbacks. However, they bring their own set of challenges. For one, they may render a lot of extraneous, and perhaps unintelligible, information, which will require extra attention and work in the analysis phase. In addition, the range of responses may be extensively wide. One way to alleviate—not eliminate—this is to make these questions as specific as possible and design them so that they relate to ends, and not just means.[3] Not only does this help respondents focus on the issue of interest, but it helps in them recalling information.

Before comparisons can be made in the analysis phase, a coding system will have to be put into place for the standardization of these responses. However, there are instances in which these additional challenges are worth facing, such as when the potential benefits of using open-ended questions outweigh the challenges they bring.

Last, it is also possible to combine both formats into one item. These items usually consist of predetermined response options as well as an additional option for "Other, please specify." If a pilot test revealed that this option was used frequently, then it would be a good idea to keep the option. If, on the other hand, a pilot test revealed that it was rarely used, it may not have to be included in the final version.

### Other Question Formats

One could argue that there are various other types of closed-ended questions. For instance, rankings are used to rank items in order of importance or priority. Here, the respondents are provided with a predetermined number of responses, while being asked to prioritize them based on some specified criteria.

Sometimes, the evaluator may be looking for more than one response on a given question. In this case, a checklist item can capture all responses that apply.

### Questionnaire Structure

Respondents are sensitive not only to the language used in each question but also the order in which these questions are asked. Keep in mind that each question can become the context for the next. Thus poorly structured questionnaires may not only confuse the respondents and cause them to provide inaccurate responses but may also lead them to abandon the questionnaire altogether.

A well-structured questionnaire should begin with straightforward yet interesting questions so as to motivate the respondent to continue. As with any relationship, it takes time for an individual to feel comfortable with sharing sensitive information; therefore save sensitive items for later on in the questionnaire.

Questions that focus on the same specific issue should be presented together, so as to maximize the respondent's reflection and recall. One way for both the questionnaire designer and the respondent is to cluster specific items around different categories. This, however, should not be confused with placing similar questions consecutively. The latter, instead of maximizing the respondent's reflection, would instead elicit an automatic response. One way to decrease the likelihood of this is to vary the type (e.g., open- or close-ended, checklist, etc.) of questions within the category.

In cases where information is required beyond what a closed-ended question can reveal, an open-ended question should follow. Usually, these types of items should be placed later on in the survey, within the restraints of following a logical sequence. Last, more general, open-ended closing questions, such as those that request respondents to add anything else that may be important but was not asked, should be used to conclude the series of questions.

### Length

As mentioned before, simplicity is key. Nobody wants to complete a long and complicated questionnaire, so the closer your questionnaire is to this description, the lower your likely response rate.

The questionnaire should include exactly what is required—nothing more, nothing less. Recall that in our previous chapter, we went over the process of identifying relevant indicators, which should be the central focus of the information collected. While there may plenty of interesting information that could be collected through the questionnaire, if it is not central to the indicators being investigated, it will only be a distraction—both for the evaluators and the respondent.

In considering the length of the questionnaire, the questionnaire crafter should think not only about the actual length of the questionnaire, but the length of time the respondent will invest in completing it. As a general rule, the entire questionnaire should take no more than 30 minutes to complete, and ideally about half that long.

- *General description of the method:* A treatment (educational program) is carried out under carefully observed and controlled conditions to see what result is obtained. This may be carried out several times to establish that any result is not a chance happening. Controls are designed to rule out possible explanations for the results other than the main treatment. Controls usually involve additional groups of subjects.

- *Strong points and advantages:* If properly designed, experiments can strengthen the assertions made on effectiveness of programs.

- *Weak points and disadvantages:* To set up control groups and carry out experiments using classic designs, the classroom setting may be altered and the resources exceed the usual limits of the classroom.

- *Measurement considerations:* Measurement is the heart of classic design.

## TREATMENT-CENTERED METHODS

Often, the kind of information required to answer evaluation questions is the by-product of activities that must take place in order for results to be obtained. This is true of most classroom activity in school programs, but sometimes we impose additional controls on the situation that are not unlike the classic scientific experiment. The controls we can impose in the classroom setting are not usually as precise as in a laboratory setting, but the social sciences can on occasion use the experimental method with some degree of success. In recent years, another treatment-centered method of obtaining useful evaluation data has been the use of simulation to monitor behavior under controlled conditions that model the conditions of a special performance situation. Treatment-based methods of gathering evaluation data are often used when there is a question of causality involved that must sort out several possible causal factors. Although this is rare due to the resources and level of intrusive control that is required, it is nevertheless a method that has a place in evaluation, especially when performance stakes are high.

## Classic Experiments

*Classic experiments* in the educational setting usually involve the comparison of two or more groups, although single-group methods do exist. The main aim of an experiment is to see what happens under specific conditions. If the design is carefully done and controls are used, an inference to cause and effect can be made. It is this aspect of classic research design that has made it attractive to evaluators when they are not sure whether the observed results of a program are in fact due to the program treatment or to some other cause. It is important to point out that establishing causality is not the same as establishing the value of the program or results. Value is assigned to obtained results when they meet the valid needs of the school system (derived from Mega on down). The program has "instrumental value" to the degree it is able to deliver consistent desired results.

Much discussion has taken place in the evaluation and research communities to draw distinctions between the disciplines of research and evaluation. Classic experiments are generally regarded as falling in the domain of research, while evaluation is concerned with the determination of worth or merit. Although widely accepted, the distinction should not prevent an evaluator from using experimental methodology when issues of causality are in question. Nor should research attempt to be value free. Ethical norms and procedural norms should be part of any research regimen. Attempts to be value free are confusions with the general aim to control bias. The results on an experiment should never be altered because the experimenter holds a bias. But the experimenter should be bound by ethical norms and methodological standards.

### Designing the Experiment

Experimental design is built on the idea that when something happens, you can observe the result directly. If you treat something in a new way and find that you have a new result (i.e., dependent variable), you assume that the change is due to the new treatment (i.e., independent variable). The problem with that arrangement is that it is not always that simple. To make sure that the observed change was in fact due to the treatment and not some other unobserved cause, scientists enlarged the scope of the design in two ways. First, they insisted on repeating an experiment several times to ensure that results were consistent, and then they began adding controls to rule out alternative explanations.

A *control* is a measure that can be understood as having two general types. First, there are the controls over conditions to ensure consistency, and second, there are additional features of the design that address the most typical alternative explanations. Experimentalists have identified several potential causative factors over time and developed ways to rule them out as a major contributing force in the experiment. Some of the most common include the effects of prior learning, age, and sex; training during the procedure; and maturation based on normal growth.

An example of a control might be the use of a second group of students who get the same conditions as the experimental treatment group except the key treatment in question. This control is designed to rule out the possibility that subjects may learn the new behavior on their own. If the experimental group that receives the new treatment shows an improvement in learning over the control group that statistical testing supports is not due to chance, we are a little more sure that the treatment is what caused the change than if we had just observed the experimental group alone. Note that this kind of comparison is not the same as comparing two different treatments to see which one works better. In the strictest sense of experimental design, comparing two treatments is less desirable than doing an experiment with one treatment and several controls. Although you may have one treatment with Outcomes that appear to be more desirable than the other treatment, the overall ambiguity of confidence in the results is no greater than when you are using the simple one-treatment design with no controls. The object of design in experimentation is to produce data on cause and effect between a treatment and the result. That data should include a statement of the confidence one can attribute to the findings. A typical experimental design for a single treatment might look like Table 5.3.

It must be noted that the two samples will not have overlapping members, but will come from the same target population. The strength of the design will increase with sample size. Statisticians have generally accepted the arbitrary number of 30 subjects as representative enough to overcome small-sample measurement error.

**Table 5.3**    Single-Treatment Design

| Random sample receives treatment. | Treatment group is tested using results measure. |
|---|---|
| Random sample from same population with all conditions the same, except no treatment. | Control group is tested using the same results measure. |

*Problems With Classic Experimental Studies in Educational Settings*

Although the classic experiment is useful to increase the confidence in findings about treatments and results, the use of classic experimentation is rare in most evaluation studies. First, the method does not address the value of the Outcome. And second, the classic experiment requires resources and time that are usually not available to the evaluator. Understanding the issues that surround the design of a classic experiment can, however, help evaluators as they observe events and consider the results. Evaluators must attempt to avoid the error of assuming that all observed results are directly traceable to the educational programs and nothing else. Evaluators must remain alert to the possibility that other causes may be operating. Some of these may be onetime events, and some of these may be built into the educational setting. When evaluators suspect that specific factors are affecting the results, they can recommend a formal experiment be used to clear up the ambiguity surrounding the educational treatment.

## Time-Series and Conventional Research Studies

On the topic of "real experiments" for evaluation and those that simply work, the literature has much to say about collecting data useful for evaluation. But no resource is as straightforward as that of Dale Brethower. Here is what he offers us about this otherwise complex topic:[4]

*People Do Not Know About a Powerful Research Design*

Time-series designs are the most powerful research designs that exist, they are used in many fields of science (including social sciences), they are almost always feasible, and practitioners in the field can use them without major cost or disruption of their work.[5]

*How Time-Series Designs Work*

The simplest time-series design is one you use regularly. Turn the light switch, and the light comes on. If it doesn't, you flip the switch a couple of times, then check the bulb. If it looks bad, you put in another bulb, then flip the light switch. Voila! The light comes on. (If it doesn't, you check the fuses or the wiring or call for help.) If I am doing some clinical work and someone describes a problem, I say "Do x," and they do x, and I ask, "Is that better?" If not, I might ask more questions or say, "Do y," and see how that goes.

*Time-Series Design*

Do something. Check to see what happens. A major strength of the design is that it supports *replications* within each study. And as any researcher knows, replication is essential to ensure that we have findings we can trust.

We can make the simple and basic design a lot more complicated. We can ask several different folks with the same presenting problem to "Do x." That is a replication across time and across subjects. Or we can check several baselines, not just what the client says hurts but any one of several other possible measures such as whether the itchy spot is red or swollen or whether the dysfunctional interaction occurs every day of the week or with everyone, and so on. We call that a *multiple-baseline design.*

We can do reversals. We say, "Do x" until a week from Thursday then "Stop doing x" and see what happens. By measuring in multiple baselines and instituting multiple treatments across time and across subjects and doing reversals and then reversing the reversals, we get a really good notion about internal validity, does "doing x" help with "condition y"? External validity is a snap because we can repeat the design in other settings, with other clients, by having other people do the treatment with their clients, and so on.

You can use the time-series design with yourself around motivational issues. What do you think might motivate you to floss your teeth regularly? Take baseline data on how well and how often you floss. Apply the motivational treatment—maybe asking a friend to monitor you and your flossing and praise you when it is working and offer suggestions when it is not. See whether the frequency or quality improves. If so, keep on with the treatment; if not, try putting $5 in your "Pay the dentist" fund every time you fail to floss when you should. Or put $10 in your "Contributions to my most hated cause" fund. Try something. The neat thing about a time-series design is that it is flexible, practical, feasible, and cheap. Another neat thing about a time-series design is that you can use it just to help you do something, or you can tweak it into a rigorous scientific study. It is a terrific design for motivational research.

When to use time-series evaluation? Use it any time you are interested in knowing the effect and impact of some program, project, activity, or intervention and are not comparing it with another program, project, or intervention. You may use a time series when you cannot run (or it doesn't make sense to run) a control group study.

For example, if you want to know whether a particular teaching technique is useful with a particular group of learners, you don't have to run a comparison group matching the learners, teachers, and environment. You may simply see whether learning and mastery took place over time. Thus the time-series approach doesn't ask, "Is Treatment A better than Treatment B?" but simply asks, "Did this treatment work in this setting?"

*Popular Designs*

Most evaluation methods books cover correlational research and double-blind crossover research, and most note the difficulties of correlational research—the difficulty of defining constructs, the difficulty of independently measuring overlapping constructs, and the fact that the correlations apply to populations, not to individuals.

Given such difficulties, you'd think people would want to know about a research design like the time-series design that would help them around, over, and through such methodological problems—but maybe not after having invested tons of money and prestige in another design.

*Here's How Double-Blind Crossover Studies Work*

"The "gold standard" of the medical research community, and indeed the "purists" in educational research, is to accept only the results of rigorous studies: double-blind or double-blind crossover studies. A double-blind study is one in which neither the people administering a treatment nor the people receiving a treatment know which treatment is being administered. For example, a nurse might deliver medicine to patients who have agreed to participate in an experiment. The nurse and the patients know that some patients are getting a potential wonder drug X and others are getting a placebo (a pill that looks like the real thing and contains substances that mimic the adverse side effects of the real thing). The researchers must use what could pejoratively be called "poison pill placebos," because most new drugs have adverse side effects. If they were given an inert placebo, the patients would know when they were getting the placebo because it wouldn't make them feel sick.

The nurse is "blind" to the treatment, as is the patient. Neither knows whether the patient is receiving drug X or the carefully crafted placebo. The crossover occurs when, unbeknownst to the nurse or patient, those patients who had been receiving the placebo now get drug X and the ones who had been getting drug X get the placebo. Rigorous, right? No chance of psychological effects from thinking you are getting a powerful drug. One has to control for such effects. A placebo works in a high percentage of cases and for a great variety of diseases. If it were patentable, it could be marketed as a wonder drug!

The double-blind crossover standard has a serious drawback. Mainstream medicine does not advertise the fact that there is no "experimental evidence" for many, probably most, medical practices. The practices are unvalidated because there have been no double-blind studies to support them.

On the other hand, practices are typically validated in use through clinical case studies, a type of validation the medical community vehemently rejects whenever a practice does not fit into prevailing notions of "best practices."

Taking the double-blind crossover study as a standard . . . leaves the medical community in the awkward position of having to acknowledge that there is no scientific evidence that amputation of one's legs interferes with walking or that decapitation is in any way harmful to one's health." The double-blind crossover design cannot be used with a powerful treatment. It works only with treatments so weak that their effects can be disguised.

## Simulations and Games

The use of simulation and game theory to build educational treatments is on the increase following successful applications in business and military settings. The objective of a simulation is to enable participants to experience the problematic factors of events but under controlled and safer conditions that occur in the real setting. Simulations have been used to teach the operation of the court system, the political system, flight training, electrical systems, and parenting and child care. In all cases, the participants experience some but not all of the aspects of the actual situation being modeled. For example, students in shop class can learn to hook up high-voltage circuits using low-voltage current. The essential cues and procedure are the same except that the consequence of error is reduced. Simulations and games have become important tools for evaluation because they allow teachers and evaluators to see students perform tasks that are not practical as real events.

- *General description of the method:* A situation is modeled using the essential cues and behavior patterns required for success in the real setting except that costly or dangerous aspect are eliminated from the exercise.

- *Strong points and advantages:* Performance can be evaluated to see how students learn under specific conditions, but the game or simulation can be controlled to stop or emphasize correct behavior without catastrophic consequences.

- *Weak points and disadvantages:* The fidelity of the simulation may be a critical factor in the transfer to the real situation. High fidelity is costly in some cases.

- *Measurement considerations:* Simulations and games provide excellent opportunities for measurement.

### Determining What to Model in a Game or Simulation

The game or simulation should contain a reasonable approximation of the setting in which the behavior is to occur, although the setting elements may model only some aspects of the real setting and not others. Only the cues and behavioral responses are important. Therefore a simulation of an electrical panel need not be energized with high voltage so long as the cues and student interactions can be performed using low voltage. A cardboard cutout of a traffic light may be sufficient as long as the red, yellow, and green lights are sufficient cues to learners to make decisions leading to the desired learning. When modeling a game or simulation, make a flow chart of the desired behavior in the actual setting, and list all of the cue response patterns that lead to correct behavior. Next, look for ways that the same cue or signal can be duplicated in the simulated environment of the game or exercise. Test the substituted elements using real students to see whether sufficient fidelity exists to obtain the level of cue response required to compete the task being modeled. After some experimentation, build the simulation model around the task flow using the substituted elements. The key is safety and control. Many simulations are made more effective when the simulation has a provision for instructor control to stop and provide coaching as students require assistance. A pilot study is normally required to arrive at a final design of a simulation.

### Using Simulation and Gaming for Evaluation

Evaluation is easily accommodated if the simulation is designed for easy observation of the learners. Since the simulation or game will have been designed using a work flow or task model, the correct behavior is specified ahead of time and evaluator observers will be able to compare learner behavior with the standard for correct performance. In addition, most simulations are designed to allow control over prompts and cues so that learners can be prompted to perform the correct sequence or act at the appropriate time. If the real setting does not include rich prompts, the simulation can be designed to gradually reduce the prompts as the learner builds internal cues and memory patterns.

- *General description of the method:* Organizational records are identified as relevant and reviewed for information on key elements of the educational program including past evaluations, meeting notes, organizational mission statements, etc.

- *Strong points and advantages:* The data exists and can often be searched using electronic means.

- *Weak points and disadvantages:* It may be hard to determine what data is relevant and what is not if data is not organized in useful categories.

- *Measurement considerations:* It is possible to use the frequency that ideas appear as some indication of the importance or time spent on an issue.

## DOCUMENT-CENTERED METHODS

### Extant-Data Review

*Extant data* refers to data that already exist in some form of organizational record. As such, it is advisable to start by considering whether these sources contain relevant and useful data. Some examples of extant data are current strategic plans, current budget records, census data, previous needs assessments reports, previous evaluation reports, past test scores, or other sources you might uncover (and there are many). One may also choose to look in records collected by other bodies, such as public and private agencies, institutions, corporations: just about any place where useful information might be mined.

While questionnaires, group processes, and interviews are traditionally associated with the collection of qualitative (soft) data, extant data tend to be associated with quantitative (hard) data. For instance, if one wanted to know the itemized financial investment for a given program or what the rate of successful completion was, asking for someone's opinion about it would not likely render the type of valid and reliable data that looking at documented organizational records might render (assuming, of course, that the data entered was accurate).

The preliminary task is the same as in the previous methods. That is, before selecting this as a viable data collection method, one must first start with the evaluation questions and the associated indicators previously identified. If relevant data can be obtained from existing records, then there is little utility in creating data collection tools to get that same data. In this case, it is most feasible to review the data that already exist. This does not mean that one should rely solely on extant data. One should still consider this data in the context of other data collected during this evaluation process.

- *General description of the method:* A list of key words and topics is used to develop data base searches to identify books and articles in periodicals.

- *Strong points and advantages:* Most libraries now utilize data bases that can be used to do electronic searches to locate titles and subjects that are related to the particular study.

- *Weak points and disadvantages:* Once a list of items is drawn up, someone has to read or scan them to glean the valuable part. This can take some time.

- *Measurement considerations:* A review may identify other measurement-based studies that have been conducted in similar settings.

## Literature Review

It is hard to underestimate the value of a well-planned review of literature. The existing literature on evaluation, school administration, program effectiveness, tactics of instruction, and decision making can assist the evaluation team in planning and implementing an evaluation. Citations from the literature may add credibility to evaluation reports. In each case of reviewing and using the literature, apply the same standards of rigor that we suggest in this book. Just because something got published does not automatically mean that it is valid. Look at each piece of literature that interests you and screen it for validity and reliability of what it offers.

It will be helpful to list topics and relate them to key words that are used in the various search programs that now augment the catalog system in modern libraries. Several special databases are now updated on a regular basis. The search librarian can help you structure your search and guide you to the appropriate database.

## Critical Incidence Technique

Critical incidents are those situations, behavior patterns, or result patterns—from actual experience—that can be proven to have a significant impact on individual performance (Micro), organizational (Macro), and societal (Mega) consequences. Many things happen in the work setting, but not all are directly related to gaps in results or opportunities for improved results. The evaluator has to use good (objective) judgment to sort out what was important and what was not. By searching the records for critical incidents or by recording critical incidents and their results, we can generate evidence about good and not-useful performance.

*General description of the method:* direct observations or self-reports of specific behaviors, situations, or results patterns that relate to an issue of interest.

*Strong points and advantages:* Can provide specific cases in point to support data collected through other means.

*Weak points and disadvantages:* If incidents provided are stated in very general terms, the data may be difficult to interpret and/or use.

*Measurement considerations:* One may want to tally the number of similar responses provided.

### What Is a Critical Incident?

Evaluators may observe many events during the course of an evaluation study. *Critical incidents* are situations, behavior patterns, or result patterns that can be proven to have a large impact on performance and organizational (Macro) and societal (Mega) consequences. Many things happen in the work setting, but not all are directly related to gaps in results or opportunities for improved results. By searching the records for critical incidents or by recording critical incidents and their results, we can generate evidence about good and bad performance.

*Standard Procedure for Recording a Critical Incident*

It is useful to develop a standard procedure and train the observation team and all other personnel who will be questioned. The following steps are recommended:

- Prepare a written definition of a critical incident.
- Prepare several examples related to the context of your evaluation study.
- Go over the examples with the evaluation team.
- Develop a common format for recording.
- Develop rules for recording.
- After a few weeks of use, review the inputs from the team.
- Make adjustments to the procedure and rules if required.

In general, things may be judged "critical" when the impact of the event changes the potential Outcome, Outputs, and Products of the program being evaluated. This can include disruptions as well as events that promote or advance the goals and objectives. Sometimes, the impact may not be evident at the time the incident happens. Here, the standard procedure is to ask respondents to think back about specific instances that illustrate what is wrong with the organization (i.e., unsatisfactory) as well as what is right or satisfactory with the organization.

These critical incidents can then be categorized as the various levels of the Organizational Elements Model (OEM) and/or for the various programs being evaluated.

## Artifacts and Work Products

This is another source of evaluation, that is, the actual result produced. If, for example, we want to check out the gaps in a teacher's performance we will check her learners' performance. If 50% of them are not reading and should be, she requires 100% to meet her standards; then we have a gap in results, and this evaluation data will identify the areas for change. If we want to make judgments about language competence, we could review learner papers and check for proper sentence structure, grammar, punctuation, and spelling. These are "artifacts" of teaching and learning.

## GUIDELINES AND CHECKLISTS FOR COLLECTING DATA

Table 5.5, based on the work of Kaufman, Oakley-Browne, Watkins, & Leigh (2003)[6] shows some basic considerations:

**Table 5.4**    Basic Data Collection Questions

---

**Some Basic Data Collection Questions**

1. What evaluation questions do you want to ask and answer?
2. What use will the evaluation data be that are to be collected and used for decision making?
3. What data already exist?
4. Are existing data hard and soft?
5. What levels of data exist, Mega, Macro, and Micro?
6. What mix of data gathering methods—tools, instruments, methods—will be used? Why?
7. What sample size provides verifiable evidence?
8. What internal data about individual and team performances gaps will be collected?
9. What external data will be collected about gaps and discrepancies in client results and expectations? In societal consequences?
10. How will the hard and soft data be collected?
11. How will the data be translated into evidence of priority Needs?
12. Who will collect the data?
13. How will the data be captured and recorded?
14. Is there a suitable questionnaire available? Can one be usefully modified?
15. Will the way data are collected really answer the evaluation questions?

---

**Table 5.5**    Evaluation Questions: What Do You Do and Deliver?

| | Questions | Notes |
|---|---|---|
| 1 | What hard and soft data will we collect? | |
| 2 | How will we collect the data? | |
| 3 | What are the available and useful ways and means to collect that data? | |
| 4 | What are the advantages and disadvantages of each available way and means to collect data? | |
| 5 | How much time is available? How urgent is the project? | |
| 6 | How much money is available for the evaluation? | |

**Table 5.5** (Continued)

| | Questions | Notes |
|---|---|---|
| 7 | What people are available to do the evaluation? How many? Where are they? | |
| 8 | What are the skill levels of the people who can do the evaluation? | |
| 9 | What are the confidentiality issues? | |
| 10 | What questions will be resisted? | |
| 11 | Are there cultural issues that impose restraints on what is gathered and how? | |
| 12 | Are there any methods that are unsuitable or suitable? | |
| 13 | What level of rapport exists between the data gatherers and the target groups? | |
| 14 | What influence, tactics, and methods are required to overcome resistance? | |
| 15 | Are the sponsors fully aware of their role? | |
| 16 | What sample size? How is the sample to be identified? | |
| 17 | Are people geographically spread? How widely? | |
| 18 | What special resources and logistics are required? | |
| 19 | What level of support can be expected from the target groups? | |
| 20 | How important is confidentiality for the target group? | |
| 21 | How will the data be captured and documented? Will the methods of collecting data be both valid and reliable? | |
| 22 | Who will compile the data? | |
| 23 | How will the data be reduced? | |
| 24 | How will the data be presented? | |
| 25 | How will questions be answered? | |
| 26 | What decisions are to be made on the basis of the evaluation results? | |
| 27 | Will the evaluation results be credible to those making the decision and those affected by the decisions? | |

**Figure 5.1**   Questionnaire Guidelines

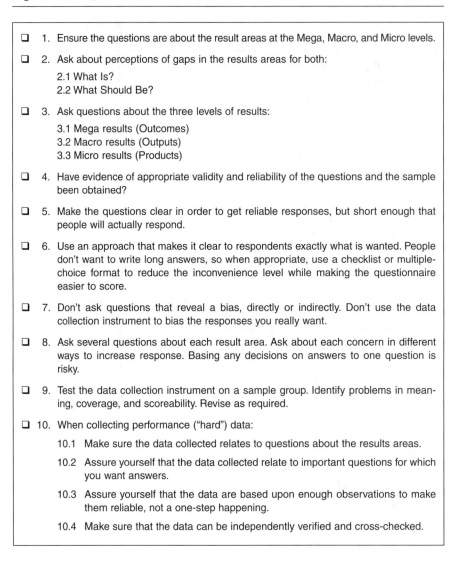

1.  Ensure the questions are about the result areas at the Mega, Macro, and Micro levels.

2.  Ask about perceptions of gaps in the results areas for both:
    2.1 What Is?
    2.2 What Should Be?

3.  Ask questions about the three levels of results:
    3.1 Mega results (Outcomes)
    3.2 Macro results (Outputs)
    3.3 Micro results (Products)

4.  Have evidence of appropriate validity and reliability of the questions and the sample been obtained?

5.  Make the questions clear in order to get reliable responses, but short enough that people will actually respond.

6.  Use an approach that makes it clear to respondents exactly what is wanted. People don't want to write long answers, so when appropriate, use a checklist or multiple-choice format to reduce the inconvenience level while making the questionnaire easier to score.

7.  Don't ask questions that reveal a bias, directly or indirectly. Don't use the data collection instrument to bias the responses you really want.

8.  Ask several questions about each result area. Ask about each concern in different ways to increase response. Basing any decisions on answers to one question is risky.

9.  Test the data collection instrument on a sample group. Identify problems in meaning, coverage, and scoreability. Revise as required.

10. When collecting performance ("hard") data:
    10.1  Make sure the data collected relates to questions about the results areas.
    10.2  Assure yourself that the data collected relate to important questions for which you want answers.
    10.3  Assure yourself that the data are based upon enough observations to make them reliable, not a one-step happening.
    10.4  Make sure that the data can be independently verified and cross-checked.

## NOTES

1.  Again, soft data are about things that are personal and cannot be validated against other things. Hard data are independently verifiable. Both are important for a useful evaluation.

2.  There are different opinions on anonymity. Some think it vital, while others suggest that people should not hide their observations, thinking, and suggestions. Choose which option based on the environment in which you are using a questionnaire.

3.  One way to cut down on the "clutter" in responses to open-ended questions is to get the respondent to focus on results and consequences, not on resources or methods.

4.  The following section is directly quoted from Professor Emeritus Dale Brethower, Western Michigan University, November 15, 2004 (personal communication to Roger Kaufman). Our thanks to Professor Brethower for this contribution.

5.  Campbell and Stanley (1966) had described them as quasi-experimental designs in their classic *Experimental and Quasi-Experimental Designs for Research.*

6.  Much of this section has been modified from Kaufman, Oakley-Browne, Watkins, and Leigh (2003). These modifications are made to target evaluation in education.

# Scenario 2

## *Finding Facts*

John Quick and his team now had a good set of questions to guide the evaluation (as described in Scenario 1). The Organizational Elements Model (OEM) helped them to make sure that they were looking at educational results both inside as well as outside.

The team was enthusiastic to get going and ask and answer the right questions. The management plan was now in draft form, and every team member had the responsibility to review and update the sections that related to their task assignments.

Dr. Mackenzie met with John to suggest some ways to further structure activity. He produced a sketch of a matrix that listed evaluation questions and, next to each, all types of data that might be relevant to answering each question. In a third column, he listed possible observation/data-gathering methods: how the performance data would be collected. John suggested that the first team meeting be devoted to expanding the prime set of questions to include the specific questions for this study. Dr. Mackenzie agreed. They started by looking at material available.

## LOOKING AT THE EXISTING "NEEDS ASSESSMENT" AND NEEDS ASSESSMENT DATA DELIVERED

The school system had a *needs assessment*, but they now questioned whether or not it was a useful one. Did it collect data on gaps in results for three levels of results and consequences? They double-checked the existing needs assessment approach and data with the model that they now believed to be most useful.[1]

It turns out that what was done was more of a "solutions assessment" that focused on teaching, learning, and resources, not upon learner mastery and competence and the usefulness of their competencies in school and in later life. What to do?

The evaluation team realized that *needs assessments* are proactive and evaluation reactive—after the fact—and they could not do a credible evaluation without useful needs assessment data. Done correctly, the *needs assessment* would provide criteria for both the current results as well as the desired and required ones. The "required/desired" part of the *needs assessment* would provide data-based evaluation criteria.

So, they did a new *needs assessment,* although some in the educational community had a bit of trouble at first understanding the differences between the gaps-in-results-and-consequences approach and the existing one, which looked at gaps in methods, processes, and resources. With discussion came understanding, for everyone really did want to be successful even if it meant giving up some previous ways of thinking.

After 3 months, the new needs assessment was conducted (they found they could use some of the existing "needs" data), but the new approach, identifying gaps in results, now provided a useful base for the evaluation. Now, to using the *needs data.*

## CONTINUING THE EVALUATION

Several community leaders were now working together, and the new approach to curriculum and teaching and learning in Cobb County was a published plan that had the blessing of the state officials. It looked as if alignment had been achieved, and it was all based on solid performance data that came from the needs assessment. So, they reviewed the original set of questions:

- Do the results we seek stem from valid needs?
- Are the mechanisms, organizations, resources, and programs designed to produce desired results effective in meeting the valid needs?
- Who are the stakeholders?
- What are the limits of this inquiry in time and resources and range of issues considered?
- What solutions are in place to meet valid needs?
- Are the solutions effective? Are the solutions efficient?
- What is the effect over time?
- What intervening variables affect Products, Outputs, and Outcomes?[2]
- How do we recognize and record or measure Products, Outputs, and Outcomes?

The first question seemed obvious now that a need assessment had been done and there were solid and measurable needs—gaps in results—upon which to base decisions, but Dr. Mackenzie urged the group to ask some related questions:

- What if the new approach does not work or work quickly enough? Will the stakeholders and the school board change their minds and go back to business as usual?
- What if the approach is working but the costs are higher than projected? Will they stay the course?

The new plan for Cobb County was based on a shared Ideal Vision— the kind of world they wanted to create for tomorrow's child—with some far-reaching purposes.

- If not all of the goals are realized or achieved only in part, will stakeholders lower their sights to a less than Ideal Vision? Will they settle for less than they had planned to deliver?

These new questions caused some deep reflection and much discussion. They soon came to a consensus that it would be a good idea to monitor the stakeholders and the school board in particular to get reactions as the school year progressed. This derivative question was added to the list:

- Will stakeholders adjust their conception of the Ideal Vision if the school programs do not succeed, or will they buckle down and work to improve the programs in order to create the kind of world they want for their children and grandchildren? Are they really committed to Mega? Will they do the right thing and not just the expedient thing?

The second question was basically asking: Do the programs work? Dr Mackenzie pointed out that the prime question illustrated a principle but now each part of the program would have to be judged by its contribution to the goals and objectives and the specific objectives that derived from them. How is each feature of the new approach working?

It was also suggested that if some adjustment had to be made in midstream, the evaluation team could assess how well Anita (recall Scenario 1) and her task force of teachers and volunteers were adjusting to the problem. Then, someone asked how it would be possible to know whether something was going wrong in midstream if the important goals and objectives relating to school ranking, standardized testing, and state testing tended to go down at the end of the school year. William DuPont spoke up and suggested looking for indicators that might be available all through the year. He noted that teacher test all the time, that the new tutorial would be a good place to get student reactions, and that the volunteers could tell us how their students were progressing on their lessons.

The team made an action item for each member to list all of the process indicators that could be tied to the eventual success or failure of the entire program. The following questions were added to the list:

- Is the tutorial period helping students learn?
- Is the individual attention that students receive making a difference?
- Do the teachers make effective use of the new 8-hour day?
- Do the volunteers make a difference in students' attitudes toward learning?
- Does the new policy on homework mean more actual time is spent on practice and learning? Does it lead to mastery?

> *Scenario Teaching Point:*
> There are more specific questions that were gradually added. We won't go into all of them. The point here is that the team realized that in a large program, questions can be asked about each feature of the program. Each part can be evaluated as a contributing part or a detriment to the overall program. Data can be gathered all along the way even if the significance of that data is not fully clear until the results are obtained.

Enter *formative evaluation.* The team read the literature of evaluation and found Michael Scriven's (1967) concept of formative evaluation. *Formative evaluation* tracks one's progress as they move from "What is" to "What should be." The evaluation team was asking questions about progress toward the final objectives. When what was being done was on track, they continued. When it was not moving toward the objectives, revisions could be made there and then, instead of waiting until the end of the program.

Once the team had expanded the set of questions, they began to match questions to the sources of information required for the answers. They divided the questions into the following sets:

- Questions that could be answered using interviews
- Questions that could be answered using tests
- Questions that could be answered using natural indicators
- Questions that could be answered by reviewing documents
- Questions that could be answered using participant observation
- Questions that could be answered by just standing around quietly observing

For the interview set, the team listed all persons who would be interviewed, and how often. For the test set, the team had to decide what tests to use: commercial standardized tests, teacher-made knowledge tests, or skill application performance tests or test runs as part of a simulation or role play. The natural indicators that they listed included class attendance, study hall noise, library checkout rate, parent complaints, and requests for transfer in or out of the school district or from school to school. The document set included review of student folders, review of school budget and accounting data, review of college entry records, and job placement records. All teachers in the program would be designated participant observers. The two graduate students would observe all aspects of the program.

## DATA COLLECTION PLAN AND SCHEDULE

Now the team was ready to plan for the observation and data collection. Each team member was assigned data collection/observation tasks, which were scheduled using a project management computer program. If a test or instrument had to be developed or purchased, that lead time was built into the schedule. Dr. Mackenzie suggested that everything they had so far should be cross-checked against the original goals and objectives stated in the newly published plan, titled "The New Approach to Schooling in Cobb County: Defining and Delivering Useful Results."

The published goals were as follows:

- Every student will graduate from high school.
- Every school in the district will achieve an "A" rating from the state.
- Graduating students will be qualified for entry-level jobs or to enter military service or college.
- The school system will be drug free, gang free, and premature-pregnancy free.
- Teachers will love their jobs.
- Students will be motivated.
- The schools' rating based on standardized national testing will rank in the upper third of the nation's schools.
- Learners will be successful in school and in later life.

Dr. Mackenzie pointed out that some of these goals were clear and had a ready criteria and data source. Others were statements of principle, but these required some operational definition that converted the goal into some observable behavior or measurable indicator or score; goals had to be converted into objectives.[3]

Teachers loving their jobs could be indicated by a self-report, but self-reports have some known weaknesses that must be considered. The team decided to approach this purpose with a combination of indicators. A teacher questionnaire would be constructed and administered three times during the first year of the new program. Teacher turnover rate and unexcused absences would be compared with the last 3 years prior to see whether a trend change had occurred. Students would be asked to comment, and some spouses and partners of the faculty would be interviewed.

## TRAPS, ERRORS, AND RULES OF THE ROAD IN THE OBSERVATION PHASE

The observation phase provides the evaluation team the information that will allow the team to analyze the data and make evaluation conclusions to be included in the presentation of findings in the reporting stage. The team may collect insufficient data due to lack of resources or other common pressures that impede normal evaluation activities. However, in addition to what could be called "normal problems," there are several traps and associated errors that are caused by inappropriate point of view or lack of perspective on the nature of evaluation in educational settings.

### The Science Trap

Some evaluators suffer from a fear that they will be challenged on findings or criticized for lack of precision that many attribute to the so-called hard sciences. We think there are many reasons to borrow from physical science as a discipline, but we also want to point out some possible errors from doing that as well. One example stems from a policy that was issued by the federal government.

In issuing a demand for "Scientifically Based Evaluation Methods" and randomized control group trials, the Department of Education has chosen language with a ring of acceptability and rigor that may gain political approval. It further seems to support the movement for increased accountability and getting the most for our education dollars. This seemingly rational request is called "face validity" because it appears, on the face, that what is asked for will work and work well. Looking valid and actually being valid might be different.

Do not assume that you are conducting a "scientific evaluation" just because you mandate procedures that are used by other scientific endeavors. This may not guarantee that your effort has the rigor, logic, and valid inference that is the hallmark of science. Your effort may not make sense, but it will sound good to casual observers (the words have a ring of science, and that sounds good)—words that have only *face validity* behind them. The problem is that evaluation efforts that depend on the marketing value of buzzwords to attempt to solve the observational methodology problems or to gain credibility are doomed to failure for a host of reasons that have been well worked out by both scientists and evaluators over the last several decades.

In our approach to evaluation, we welcome opportunities to apply science and research to evaluation. But the benefits of science cannot be obtained by just "talking science" that turns out to be only superficial application of buzzwords or marketing flair. What we use, do, and deliver must deliver useful results—not just seemingly appealing approaches. The following are some common errors that can and should be avoided.

### Error of Association

When we have confidence in propositions that fly in the face of facts because a noted personality took part because of the past reputation of participants, or because of advertising, that is the *error of association* (most advertising depends on us making the error of association). When evaluators use terms that sound scientific or produce reams of computer output because scientists use computers a lot, they must take care to do real science and to use statistics that are relevant to the question at hand. Science is not based on credibility by association. Science is not done by endorsement of the elite, nor is science the storage of enormous quantities of computer information (just storing information by itself does not make it scientific). There are many observational methods of science that also apply to evaluation, but they must be used correctly and appropriately. They must not be "window dressing."

### Error of Relevancy

The aim of science is to expand knowledge and understanding about the natural world by using theory building, hypothesis testing through experimentation, which is a very special type of observation. Science has rules or "canons" for observation and the use of controls, which are attempts to rule out factors that could enter into a cause-and-effect relation. Some of these can apply to evaluations. An evaluation of a treatment (reading program) might ask whether it was indeed the reading program that caused the reading gains in the students.

A scientist may well ask the same question, and the way the answer is obtained will be subject to rules like these: A rule that calls for observations to be repeatable, forming a conclusion based on a nonrepeatable, onetime event, is called the "error of the artifact." Hence the Canon of Repeatability. The scientist will look for the simplest answer that explains all that has occurred.

The Canon of Simplicity *(Occums razor)* states that the simplest explanation that explains all of the realities is the best to use. There are, however, some important differences between scientific experiments and educational programs being evaluated. The evaluator not only wants to know that there is a cause and effect between the reading program and the students reading improvements, but the evaluator is also looking at the value of the program in relation to a community need—a gap in results rooted in the community. The evaluator is less able to do things over and over, while the scientist commonly does one experiment after another. Perhaps the most striking difference is that to the scientist, literally every phenomenon is of potential interest. Odd bits of data may at some point result in a new theory. The search never ends.

Evaluators, however, have a different focus (and usually a resource limitation). Evaluators are looking at the results of programs and structure their inquiry to consider only those factors relevant to the program (factors in the cause-and-effect chain).

Evaluators who practice the inductive logic of science (to gather as many facts as possible) may run out of time and money before they have answered the evaluation questions at hand. To do this is to commit the *error of relevancy*.

### Other Errors of Procedure Logic

There are errors of logic that lead to false conclusions. We will cover some of those errors of logic in the next scenario. There are also logical errors that occur in observations and procedures. These errors are often committed in evaluations that try to mimic the procedures of science without really doing good science. Here are a few of the most common. The *error of the forked path* occurs when procedures that lead to two different end products start with the same steps in common: It is possible to start to do Procedure A and end up doing Procedure B. This is particularly true if you are behind schedule, under pressure, or have just completed Procedure B on a prior task. This error can affect evaluators in collecting or transcribing data, giving examinations, grading tests, and documenting results. This error can be reduced by creating a "pause and consider" cue just ahead of the branch point.

Another common procedure error is the *error of false randomization*. To make an inference about a population from a sample, that sample must be drawn at random. However, many times in evaluation situations the so-called sample is not representative of the population, but statistics that rest on that assumption are used anyway. It is also very common in evaluation studies to commit the *error of not controlling for bias* in making observations. Bias on the part of observers is sometimes difficult to eliminate, but there are ways to reduce the effects of bias, such as using multiple observers who compare findings.

## The Methodology Trap

Observation methods are developed to answer questions and avoid errors of logic, errors of technique, errors of omission and commission, and errors of bias. Many approaches have been codified and highly valued for the contributions in sociology and educational research efforts. Unfortunately, an expectation has developed that requires the use of methods and approaches to gain respectability and acceptance independent of the suitability of the method to answer the questions at issue. Here are some errors related to methodology.

### Error of the Instrument

We often use instruments (electronic and mechanical as well as paper or computer-delivered tests and exercises. It is very wise to keep in mind that all instruments are subject to failure or loss of calibration or incorrect use. Some electronic instruments require setup procedures that are complicated and must include warm-up time. Hook up of attachments may require particular care and correct placement. Written instructions may be confusing. Tests may be unreliable or invalid. Language usage may differ between groups, as when a test using complex medical language is given to persons with no medical background. All of these potential problems should increase the care devoted to the use of instruments. Failure in this area will compound errors of measurement.

### Error of Measurement

We measure things in order to make generalizations about phenomena in the programs that we are evaluating. But we must always consider what is being measured. Are we measuring the right things (called "validity")? What can we claim based on what we measure, and what does that measure stand for in the complete system of events and mix of intention and results? We must ask why each measurement is important to our conclusions. We must consider how often to measure, what to measure, and what scale to use in measurement. Measurement can add precision to a study, but incorrect measurement due to flawed procedures can lead to a false sense of precision where none is warranted. For example, the use of the wrong scale and subsequent mathematical treatments of the data can lead to enormous distortion.

### Error of the Model

Models can be powerful and useful for planning and executing evaluations. But all models are approximations or representations that may or may not fit the events and situations being modeled. When we create a model either for procedure or for explanation or for mapping, we often use the model to predict events in the program being evaluated. If the model is a good fit, it may be useful in predicting results. However, we must always keep in mind that the model is not the real thing, and when we base our conclusions and plans on the model only, without confirming the prediction with corroborating information from other sources, we commit the *error of the model.*

### Error of the Artifact

Occasionally, we observe something in an evaluation study that happens only one time and cannot be repeated by any direct manipulation of the program under study. Sometimes, the single event (artifact) is good, and sometimes it is bad. It is important that the onetime occurrence stimulate additional study. However, it is equally important that conclusions about the program not be based on a single result. To do so would be to commit the error of the artifact (failure to replicate).

### Error of the Blind Spot

We have stated the importance of using the results of a program as the key focus of evaluation, but we do not at the same time imply that evaluators do not pay attention to the entire execution of the program. For example, in the event that program results were not what was intended or were in some way detrimental to the larger societal well-being, we would want to discard what did not work. But does that mean the entire program must be scrapped and a totally new program put in place? This might be the case if no observation took place during the program. The total penetration of the program in as many observational modalities as possible provides clues as to what parts of the program could be changed or modified.

*Error of Displacement Shift*

When observing events in an evaluation of a program, we tend to look where we can look and not always were we should look. If we limit our observations to only the easy parts, we may miss critical aspects of the program. There is an old joke about a man who loses his car key in a dark parking lot. He begins to search for the key out in the street. When asked why he is looking in the street and not in the parking lot, he replies that the streetlight makes it easier to see in the street. Another type of displacement occurs when we write educational objectives that cover only the parts of the performance that lend themselves to easy objective writing. The classic example is trying to evaluate a complex skill by asking questions about the names of the steps in the performance. If you limit your evaluation to that aspect only, you have committed the *error of displacement shift.*

*Error of Population Masking*

If a subgroup (students in Introductory Statistics) of a general population (all students in the university) have difficulty understanding the teacher, interviewing them may reveal the problem. However, if data on student dissatisfaction in one class were lumped with the general population to get an average level of student dissatisfaction, the particular subgroup problem would be submerged in the general data pool. If you base conclusions about the existence of problems on the average data only without further analysis, you run the risk of committing the *error of population masking.*

*Error of the Average Person*

We often talk of the average student. However, the limits posed by the class of measurement used and the characteristics measured must be made explicit. The study of ergonomics has profited from the use of data on populations, but in most cases, the extremes are used to capture most of the population.

## RULES OF THE ROAD FOR THE OBSERVATION PHASE

*Rule 1.* Time and resources must be devoted to observation (see Figure 2.A).

*Rule 2.* The target of observation is results. The most central theme of this book is that the main focus of evaluation activity should be to check results of your programs and educational endeavors and see whether they deliver results for all stakeholders, including our shared communities and society. Looking at results is not just a slogan; it profoundly separates our approach from other forms of evaluation.

*Rule 3.* Establish a clear path between program activity and results. There are two rules of the road associated with the concept and the practice of looking at results. The first of these we call the *clear-path rule*. The concept of results implies that a cause-and-effect chain exists between your intention for the program being evaluated and student learning. You intend that teaching and learning activities will achieve the results that you desire for the students. In most educational settings, educators have some control over the environment and the possible list of interruptions that could break the chain leading to the result. As educators, you recognize that in modern times, the list of factors that can impinge on the teaching-learning process has grown. We now have security issues, cell phones, dress codes (or lack of dress codes), drugs, gangs, poverty, and budgetary pressures that did not exist a decade ago. The point here is that the clear path can be corrupted. Therefore evaluation must include assessment of the Process, which leads to the Product (resulting learning or lack of learning). We have focused on the Product (results) in order to steer clear of the danger of valuing a Process that leads nowhere. We value a carpenter who hammers, saws, and nails lumber together to build a house, not for the simple actions of hammering, but for the proper assembly of the components to stand the test of wind and rain[4] to provide warm, dry shelter. The carpenter follows a blueprint. What happens if the carpenter does his part correctly but the blue print is wrong? In evaluation of the results, we still want a structure that meets our criteria, but in the example of the carpenter, we see that more than one factor can influence the result. In this example, we can still do meaningful evaluation because the clear-path rule applies. That is, we can identify all of the contributing factors and trace our steps to each factor in the event that the results are other than expected. In education, that can be a lack of learning or undesirable side effects. As in other rules, there is a proper order to be followed in their application. First, keep your focus on results, and then apply the clear-path rule.

*Rule 4.* Use valuable observation resources sparingly, but widen the focus when emerging issues have a reasonable probability of influencing program results. If a clear path cannot be established, apply this rule to widen the focus of the study. When results are not as expected or undesirable side effects are observed, it is necessary to widen the pattern of observation. The *focus rule* provides a way to expand your evaluation. The focus rule is to start with a narrow focus on your evaluation, focusing first on results, and apply the clear-path rule. If a clear path cannot be established or the results are not as expected, increase the scope of the evaluation to a wider focus. Now, your evaluation task includes discovery of issues and factors that affect achievement of desired results. Note that looking for competing program goals that set up a zero-sum gain situation is a good place to start. To widen the focus of evaluation, you will have to consider your resources.

*Rule 5.* When you identify an issue that may shed light on the factors leading to outcomes, use a sufficient number of evaluators and the time invested in the evaluation to reach full understanding of the issue. We make this point with a hypothetical chart. If time is charted on one axis and number of evaluators (along with their instrumentation) on the other, we believe that the resulting information gain will result in four stages. The first is the *zone of first impression,* the second is the *zone of emerging issues,* the *third is the zone of discovery,* and the last is the *zone of understanding.* The point is that you must invest enough time and resources to an evaluation study to reach a true understanding of events and factors. If you stop at first impressions, you may form the wrong conclusions later on in the study.

In the beginning of an effort to widen the scope of an evaluation, the evaluation personnel are able to see the obvious elements of the situation.

**Figure 2A**    The Importance of Sufficient Time and Resources

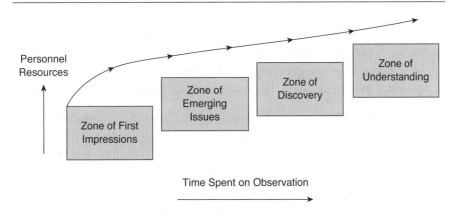

NOTE: The data accumulation curve is imposed on personnel resources plotted against time in observation.

The *zone of first impressions* is the area of the chart that covers initial data collection of everything that is easy to see. However, first impressions can be misleading, and it is highly desirable to stick with the observation long enough to reach the *zone of understanding.* This is the point at which the observation team can be confident that their findings are both relevant and accurate. But the team must first pass through the *zone of emerging issues* and the *zone of discovery.* In these phases of the investigation, data leads are developed and followed, hidden agendas are uncovered, and factors that bear upon the Products, Outputs, and Outcomes of the program are identified.

> *Rule 6.* Organize and cross-check your data. Organize your data to support each of the questions in your study. As you discuss issues among your evaluation team, keep notes on these discussions, with an eye to later using some of this material in the final report and recommendations.

Periodically in your study, compare emerging findings across the entire study to match information with timelines and with intermediate Outcomes like progress tests, special events, problems, disruptions, and changes in policy or procedures.

## ORGANIZATION AND CROSS-CHECK LIST

*Checkpoint 1.* Was the evaluation team in position to gather information and record data? Can you provide meaningful evaluative findings regarding the results of educational efforts?

*Checkpoint 2.* A simple description of results is not evaluation of results. Results are valued according to the goals and objectives of the educational system and larger society that support that system. Results may be as planned or not, depending on the success of the program or methods used to achieve them. Do you have data that links results to needs?

*Checkpoint 3.* When the results are not as planned, the evaluator may or may not be in a position to provide evaluation data to support the decisions to change, adjust, or start over. The guidance that the evaluator can render is a function of the general understanding of what went on, which, in turn, is a function of the information gathered. Do you have data on the cause of unplanned results?

*Checkpoint 4.* We shall use the term *data* to refer to any information that has been collected through observation (of several kinds) and has been recorded in some way. Do you have data on instructional activity, environmental factors, teacher skills and attitudes, milestone indicators, progress tests, and final results?

*Checkpoint 5.* Data can be the notes, records, recordings, and so on that have been collected either by the evaluator or his or her team and any other recorded information that is relevant to the issues at hand. How well has the team documented its findings?

*Checkpoint 6.* Information sources, on the other hand, are for practical purposes limitless, for there is an infinitesimal range of things that could be looked at. That range is narrowed a bit if we limit looking to those areas that have potential or actual relevance to all of the goals, objectives, and strategies that were set in place to reach the desired results. Has the team overlooked any important information resources?

*Checkpoint 7.* To capture the idea of potential information sources, consider the following: Between any two points in time t1 and t2, there are numerous events, which can be summarized as:

- Events under control of the program team that affect program results (evaluator observes)
- Events under control of the students that affect program results (evaluator observes)
- Events under control of the teachers that affect program results (evaluator observes)
- Events under control of the evaluation team (observations and recommendations)
- Events not under control that affect the program results (evaluator tries to identify)
- Events not under control that are irrelevant to program results (the evaluator tries to avoid spending resources to observe here)
- Unknown factors (evaluator may get lucky and discover relevant factors)

Were each of these provided for in your data collection plan?

*Checkpoint 8.* If the evaluation team is to base recommendations on findings related to the actual events of the situation in question (as opposed to basing recommendations on preexisting ideas and/or biases) and if the recommendations are a function of understanding the unfolding events, then the collection of information and subsequent conversion to data that will be used to support conclusions and recommendations is one of the most important functions of the evaluation effort. Will you be able to make sense out of your data when you start the analysis process and arrive at a conclusion to put into the report?

*Checkpoint 9.* Planning for observation and data collection (assuming that observations are converted to notes and records) can draw on several observation methodologies, all of which can result in data collection. Can you answer the original evaluation question set with your data?

*Checkpoint 10.* Did the evaluation team wisely use all possible information-gathering resources in such a way as to gather sufficient meaningful data and yet remain on schedule and on budget, the two biggies of project management (and evaluation management)? Are you on schedule and on budget?

## NOTES

1.  Kaufman's needs assessment process (Kaufman, 1992a, 1998, 2000; Kaufman, Oakley-Browne, Watkins, & Leigh, 2003; Kaufman, Watkins, & Leigh, 2001).

2.  Please note our modeling what we would like you to do: differentiate among and align the three levels of results. While it is conventional to call all results "Outcomes," we reserve that label only for societal consequences.

3.  *Goals* are measurable on a nominal or ordinal scale, while *objectives* are measurable on an interval or ratio scale.

4.  We have, as authors, a very good appreciation for this. The work of this book was disrupted by the occurrence of four hurricanes that crossed Florida and thus our work. These acts of nature set us back several times.

# Part III

# Results

**Figure III**    A Phased Evaluation Plan for Evaluation

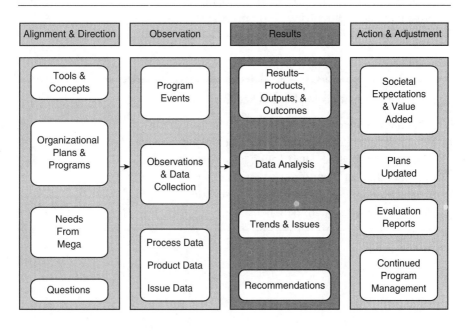

This section addresses the use of the evaluation data you have collected. Data that are not valid or reliable are dangerous, or at the very least useless. Once we have collected data, we have to make sense of the information so that useful decisions can be made about what is working, what is not, what to change, what to add, and what to delete. Here, we provide:

Analyzing primary results data

Looking for explanations

Using statistics

Looking for patterns and trends

Meta-evaluation

---

**Prime Questions for Results Section**

Did the actual results line up with the goals and objectives?
What unexpected events changed the Outcome?
What unexpected events changed the Outputs?
What unexpected events changed the Products?
What causes of change and deviation were observed?
Is all of the information collected free of bias?
What patterns and trends were observed?

---

**Secondary Questions for Results Section**

What are the measurement data for each observation?
What are the measurement data for each result for each objective?
What are the specific data relating to unexpected events?
Are all of the facts supported by evidence and verification?
Are there any gaps in our observation schedule?
Have all problems been identified?

# Analyzing and Interpreting the Data

**6**

E valuation is much more than the data collection. There is a considerable amount of planning that should take place prior to observation and data collection, as well as analysis, synthesis, and interpretation of the data afterward. In this chapter, we will take a closer look at what we do with the data once they have been collected.

The term *analysis* is often used in a casual context to mean any number of things, from breaking a subject down into parts, to solving a problem, to discovering the nature of the world around us. In our use of the term, we are going to be more specific. The *analysis* of data as part of an evaluation effort is the organization of information to discover patterns used to support hypotheses, conclusions, or evaluative claims that result from your evaluation study.

If you have quantitative data, various statistical operations can help you organize your data as you sort through your findings. Qualitative data are also subject to analytical routines. Qualitative observations can be ordered by source and by impact. Checking the frequency of qualitative observations will begin to merge qualitative into quantitative data. Both qualitative and quantitative data sets should be obtained from relevant— valid and appropriate—information sources. Once that is done, you examine the information obtained to make sure it is relevant to each issue or evaluative question in the study.

## ANALYZING EVALUATION DATA

Let's now assume that enough time has passed to allow the program, or whatever it is you are evaluating, to have noticeable impact. The data

*Note:* Gaps between expectations and obtained results do not always have to be negative. You may have the happy task of finding out why goals and objectives were exceeded! In either case, positive or negative, your analysis should lead to recommendations that are backed up by sound data-driven arguments that will support management decision making.

collection stage, as all evaluation stages, should have been based on the needs assessment findings, particularly the identified needs that were used to define the objectives that were set at that time. This is basing what we use, do, produce, and deliver on performance data and is perhaps the biggest reason for deriving measurable and precise objectives based on needs. When derived correctly, they tell us exactly what result is to be achieved, when it will be achieved, under what conditions it will be achieved, and what criteria will be used to determine whether it was satisfactorily achieved. Those very same objectives become the basis for the core evaluation questions.

You also wisely gathered data on the implementation of the tactics and methods for the educational enterprise to deliver the desired results. Now you are in a position to look at the results and compare the results obtained with the results desired. In the event there is still a gap, you look at the implementation data for clues to what caused the deviation.

## Analyzing the Data on Core Results

*A Core Evaluative Question*

This question is based on one of the objectives established during needs assessment: *Will the new curriculum and new teaching programs, by the end of the school year, enable 100% of Sterling High 11th graders to meet or exceed the criteria required to advance to 12th grade, using promotion criteria reflected in official promotion records?*

Goals (measured at a nominal or ordinal scale) and objectives (measured at an interval or ratio scale; refer back to Chapter 4 for more on scales of measurement) can be made measurable or observable by using "operational definitions," which can often be a set of specific measurable indicators so long as the indicators have a valid and reliable relationship to the goal or objective. There might be several different indicators for one single objective. In the case above, "meet the criteria" opens the door to a host of indicators. What are all the criteria required of Sterling High 11th graders to be promoted to seniors? Each of these criteria would become an indicator, as such:

Criteria A: Grade of C– or better in Math

Criteria B: Grade of C– or better in Natural Sciences

Criteria C: Grade of C– or better in History

Criteria D: Grade of C– or better in Economics

Criteria E: Grade of C– or better in Health and Fitness

Criteria F: Etc. . .

*Some Related Evaluation Questions*

This question is also based on the needs-assessment-driven goals relating to the purpose of school in the first place. School progress must be meaningful advancement based on learning and learner performance. Do the grades obtained reflect learning? Is that learning building toward a self-sufficient and informed graduate who can function in society? Because the evaluation team asked these additional questions, they also obtained data that related to the answers.

> *Note:* This could be a trick example. We all agree that setting a goal for all students to move on to the next grade seems reasonable. But you must include the idea that meaningful learning took place and that grades were not artificially assigned to move students through the system. Adding Mega criteria to evaluation can help prevent you from truncating your criteria and losing insight into the three levels of results. Behind the grades, there must be performance that is relevant to the larger objectives. What can the students do to obtain jobs and contribute to society?

## METHODS OF QUALITATIVE ANALYSIS

### Examples of Qualitative Data

- *Teacher interviews about the new tutorial:* Teachers can be interviewed asking a set of questions to get at specific issues, or teachers can be allowed to comment on events from their point of view. Often, valuable insights can be gained on how programs work under actual school conditions.

- *Teacher interviews about student work:* Teachers can comment on students and the lessons and exercises that have been completed. Teachers will know what parts of the lessons were difficult to get across to students and what parts seemed to work well.

- *Student interviews about the new tutorial:* Students can be asked to directly comment on aspects of a program that they were required to execute. Effective domain data can be obtained as well as more objective aspects of programs.

- *Student interviews about teacher assignments:* The student point of view about the assignments is valuable. Are lessons too hard, too easy, and do they have all of the reference materials required?

- *Outside observer reports:* Outside observers can provide insight without the burden of having been part of the implementation. Often, they can see things that participants miss.

- *Judgments about samples of student work:* Students and teachers can render judgments about the quality, quantity, and difficulty of student projects.

## A Word on Analyzing Qualitative Data

Not all the data collected will come neatly measured. Recall from the previous chapter that a variety of methods for collecting qualitative data may have been used (e.g., observations, interviews, focus groups, among several). Methods for analyzing qualitative data range from narrative descriptions to quantitative analysis of such descriptions. Ordering responses in a framework related to the evaluation questions will allow you and others to make sense of the results more efficiently.

## Analysis of Models and Patterns

Continuously searching for patterns within the data even while the data collection process is still going on can help evaluators proactively adjust and refocus their data collection to render useful information. This revise-as-required approach can save you time and frustration. Be sure, however, that you are not revising in order to get data supporting a preexisting bias or hidden agenda.

Below are some general steps that should guide the analysis of qualitative data:

1. Use a framework for scoring the observations based on the evaluation questions to be answered.

2. Review notes as you carefully reflect on the impressions they make on you.

3. Recognize recurrent themes and code them accordingly.

4. Organize data according to the themes you have identified.

5. Look for potential relationships among the themes, if any.

6. Identify explanations, possible causal factors, and events with potential impact, and the like for each theme.

7. Validate preliminary interpretations by triangulating data (using three or more sources) to support or disprove your hypotheses (this is a good time to entertain alternative explanations).

8. Draw conclusions.

For some excellent resources to learn more about analyzing qualitative data, see Miles and Huberman (1994); Richards and Richards (1994); and Weitzman and Miles (1995).

## Qualitative Analysis of Models Can Set the Stage for Quantitative Analysis

Qualitative inquiry is often a good way to identify factors, issues, and players that may be acting within and around the environment of an evaluation study. Cooley and Lohnes (1976) referred to what they call the "Context Principle" to describe the set of variables that seem to be acting in a given setting. Noting the large amounts of unexplained variance from large studies of the past, they cast a wider net to include things like community culture, family influences, school resources, policies, instructional activities, and peer groups and the motivations and abilities of the learners. All of these interact.

*Path analysis* can be used to chart the relationships and effects. Assumed causal relationships are tested using path coefficients, which are standardized partial-regression coefficients. A multiple-regression equation is used to estimate the dependent variable or learning outcome.

## Analysis Using Structured Discussion

From time to time during the course of an evaluation, the evaluation team leader may gather observers to participate in a discussion of the observations made at that point in the study and later to discuss results in relation to observed events. The purpose of structured discussion is to clarify issues that have emerged in the study and to identify possible cause-and-effect relationships regarding events and results. Each issue is identified and sorted according to relevancy to the study and possible influence on programs and results.

- *Description:* Observers discuss and identify issues that appear to bear on the study under the guidance and control of the team leader. Issues are sorted by relevancy and impact. Structured discussion can be used during and at the conclusion of a study.

- *Advantage:* All issues can be entertained even if they are not antici-
pated in the planning stage of a study. Issues can be modified as
additional data become available. Hypotheses can be formulated
for continued review and confirmation between events and results.
Data can be organized using this method of analysis using both
new emerging as well as initial data collection categories.
- *Disadvantage:* The method is not good as a method of strong proof.
Observers cannot vote to make something true or false; they can
only identify issues that must be investigated and subjected to
further testing or inquiry. Discussions that are not conducted with
discipline and leadership can generate abundant red herrings.
Strong leadership, on the other hand, can introduce strong bias.
*Measurement Considerations:* Structured discussion is a good way
to identify candidate (potential) observation targets for measurement. Formal measurement will usually be made only after appropriate metrics are selected and subsequent follow-up observations
are made.

### Imposing Structure on Emerging Issues

The structure of this type of analytical discussion comes from the rules
of conduct that are imposed by the evaluation team leader. A structured
discussion is not a free-for-all, with each observer bringing up all of the odd
tidbits that happened during observation. The team leader begins each discussion with a question designed to focus on a specific part of the study.

An example of a structured discussion question would be, "Does anyone have an observation that is relevant to the use of the tutorial period
as part the support of the classroom teaching and helping make it successful?" At this point, each member of the group would get a chance to
comment on their observations that bear on the question. The first rule of
conduct is to stick to the topic.

The second rule of conduct is that no observations are discarded or
discredited in the first round of questioning. The third rule is that all comments are written down. The team leader then opens the forum to general
discussion, and the group rates all observations for potential as explanations of causes and effects, for potential for further investigation, or for
relegation to the "Not sure what this means category." At this point, the
leader moves on to the next question, and the process is repeated. After all
of the questions on the leader's list are explored, each participant in the
discussion may add a question about something he or she feels was left out
of the initial discussion.

The product of structured discussion is a list of observed events or issues
that may bear on the study, a set of possible cause-and-effect relationships,

and areas that require more investigation. These are organized by the question structure and general relevance. These can be helpful in understanding other results data collected.

### Understanding Relevancy

Relevancy is decided on the basis of the potential or demonstrated bearing on the main focus of the evaluation study: Is it important, and will it make a difference? The shorthand logic of our approach to evaluation is that *organizational* solutions like school system programs flow from valid needs—gaps in results—of the community and that our primary focus of evolution is to ensure that program results meet those needs. The secondary focus of evaluation is to identify program factors that contribute to or interfere with the desired results. Therefore all information that helps us make sense of this chain of logic is relevant. When evaluators note that teachers have deviated from prescribed program methods, that observation is bound to be relevant to later discussions of the results and what caused them. If an evaluator was to take it upon himself or herself to jot down the location of the parking place that teachers use each day, that bit of data is more than likely not going to be relevant to the main focus of the evaluation.

To be considered relevant, data must bear on the study with some plausible tie to the main events of teaching and learning. Both learning-disruptive and learning-enhancing events will count as relevant.

A word of caution: Not all events will have a clear relationship to the mainstream. It takes time and repeated discussions and periods of observation to gradually assign greater or lesser relevance to data. The team leader must balance data collection resources against the continual search for explanation. Relevancy is one factor that enters into the calculation of that balance. The evaluation questions should remain in central focus at all times.

### Formulating a Hypothesis

As issues emerge, the evaluation team can formulate ideas on what appears to be working and what is not, and why. These ideas will later play a role in formulating recommendations at the conclusion of the study. Such hypotheses are different from those defined before the evaluation that were based on the needs assessment data and the basic evaluation questions. We are noting that as data collection is being conducted, new insights might be discovered that give us the opportunity to develop *en-route hypotheses.*

*En-route hypotheses* may be constructed prior to final results and take the form of postulations such as, "The extra coaching during tutorial may have a positive effect on test scores." Once testing has been conducted and the results are available, we can test the en-route hypothesis to determine that "the extra coaching during tutorial did contribute to higher test scores." Thus the en-route hypothesis was testable.

Educators may well construct controlled experiments to confirm that the relationship exists and to rule out alternative explanations. But such tests are rare in evaluations because it is hard to set up a control to rule out each alternative explanation, and many factors contribute to test performance. For this reason, it is more common in evaluation studies to use a form of logic called "analytic induction" (see Robinson, 1951). This type of study is a *time-series* activity that looks at results over time for a student or a group of students (or other groups). In this approach, a hypothesis is not tested using an experiment with treatment and control groups, but is subjected to a continued process of observation of results during the course of a program, project, or activity. As new data are collected that support the hypothesis, the hypothesis is preserved. But if data do not support the hypothesis, the hypothesis is modified or discarded. This process is continued throughout the study—over the time of the study—until only those ideas that have stood up to continued review and adjustment remain. Only these ideas will be considered to bear on the conclusions and recommendations.

Here is an example of the type of factor that could provide the basis for a hypothesis in an evaluation study. Evaluators note growing evidence that peer coaching is making a contribution to learning. They continue to add observations to this evidence, culminating with measurement data on achievement tests. If this data also support this hypothesis and no counterevidence has been collected, the hypothesis will stand and be used as part of the general findings. While the inference is not as strong as controlled experimentation, it is usually strong enough to warrant consideration as part of the findings. This *time-series method* (refer to Chapter 5) has the advantage that it is usually more convenient and doable in an ongoing educational setting.

Another source for formulating hypotheses is basing them on needs, or gaps in results. When gaps are identified and documented, these provide good opportunities to ask questions such as "Why do these gaps exist?" and "Where do they come from?" One can look to the literature for possible answers, brainstorm with educators on the evaluation team, and spring from insights and experience. No matter, possible causes of the needs and possible ways to close them can serve you to form hypotheses.

### Controls on Structured Discussion

Structured discussion works best when guided by a strong leader who is knowledgeable as an evaluator and is respected by the group. The main tools to keep the discussion focused and productive are a set of rules of conduct and the respect of the group for the discussion leader. The rules include:

- Always prepare an agenda with topical questions based on the evaluation questions to focus discussion.
- Keep discussion to the questions at hand until the end when the forum is open to new questions.
- Each participant gets a turn at presenting issues and observations.
- No issues are ruled out that bear on the question.
- Each issue is checked for relevancy.
- Issues are ranked according to relevancy and potential causality.
- Hypotheses are formulated only after all issues are presented.
- Written records are kept for each discussion.
- Further observations are assigned as action items.

## Analysis Using a Fidelity Matrix

Evaluations of solutions that are designed to meet the needs of society are based on the Ideal Vision. All aspects of that solution must be in alignment in terms of the value added at each level.

### Key Dimensions of an Intervention

The implementation can be broken into at least three areas where judgments can be made that compare the intent of a program as expressed in goals and objectives to the actual results obtained. It is not always enough to identify what you want to achieve: The plan must be the right plan to get the job done; the plan must be carried out well; and all of the players must behave as predicted. The difference between a plan on paper and the activity of plan implementation is often the difference between success and failure. This difference requires a focus on the logic of intervention. Evaluators must consider the following key dimensions of an intervention in order to make meaningful judgments about the results:

1. A plan has *high situational fidelity* when the plan or model correctly provides a course of action that will achieve a desired result, correctly matching the solution to the problem; the plan or model has *low situational fidelity* if it is flawed from the outset. The design will not achieve a desired result.

2. Assuming independence between the plan and the way the plan is executed, there is a second dimension of *executional fidelity*, in which the plan can be carried out well or corrupted in the execution by unplanned events and interruptions.

**Table 6.1**    Fidelity Matrix

| Situational Fidelity High | Situational Fidelity Low |
|---|---|
| Executional Fidelity High | Executional Fidelity Low |
| Behavioral Fidelity High | Behavioral Fidelity Low |

**Table 6.2**    Fidelity Matrix Example

| *Situational Fidelity High* | *Situational Fidelity Low* |
|---|---|
| Clear valid goals and objectives<br>Problem matched to solution<br>Appropriate choice of means | No goals and objectives<br>Problem unrelated to solution<br>Poor choice of means (quick fix) |
| *Executional Fidelity High* | *Executional Fidelity Low* |
| Objectives are operational<br>Follow the plan well<br>Stable situation | Objectives are over general<br>Deviate from the plan<br>Unstable situation with distraction |
| *Behavioral Fidelity High* | *Behavioral Fidelity Low* |
| Teachers competent<br>Students motivated<br>Community supportive | Teachers less than competent<br>Students distracted<br>Community nonsupportive |

3. A third dimension consists of the human element: instructors, students, and administrators who behave as predicted and required or not. This we call *behavioral fidelity.* The last dimension can include social forces generally outside of the planned area of engagement but capable of imposing change by supporting or undermining the effort.

Any educational program can be analyzed using the three fidelity dimensions listed above. Using the high and low ends of the fidelity continuum, a six-cell matrix can be created to model a given case. The six cells of the matrix are *high* and *low situational fidelity, high* and *low executional fidelity,* and *high* and *low behavioral fidelity* (see Table 6.1). Table 6.2 shows examples of findings that would be classified as either high or low fidelity in each of the three fidelity dimensions.

*Using the Three Dimensions of Fidelity*

The high/high/high side is the "side of success," and the low/low/low side is the "side of failure." The analysis may appear simplistic when everything is going right or everything is going wrong. The mixed levels of fidelity are what lead to errors in judging programs. Several patterns are possible, and the benefit of this type of analysis is to prevent wrong decisions when it comes to making changes to keep what is working and change what is not. An unsatisfactory result may be due to low fidelity in one or more dimensions, but corrective action must target the specific cause. We should not throw out a good plan because of poor execution. Neither should we keep a bad plan that was faithfully executed to the letter. There is only one pattern that leads to success (high/high/high), but there are many possibilities that lead to failure. Each of the cases leading to failure, however, will require a different corrective strategy (see Table 6.3).

## METHODS OF QUANTITATIVE ANALYSIS

### Examples of Quantitative Data

At this point, you have collected data for the relevant indicators you identified for each of your evaluation questions. Recall from Chapter 3 that data can be measured on a nominal, ordinal, interval, or ratio scale, as appropriate. Below are some sample indicators, along with the level of measurement appropriate for each. This is important, because the level at which your data are measured also impacts the statistical methods appropriate for their analysis, as discussed later in this chapter.

- Student test scores for the target year (ordinal/interval[1])
- Student test scores for the previous 3 years (ordinal/interval)
- Student scores on standardized tests (ordinal[2])
- Frequency count of missed assignments (ratio)
- Frequency count of missed days of school by individual students (ratio)
- Teacher contact hours count in classroom (ratio)
- Teacher contact hours in tutorial (ratio)
- Number of completed assignments by student per day (ratio)
- Number of students applied for college track (ratio)
- Number of students who get into higher-educational institutions of their first, second, or third choice (ratio)
- Demographic data from student, faculty, or other stakeholder questionnaires (nominal)
- Likert scale items data from student, faculty, or other stakeholder questionnaires (ordinal)
- Questionnaire data from community stakeholders (ordinal)

**Table 6.3**    Using The Three Dimensions of Fidelity

Success Case 1:

| High-Fidelity Plan | |
| --- | --- |
| High-Fidelity Execution | |
| High-Fidelity Behavior | |

Failure Case 2:

| High-Fidelity Plan | |
| --- | --- |
| | Low-Fidelity Execution |
| High-Fidelity Behavior | |

Failure Case 3:

| High-Fidelity Plan | |
| --- | --- |
| High-Fidelity Execution | |
| | Low-Fidelity Behavior |

Failure Case 4:

| High-Fidelity Plan | |
| --- | --- |
| | Low-Fidelity Execution |
| | Low-Fidelity Behavior |

Failure Case 5:

| | Low-Fidelity Plan |
| --- | --- |
| High Fidelity-Execution | |
| High Fidelity-Behavior | |

Failure Case 6:

| | Low-Fidelity Plan |
| --- | --- |
| | Low-Fidelity Execution |
| High-Fidelity Behavior | |

Failure Case 7:

| | Low-Fidelity Plan |
| --- | --- |
| | Low-Fidelity Execution |
| | Low-Fidelity Behavior |

There are a number of quantitative analysis techniques available, but selecting the appropriate technique depends not only on the scale used to measure the data but also on the specific purpose of your analysis. Below are some samples of such purposes and the types of appropriate quantitative analysis techniques for each.[3]

- To show the relative position of an individual in a group (measures of central tendency)
- To describe the shape of a data set (measures of variability)
- To show relative ranking (measures of central tendency)
- To compare two sets of data (measures of variability)
- To discover relationships (measures of relationship)
- To compare two factors with multiple conditions (statistical testing)
- To show cause and effect (statistical testing)
- To make statements of likelihood (statistical testing)
- To make a prediction (statistical testing)
- To show relative effect size (statistical testing)

Having raw data is one thing, and answering questions with that data might be another. For data to reveal the answers to our evaluation questions, they must be represented in a way that is meaningful to those viewing them, using them, and making decisions based on them. We have to turn data into information that will lead to useful decisions. Statistics—correct statistics—can help us best ensure that what we found in the evaluation makes sense and that our conclusions and recommendations are defensible. Over the years, various types of statistics have evolved to refine raw data and help us make sense of the findings. The following section is a short overview of some useful statistics.

## STATISTICS

While the mere mention of the term *statistics* may be intimidating for some, we all—every one of us—are truly more familiar with them and the basics of statistics than we think. Let's see.

We hear it advertisements all the time: "Ninety-five percent of dentists surveyed recommend . . ." Or you may have heard someone ask how many miles a given vehicle averages per gallon. Understanding statistics serves beyond formal data analysis and evaluation. It truly helps us be more aware consumers of knowledge, products, services—everything in everyday life—so that we can make good decisions, and so we can do evaluation without any fear that our evaluation efforts will make the situation worse with unsupported conclusions.

There are two main types of statistics: *descriptive* and *inferential*. The first step in making sense of data is to summarize or describe them. As the name implies, descriptive statistics are used to this end. They allow us to summarize an almost endless list of individual scores into one, or various, indices. In some instances, obtaining descriptive statistics is the sole data analysis procedure to answer evaluation questions, for example, "What was the average score of my class on the Terra Nova Test this year?" One may also want to find out how well a particular individual did in relation to that average or how spread out the scores are from that average.

Inferential statistics allow us to make generalizations from a sample to a population. As the name implies, we are *inferring* that the sample is representative of the population. Thus one of the prerequisites for using inferential statistics in a meaningful way is to have data from a representative random sample. While the main focus of this section will be on descriptive statistics, some inferential statistic tools will be briefly described later in this chapter.

The most commonly used descriptive statistics are measures of central tendency, measures of variability, and measures of relationships.

## Measures of Central Tendency

Measures of central tendency are probably the best way of describing data when we must rely on a single number to represent—provide us with a "snapshot" of—an entire set of scores. There are three measures of central tendency: the mean, the median, and the mode.

### The Mean

The *mean*, perhaps the most frequently used measure of central tendency, is essentially the average of a set of scores. It is calculated by adding up all the individual scores and dividing that total by the number of scores in that data set.

One of the characteristics that make it so commonly used is its stability. Because all the scores are included in its calculation, it is more stable than those measures of central tendency, which use only some of the individual scores.

However, the flip side to using all the scores is that it is also susceptible to the effects of extreme scores. For example, take a look at the following set of scores:

18

19

17

18

18

18

16

16

18

19

16

17

16

18

16

99

The mean for this set of 16 scores is approximately 22, yet all but one of the scores ranges from 16 to 19. Does this mean truly represent the average score? Were it not for that one single outlier, or extreme score, of 99, the mean would actually be approximately 17. Since the mean is affected by extreme scores, it is usually not the best choice when dealing with a set of scores that contains one or two (or even a few) extreme scores.[4]

It is appropriate to use the mean when the data are measured at either an interval or a ratio scale. Unfortunately, the mean is often inappropriately used without regard to the type of data measurement used. An example of this is seen when we are provided with mean scores of questionnaire items, which tend to be measured on a nominal or ordinal scale, even if we attribute a numerical value to it. For example, Likert scales range from (1), strongly disagree, (2), disagree, (3), neutral, (4), agree, to (5), strongly disagree (see Figure 6.1).

It is of little usefulness to add up a variety of responses such as strongly disagree, agree, neutrals . . . and then say that the average response was "agree and two tenths (or 4.2)." For ordinal data, the median or the mode (described below) are more appropriate measures of central tendency. Specifically, for data measured with a Likert scale, even percentages of each response may be a more accurate and useful way to summarize results.

**Figure 6.1**   Sample Likert Scale Format

| Describe how you see the Smart Start Program *currently* operating.<br><br>Please indicate your level of agreement with the following statements by providing <u>one response </u> to each question. | Select One Option |
|---|---|
| | Strongly Disagree   Somewhat Disagree   Somewhat Agree   Agree   Strongly Agree   Not Applicable |
| The confidentiality of participants is adequately maintained. | 1  2  3  4  5  6  7 |
| Instructors have adequate knowledge of the content they teach. | 1  2  3  4  5  6  7 |
| The skills of instructors are adequate. | 1  2  3  4  5  6  7 |
| The content of this program is up-to-date. | 1  2  3  4  5  6  7 |

*The Median*

The *median* is the midpoint of a distribution. Since half the scores are above it and half the scores are below it, it is also referred to as the "50th percentile." In cases where there is an odd number of scores, the median is the middle score when they are arranged from low to high. In cases where there is an even set of scores, the median would be the average of the two middle scores. The best way to recognize the middle score(s) is by arranging the set of scores in numerical order, either ascending or descending. For example, take the following set of scores: 18, 17, 16, 19, 20.

These are first arranged in numerical order:

16

17

18 x                          The middle score then becomes obvious

19

20

If there were an even number of scores:

15

16

17 x

18 x          The two middle scores would be averaged as such:

17 + 18 ÷ 2 = 17.5

19

20

As you can see, the median does not necessarily have to represent an exact score from the data set.

The median is the most appropriate measure of central tendency for data measured at an ordinal scale (e.g., Likert scale responses from an attitude questionnaire, as described earlier.). Because it is the midpoint of a set of score, the median is not necessarily affected by every single score. In relation to the mean, it is not sensitive to outliers and thus is a better measure of central tendency when the distribution of scores is skewed by an extreme score. Thus it could potentially be used for data measure at an interval and ratio scale, particularly in cases where the distribution of scores is significantly skewed and the mean misrepresents the typical score.

### The Mode

This is the least-used measure of central tendency. The *mode* is simply the most frequent score. No calculation is required to identify the mode. Instead, it is established by looking at a data set or a graphical representation of it to see which score occurs with most frequency. The mode brings with it a significant limitation, namely, that it is quite possible for a distribution of scores to have more than one mode. If two scores are tied for the highest frequency, then it is said to be a *bimodal distribution,* and if three or more scores are tied for the highest frequency, it is said to be a *multimodal distribution.* Finally, if each score occurs with the same frequency, there is no mode and it is referred to as a *rectangular distribution.*

The mode is the most appropriate measure of central tendency when using data measured at a nominal scale.

### Numbers Don't Lie?

If someone tells you that "Numbers don't lie," don't believe any set of numbers they put in front of you! Numbers can indeed be used to lie. A measure of central tendency can be misused to render the most favorable index rather than the most accurate. Thus it is important to consider the characteristics, limitations, and appropriate uses of each measure of central tendency because each will inevitably impact our representations of a given data set and, in turn, the conclusions we draw from them.

## Measures of Variability

While measures of central tendency are very useful for describing a data set, they do not tell all. Before we can make sense of those descriptions, we also have to have an estimate of the spread and variability—how much the data vary—of that data set, both within a given distribution and between distributions. The indices used to make these estimations are called *measures of variability.* The most commonly used measures of variability are the range, the quartile deviation, and the standard deviation.

### The Range

The range is often the easiest and quickest of the measures of variability to estimate. It is defined either as the difference between the highest and lowest score ($R = H - L$), or as the difference plus one ($R = H - L + 1$), which is more specifically referred to as the *inclusive range.* For example, the range for the following two sets of data are determined as such:

| | |
|---|---|
| 90 | 40 |
| 94 | 55 |
| 93 | 60 |
| 96 | 80 |
| 95 | 95 |
| Range = 95 − 90 = 5 | Range = 95 − 40 = 55 |

Thus a small range represents a set of scores that are clustered close together, while a large range represents a set of scores that are more spread out. A potential drawback is that since it takes into account only the highest and lowest scores, an extreme score (either at the high or low end) can result in a misleading range. For example:

| | |
|---|---|
| 90 | 38 |
| 93 | 93 |
| 95 | 95 |
| 97 | 97 |
| 99 | 99 |
| Range = 99 − 90 = 9 | Range = 99 − 38 = 61 |

As you'll notice, only one score distinguishes each of these data sets, yet the change in that one score for an extreme score (90 for 38) has a profound effect on the range.

### The Semi-Interquartile Range

The *semi-interquartile range,* or the *quartile deviation,* as it is also known, is estimated by the middle 50% of the scores, and as such, it is not as sensitive to extreme scores as is the range. The formula is as follows:

$$\text{SIQR} = \frac{Q_3 - Q_1}{2}$$

Here, $Q_3$ represents the third quartile, the point below which 75% of the scores fall, while $Q_1$ represents the point below which are 25% of the scores. Recall that the median is the midpoint of scores and as such, it corresponds to $Q_2$, or the second quartile. In fact, the median is usually used along with the SIQR.

For example, if we have a data set with 40 scores, $Q_3$ is the score below which are 30 scores (75% of 40 = 30), and $Q_1$ is the point below which are 10 scores (25% of 40 = 10). If you arrange each score in numerical order, you can quickly identify each quartile. In the case of even distributions, each quartile can be estimated as we did with the median ($Q_2$).

The same characteristic that makes it less sensitive to extreme scores (i.e., estimated by the middle 50% of scores) can also be considered a drawback. After all, 50% of the scores are being excluded in its estimation. So, while the range is a better estimate of variability than the range, it is not the most stable. Perhaps the most stable measure of central tendency is the standard deviation.

### The Standard Deviation

The *standard deviation (SD)* is the most commonly used measure of variability and is most appropriate when the data are measured at an interval or ratio scale. Recall that the mean is the most appropriate measure of central tendency with these scales, and thus the mean and standard deviation are usually reported together. Like the mean, the standard deviation is estimated with all scores in a given data set, and as such, it is the most stable measure of variability. If you have both the mean and standard deviation of a data set, you have a pretty good idea of how the scores are distributed.

There are plenty of software packages that allow us to estimate the standard deviation (and basically any statistic) with the touch of the button.

For your own curiosity and understanding, the formula for calculating the standard deviation is:

$$SD = \frac{\sqrt{\Sigma(X - \bar{x})}}{N} \quad \text{or (because } X - \bar{x} = x^2) \quad SD = \frac{\sqrt{\Sigma x^2}}{N}$$

The uppercase $X$ stands for score, while the $\bar{x}$ (pronounced "X bar") stands for the mean, and lowercase $x$ stands for the deviation of a score from the mean of its distribution. Thus one must first calculate the mean and then subtract the mean from each score. Then, each deviation is squared and then added (as indicated by $\Sigma$). The value of this formula is then divided by the number of scores $(N)$ and the square root calculated. For example:

$$X$$
$$14$$
$$16$$
$$18$$
$$18$$
$$19$$
$$11\bar{x} = 17$$

$$x$$
$$14 - 17 = -3$$
$$16 - 17 = -1$$
$$18 - 17 = 1$$
$$18 - 17 = 1$$
$$19 - 17 = 2$$

$$x^2$$
$$9$$
$$1$$
$$1$$
$$1$$
$$4$$
$$\Sigma x^2 = 13$$

$$SD = \frac{\sqrt{13}\,\sqrt{2.6}}{5} = 1.6$$

As with the other measures of variability, a small standard deviation value represents small variability; that is, scores are closely clustered together: The bigger the value of the standard deviation, the bigger the variability.

One important fact is that in a normal distribution (next section), 99% of all scores fall within 3 standard deviations above and below the mean. In other words, each distribution has its own mean and standard deviation; if you multiply that standard deviation by three, add it to the mean on one end, and subtract it from the mean on the other end, this will give you the range that includes practically all scores. This is noted as follows:

$$11\bar{x} \pm 3SD = 99.9\% \text{ of scores}$$

For example, let's say for a given distribution, the mean is 51 and the standard deviation from this mean is 4.

$$51 + 3(4) = 63$$
$$51 - 3(4) = 39$$

Thus we can say that 99.9% of scores in this distribution fall between 39 and 63. As you can see, the mean and standard deviation together describe the data set incredibly well. Let us now turn our attention to a central topic, the normal curve/distribution.

### The Normal Curve

The *normal curve,* also known as the *bell-shaped curve,* is a hypothetical concept based on mathematical principles that allows us to make comparisons among scores. While no actual distribution fits this model perfectly, they can come close enough (particularly those in education) and thereby still allow us to make decisions. In fact, this distribution shape is often found in our environment (e.g., height, weight, IQ scores). For example, most people's height clusters around an average. You have fewer people who are either taller or shorter than that average, and you have even fewer people who are considerably taller or shorter. The further away we get from that average, the fewer individuals we will find. Take a look at Figure 6.2 for an illustration.

The curve that appears in Figure 6.2 represents the *normal distribution.* In such a distribution, the mean, median, and mode all coincide. As mentioned before, 99.9% of cases fall within ±3 standard deviations (add up the percentages of each interval to get this figure). It does not include 100% of scores to accommodate the potential for extreme scores. If you take a look at this distribution, you can see that we can follow the same procedure we used to calculate the range of scores that fall within 99.9% of the cases in the previous example to calculate the percentage of scores included within

**Figure 6.2**  Bell Curve

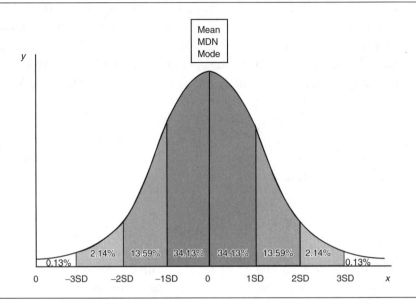

each, or more, standard deviations. For example, if we used the normal curve to illustrate a distribution with a mean of 50 and a standard deviation of 5, we could assume that 34.13% of scores fall between 50 and 55. Because the same percentage of scores could be found between 45 and 50, we could also claim that 68% of scores fall between 45 and 55.

### The Usefulness of the "Normal" Curve

The normal curve is often assumed to be useful in education, for it is thought that it represents reality. Professors and teachers still often "grade on the curve," meaning that they distribute all learners proportionally within the standard deviations (more Cs than As or Fs). This might be misleading.

The normal curve shows what happens when nature has its way. But education intends to intervene so that this doesn't happen: We help learners learn, master important content, and be able to prove what they have learned. The very act of teaching (and programs, projects, and activities) should, if it is effective, skew the curve in a negative direction. The more effective our teaching and programs, the more learners will perform above the average. Thus there is a continuing shift from "norm-referenced tests," which are meant to spread students out to adhere to the normal curve, to "criterion-referenced test," where the exact required performance is assessed.

Does this mean we should "teach to the test?" The answer is "yes" if (and only if) the criteria are valid, based on valid needs. If our objectives and criteria are correct, useful, and aligned, then we certainly want every learner to master all objectives and provide themselves and us with the evidence that they have mastered the learning materials.

## Standardized Scores

Up until this point, we have been discussing raw scores, numerical values that summarize the actual responses made on a given evaluation instrument. These raw scores have their limitations, however. Such is the case when we want to compare scores across different evaluation instruments. To make fair inferences from such comparisons, we must ensure that we compare apples to apples, rather than apples to oranges. To this end, we can use a method of converting raw scores (provided they are based on interval or ratio scales) into standard scores that can be used to make comparisons across different measurement instruments or scales. Standard scores express how far a given raw score is from a given point, such as the mean, based on standard deviation units. It should be noted that standard score equivalencies are based on a normal distribution, though the actual distribution in question may not be. Thus we must use a procedure to ensure that we transform a set of raw scores into normally distributed standard scores.

One of the most commonly used standard scores are $z$ scores. A $z$ score tells us how far above or below the mean in standard deviation units a raw score lies. The formula for converting raw scores into $z$ scores is as follows:

$$z = \frac{X - 1\bar{x}}{SD}$$

$$z = z \text{ score}$$
$$x = \text{raw score}$$
$$\bar{x} = \text{mean score}$$
$$SD = \text{standard deviation}$$

Here is how it works:

1. A raw score that falls exactly on the mean corresponds to a $z$ of 0.

2. A raw score that is 1 standard deviation above the mean corresponds to a $z$ of 1.

3. A raw score that is 2 standard deviations below the mean corresponds to a $z$ of $-2$.

4. Etcetera . . .

If we have the mean and standard deviation of various distributions, we can easily plug them into the formula above and compare them on the same scale, which, in turn, can allow us to make more accurate comparisons.

The other commonly used standardized scores are $T$ scores. They function exactly as $z$ scores; however, they have a mean of 50 and a standard deviation of 10. A $z$ score is converted to a $T$ score by multiplying the $z$ score by 10, and adding 50. Because $T$ scores probably seem more tangible than $z$ scores, they can be more effective in communicating comparisons to stakeholders with little to no statistical background. (Note that a "$T$ score" is not the same or even related to "$t$ test," which is a statistical operation to compare the size of the effects of two or more sets of variables.)

## Measures of Relationship

In some instances, our evaluation questions will be focused on the relationship between two scores, or factors. For instance, we might want to know whether high performance in one teaching-learning area is related to high (or maybe low) performance in another area, or perhaps whether one participant characteristic is related to another characteristic. For example, is gender related to performance in math, or is truancy related to economic status? These might be related to decisions about admission of potential participants into a particular program or differential learning opportunities depending on entry characteristics.

What we want to know here is whether performance in these two different areas is correlated. To answer this question, we compare the two sets of data by using a correlation coefficient, or $r$.

The correlation coefficient is a number ranging between .00 and 1, which indicates the degree of relationship between the two sets of scores. The closer the coefficient is to 1, the stronger the relationship, and vice versa. The closer to .00, the weaker the relationship.

It is important to note, however, that what we are talking about here is not a causal relationship (you may have heard the expression "Correlation does not imply causality"). The fact that two factors may be related does not provide us with the evidence that one is affecting or causing the other. It is entirely possible that a third, unidentified factor may be causing the effect. Yet a common interpretation mistake is to assume that if two variables are correlated, one must be causing the other (e.g., many superstitious beliefs and behaviors are based on this fallacy). One example is that teacher salaries are positively related to the sale of alcoholic beverages, a correlation that exists; however, the two variables really have nothing to do with each other. They are independent.

While there is no universally accepted rule as to what precise coefficient constitutes a strong correlation versus a low one, there are some general guidelines (though these will likely vary across different fields or areas of study):

.00 to .20 = Weak

.30 to .40 = Moderate

.50 to .60 = Moderate-Strong

.70 and above = Strong

Relationships can be positive or negative and can range from −1 through 0 to +1. A positive relationship is one in which both factors vary in the same direction. For instance, performances across two different programs may both be high or may be both low. A positive relationship can have a coefficient anywhere between 0 and +1. A negative relationship is one in which each factor varies in the opposite direction. For instance, high performance in one area may be correlated with low performance in another area. A negative correlation is expressed with a coefficient ranging from .00 to −1.

Here are some sample interpretations:

$r = .25$: Low Positive, meaning that while the two factors vary in the same direction, they don't appear to have a strong relationship.

$r = -.40$: Moderate Negative, meaning that the two factors appear to be inversely related to one another, with this relationship being neither too weak nor too strong.

$r = -.05$: Very Weak Negative, meaning that there probably isn't much of a relationship between the two factors, even if there are traces of a potential relationship being inverse.

$r = .76$: Strong Positive, which suggest that the two factors are strongly related and vary in the same direction.

While there are numerous ways to estimate a correlation coefficient (and the appropriate one, once again, depends on the scale of measurement), two of the most commonly used methods are *Pearson r* (also referred to as *product moment correlation coefficient*), which is most appropriate when data to be correlated are measured in an interval or ratio scale, and *Spearman Rho,* which is appropriate if at least one of the factors being correlated is measured on an ordinal scale.

## Inferential Statistic Tools

When we must take our data further than a simple description, we use *inferential statistics.* For instance, we might want to predict student performance on a given program or level. While inferential statistics (also referred to as *statistical tests*) do not provide us with definitive answers, they can provide us with a rigorous way to determine the probabilities that our data findings did not occur by chance alone.

A central concept here is *hypothesis testing.* For any formal testing, we should specify a null hypothesis and an alternative hypothesis. The *null hypothesis* expresses that no differences or associations will be found in the data set, while the *alternative hypothesis* is the opposite and expects that a difference or association will indeed be found within the data.

For example:

Null: There is no difference in science achievement between the group completing the U-Discover Program compared with the group that did not participate in the program.

Alternate: There is a difference in science achievement between the group completing the U-Discover Program compared with the group that did not participate in the program.

How do these relate to our evaluation questions? For each appropriate evaluation question, both a null and an alternate hypothesis should be derived. For example, a general evaluation question for which the above null and alternate hypotheses would have been derived may be:

Do U-Discover Program participants perform better in science?

## Parametric and Nonparametric Statistics

There are two main types of inferential statistics: *parametric* and *nonparametric. Parametric statistics* is mathematical procedure for hypothesis testing that assumes that the distributions of the variables being assessed have certain characteristics. For instance, analysis of variance (ANOVA) assumes that the underlying distributions are normally distributed and that the variances of the distributions being compared are similar. While parametric techniques are generally robust, that is, they have substantial power to detect differences or similarities even when the assumptions are violated, some distributions violate these assumptions so strikingly that nonparametric techniques are warranted in order to detect differences or similarities.

*Non-parametric* statistics is a branch of statistics that was developed to create test statistics that did not require that the population of interest be normally distributed. Thus, the non-parametric statistic for comparing the center of two populations, the Mann-Whitney, Wilcoxon two independent samples test does not require normality, as does the two sample t-test. However, non-parametric statistics are not assumption-free. For example, the Wilcoxon two sample test requires that the observations be independent and of the same shape. One situation in which non-parametric statistics are widely used is when the researcher has small sample sizes from populations that are clearly not normally distributed (Doug Zahn, personal communication, April 22, 2005).

Selecting the right inferential statistic tool depends on a number of things:

1. The scale used to measure these variables (nonparametric tests tend to be appropriate for nominal and ordinal data, while parametric tests are used for interval and ratio data).

2. The number of groups being compared.

3. Whether groups are related (e.g., pretest and posttest for one group) or independent (e.g., a control group receiving no treatment, such as participating in a program, and an experimental group receiving the treatment).

While an extensive list of statistical tests will not be covered here, Table 6.4 should be helpful in selecting the right tool.

After computing the appropriate statistical test, we must determine whether the results are significant (i.e., the results were not due to chance, resulting in a rejection of the null and consideration of the alternate) or not (fail to reject the null, which basically means we don't have evidence to claim that our treatment had an effect).

At this point, we are still not ready to draw conclusions. As we shall see in the next section, statistical significance is one piece of information, one that differs from practical significance.

## INTERPRETATION

While data analysis focuses on organizing and summarizing information, interpretation attaches meaning to such organized information in order to draw plausible and supportable conclusions. In this sense, data analysis

**Table 6.4**    Some Statistical Tests

| Number of Groups Being Compared | Interval or Ratio | Ordinal | Binomial (Two Possible Results) |
|---|---|---|---|
| One group to a hypothetical value | One-sample t test | Wilcoxon test | Chi-square or binomial test |
| Two independent groups | Unpaired t test | Mann-Whitney test | Fisher's test (chi-square for large samples) |
| Two related groups | Paired t test | Wilcoxon test | McNemar's test |
| Three or more independent groups | One-way ANOVA | Kruskal-Wallis test | Chi-square test |
| Three or more related groups | Repeated-measures ANOVA | Friedman test | Cochrane Q |

deals with the facts, while interpretation is related to value judgments. Because this is an innately subjective process, careful attention and effort should be placed on ensuring fairness, openness, and as much objectivity as is realistic under the circumstances. Even the most fair and well-meaning evaluators will be biased to some extent. Our perceptions are impacted by our past experiences, preferences, values, and habits (e.g., noticing some details while being unaware of others). Thus it is helpful to clearly articulate our rationale for the interpretations we make and to justify our decisions based on valid data and sensible analysis and conclusions from that data.

Another helpful tactic is to involve others in the interpretation. Including stakeholders in the interpretation of data provides the opportunity to consider the data in a variety of different perspectives. Also helpful in incorporating other perspectives is reviewing results from other relevant projects. These can provide helpful insights that may have been missed in this evaluation.

Even perfectly quantifiable data require interpretation. Suppose that your results are statistically significant—now what do we do? One of the basic questions that you will have to ask yourself is whether the results that were observed were of practical importance. For instance, suppose the data for one of your evaluation questions, one dealing with relationships between two variables, yielded a correlation coefficient of .22, which was found to be statistically significant. While it was found to be statistically significant, that is, not occurring by chance, is it of practical significance? You and your stakeholders will have to make that call. Is the actual relationship strong enough for you to base important decisions on it? Perhaps not, and thus one data-driven decision, in this case, would be to look for other data upon which to base your decisions. Remember, the whole point of evaluation is to make decisions for continuous improvement.

In interpreting results, it is also important to keep the purpose of the evaluation in mind, as well as the evaluation questions that were to be answered with the data. These, of course, should be linked to needs— gaps in results—identified during the initial needs assessment. These pieces of information will be instrumental in making relevant interpretations and conclusions. Based on these inferences, a detailed list of applicable recommendations should be derived. Such recommendations for action provide the central basis for decision making and thus are the drivers for the evaluation in the first place. You can see why this might be the section of the evaluation report that draws the immediate attention of decision makers.

In sum, there are a variety of considerations and approaches to making sound interpretations. Below is a list of general guidelines to consider in this process:

1. Involve stakeholders in the process.

2. Consult various perspectives (such as people, other evaluation reports, different related studies, etc.).

3. Review the purpose of the evaluation: What questions have we asked and answered?

4. Determine whether the evaluation questions have been satisfactorily answered by the data collected (and remember that these should be linked to the needs identified in the needs assessment process; in other words, determine whether needs—gaps in results—have in fact been reduced or eliminated).

5. Determine the value and implications of findings.

6. Look for consensus where appropriate, but don't force it if none exists.

7. Distinguish between statistical significance and practical significance.

8. Be forthcoming and explicit about limitations of the data and its interpretation.

## RECOMMENDATIONS AND DECISION MAKING

While evaluators may have done quite a bit of work by this point, their clients still have a long way to go. The client must still determine the value and feasibility of the conclusions and recommendations and decide what next steps to take. Some of the relevant questions remaining include: Which alternative recommendations are selected? What other information is still missing before we can make sound decisions? What questions should we have asked but did not? Do we have confidence in the data collection, assessment, and conclusions?

In fact, the recommendations should really be derived as a team effort. Decision makers, as the responsible parties for future changes, should be involved in defining what recommendations and next steps are appropriate and feasible based on the organizational objectives and the value they intend to add to their clients, their organizational culture and climate, and a host of other realities they face. Such recommendations, especially when principally proposed by the decision makers, have a better chance of being implemented.

Worth noting is that data should not automatically dictate the decisions, but rather should serve as key input into the decision-making process. A helpful list of steps for sound decision making follows:

1. Define the type of decisions to be made. To what results are they related (this should be the evaluation questions that drove the evaluation process)? What factors do they involve? Students? Staff? Programs? Funding/budget issues? Other resources? This may seem obvious, but being clear about the types of decisions to be made will make life much easier for all involved. What are the costs and consequences for being wrong and being correct?

2. Identify the possible alternatives. It is uncommon to have a shortage of ideas about "how" we might accomplish something, especially when working in a team. Here is the chance to not only come up with some insightful and original ideas but also to get buy-in from the entire team. The more people feel they were involved in creating solutions, the higher their personal investment in the success of that solution. One key driver in the generation of these alternatives should always be the results we are after.

3. For each alternative, create a list of pros and cons, as well as costs and consequences; it is essentially what we do when we interview candidates for a job. We don't hire the first one to show up; rather, we careful review the qualifications, strengths, weaknesses, and drawbacks associated with each and then hire the best match.

4. With this information at hand, we are in the position to rank the alternatives in order of appropriateness and feasibility. What is appropriate and feasible will vary from organization to organization. Stakeholders must come up with a list of pertinent criteria that makes sense for their own organization and purposes. Criteria might include effectiveness of the alternative, cost, previous experience with it, and any political considerations.

5. Once ranked, decisions makers will have to do what they do best: decide. They will have to decide which alternatives make the most sense. The previous step may have facilitated this stage quite well or may have left decision makers with more questions than before. Even considering taking no action at that point in time with regard to a particular decision may be a wise decision. All alternatives and their potential impact should be carefully considered.

Usually, evaluators tend not to be involved in the actual selection or implementation of recommendations, unless of course their evaluation project is ongoing. For instance, they may also be responsible for creating the evaluation framework for whatever alternatives were selected for implementation. In addition, they could be involved in the design, development, implementation, and formal evaluation after implementation.

The evaluator's involvement at every stage allows everyone to stay focused on the measurable results and improvement that the recommendations are meant to deliver and better ensure that we have asked and answered useful questions.

## NOTES

1. Depending on "what" is being measured and "how," a test could represent either ordinal or interval data. Be sure to refer to Chapter 4 for the unique characteristics of each scale.

2. While some may consider this data to be measured at an interval scale, it is actually ordinal. Consider that the basis for a given score is relative to other scores on the distribution.

3. We don't quote references to these because any contemporary statistics book will provide information on each.

4. Of course, make sure you find out the reason for any extreme scores; that could be important.

5. References are provided at the end of this book. We encourage you to consult them and use the useful information they contain. For now, realize that there are useful statistical tests and tools for you to use.

# Communicating Results and Recommendations to Stakeholders

# 7

The whole point of evaluation is to use the findings to inform decision makers and stakeholders so they may take action—appropriate and useful action. That action should be the right action for the right reasons. Failures in communication following an otherwise sound evaluation can lead to wrong actions based on incorrect interpretations of your evaluation report. What is found in an evaluation can and must be clear, concise, convincing, and right.

## THE IMPORTANCE OF LANGUAGE FOR CLEAR COMMUNICATION

### The Right Language for the Right Audience

The role of language is an important issue.[1] Language is too often taken for granted. We want to prevent confusion or miscommunication and make sure that the evaluation findings you worked hard to obtain do not cause your audience to make decisions that are not supported by the data.

An evaluation report is designed to communicate. In school systems, this communication is expected to provide program decision makers with clear and concise information required to make correct, productive, and useful program decisions.

At issue is that a decision maker could make an incorrect decision based on misinterpretation or overreaction to report language. The idea that evaluation may appropriately support decision making is not new.[2] One noted evaluator (Weiss, 1972) pointed out, "In its ideal form, evaluation is conducted for a client who has decisions to make and who looks to the evaluation for answers on which to base his decisions" (p. 6). The worlds of the administrator and the classroom teacher are often described using special local meanings of terms containing political, technical, and unique language sets that can vary from the norms in use by evaluation teams grounded in academic and educational settings. Terms like *validity*, for example, are used in different contexts, with different technical and lay meanings.

The University of Illinois Center for Instructional Research and Curriculum Evaluation (CIRCE) is one of several professional evaluation organizations that checks the impact of results and language of presentations by using reviews by a professional evaluator outside the immediate investigative team (Davis et. al, 1999, 2000). This review, a form of "meta-evaluation," can be used to spot words that trigger hot issues and tender feelings that could lead to unwarranted programmatic actions. But how can evaluators determine whether the report communicates well? That is, how can evaluators assess the likelihood that decision makers who read an evaluation report will interpret it as the authors intended? One variation on the meta-evaluation is to use a surrogate (substitute) decision maker to review findings and courses of action that follow from the findings. The aim is to reduce the risk of communication error.

Some review questions:

1. Are the findings stated in the correct order of importance (misprioritization of findings)?

2. Are the format and organization poor for client use?

3. Is phraseology overly emotive (i.e., "loaded" words)?

4. Is wording ambiguous (a phrase easily taken two ways) and imprecise (vague terms or phrases)?

## The Two-Path Tactic

We suggest that at least two types of review take place as you begin to write the evaluation report. An outsider should review the language and presentation effects to make sure there are no possible terms and ideas that could confuse or mislead decision makers. This could be formal language impact review using a surrogate decision maker. For the second review, we propose use of a questionnaire similar to the one outlined below to assess whether actions likely to result from the publication of the evaluation are consonant with the intentions of the evaluation team. For example, if a language impact review indicates a decision maker would cancel a program based upon an evaluation report, that decision should seem reasonable to the evaluation team in terms of their intent, understandings, expectations, and meanings as they wrote the report. If impact review indicates that a decision is likely to occur that is not consonant with the intent of the evaluation team, the evaluators may then consider revisions to reduce the risk that the decision makers will overreact to words, terms, phrases, or presentation of information.

The following sections provide more detail on these two paths.

### Iterative Exchange of Impressions, Ideas, and Meanings

Once the evaluation is under way, we recommend an *iterative* approach, in which the evaluator provides draft sections likely to be used in the report. These sections are subjected to shared reviews (stakeholder representatives and evaluation team members). Then, as the requirement for strategic thinking about the future evaluation activities and the report itself emerges, the evaluator can arrange for face-to-face discussions with reviewers.

When a draft is provided, the evaluator may supply at the same time one or more questions for the stakeholder reviewer to answer about the report. The question(s) may ask the reviewer to paraphrase the meaning of key marked parts of the excerpt or of the whole. Or the evaluator may provide questions that ask the reviewer to answer specific questions on meaning, tone, or emphasis. The reviewer should also be asked to provide any additional comments he or she believes to be appropriate. This approach is similar to usability testing and cued-response protocol testing, used by a wide variety of government and corporate agencies to improve documents of all types (Daniel, 1995; Dumas, 1999).

### Facilitating a Language Impact Review

A formal assessment of some polar opposites can be a starting place in assessing language from both the client's and the evaluation team's perspective. An active dialogue to discover where each party falls, and the implications expressed in language, can reveal much.

Table 7.1 contrasts some examples of polar terms and positions that can relate to the way observations are made and couched in language. The table is a set of some possibilities—it is neither exhaustive nor representative of any particular evaluator or client.

The intent is to show that orientations and preferences may differ. Early and continuous discussion using these common opposites may lead to more sensitive use of terms and better understanding of underlying program activity and structure.

**Table 7.1**    Possible Conflicting Evaluation Report Presentation Techniques
and Orientations

| Polar Positions | |
|---|---|
| Supports thought and consideration of complex "whole picture" issues | Support specific decisions |
| Whole (extensive description and interpretation) must be read | Executive summary/briefing |
| Comprehensiveness | Brevity |
| Goal free (without reference to any existing objectives) | Goal driven |
| Qualitative | Quantitative |
| Considers *all* dimensions seen as relevant by the evaluators | Focuses on main issues of interest to the client |
| Detailed description of methodology | Summarizes methodology |
| Book-like organization, with chapters, brief appendices | Shorter report body, with appendices for details |
| Language is professional, maintains standards in the evaluation community | Language is corporate or governmental, suitable for use in the client organization |
| Sequence is set to show gradual development or sequence of evaluation | Sequence is set by priority order of the major findings |
| Emphasizes limitations in data collection and conclusions that can be drawn | Emphasizes findings and trends, notes limitations |
| Data presented with mostly equal weight in terms of visual presentation and overall organization | Most important data emphasized by sequence, subtitles, boldface, and other techniques |
| Emphasizes program weaknesses and limitations to avoid the risk of "over-positive" presentation of results | Addresses weaknesses and limitations, but also strengths and accomplishments achieved |

Several approaches for discussing communicative techniques and orientations are available. One simple approach is for the evaluator to provide samples of previous reports completed, so the client can get a feel for the evaluator's style. In most situations, this will provide a sufficient basis for discussion and resulting guidance for the look and feel of evaluation reports.

In a few cases, client organizations may have specific communicative guidelines they desire the evaluator to apply. For example, federal agencies may desire that reports use techniques of the U.S. President's Plain Language initiative. The client may have specific requirements concerning basic report structure: active versus passive voice, readability, paragraph unity, avoidance of loaded words and phrases, tone, use of headings and subheadings, use of summaries, and use of highlighting and prioritization techniques, such as use of tables, figures, bolding, and bullets. Any such specific requests should definitely be discussed before the evaluator and the client agree to proceed with the evaluation; some evaluators may find these requirements too restrictive and decline the work.

## The Language Impact Review Process

To support language impact reviews of evaluation reports, a follow-up on procedure can be added to the meta-evaluation. We suggest the following steps:

1. The client organization selects one or more client representatives to review the draft evaluation report sections or the entire report. The representative will be a surrogate for the client's senior decision maker(s).

2. The surrogate reviews the draft materials, using a language impact questionnaire (below) or similar tool. The surrogate also provides any additional comments he or she believes to be appropriate. At this time, no discussion occurs between the surrogate reviewer and the evaluation team.

3. The evaluation team reviews the results of the language impact questionnaire to determine whether the reactions of the surrogate are in consonance with the intent of the evaluation team—is what they thought they wrote what the surrogate understood?

4. If it appears that miscommunication may have occurred, the surrogate and the evaluation team engage in discussion to discuss reporting strategy and identify possible sources of miscommunication.

5. The evaluation team prepares a revision if required by Step 4.

6. The evaluation team and the client organization repeat the language impact review with a different surrogate. The process is repeated until consonance is reached.

Figure 7.1 provides one possible example of a questionnaire for language impact review of an evaluation report (section or whole). A caveat: We are not proposing that this specific questionnaire be used as is; rather, we are proposing that questions of this type be used. The questionnaire should be modified by the evaluator and the client to address their specific evaluation situation.

## THE EVALUATION REPORT

All of the work that you have put into the evaluation planning and observation phases must now be converted into a report that clearly communicates the results of the evaluation effort that are related to the results of the program being evaluated and the events (and processes) that led up to the program results obtained. The report must also reflect the discipline, rigor, and scope of the evaluation. A wide-ranging evaluation study will require a larger report than a tight, small study designed to answer fewer evaluation questions. We have found that the following four types of written reports and three types of oral reports will serve most of the situations. An evaluator who is engaged with a school system on a continuous basis will have the opportunity to use more than one of these types of reports.

### Types of Written Reports

The type of report must support the type of evaluation. As we have noted in other sections of this book, our main emphasis is on confirming that results obtained are the ones intended. That is, the results that were predicted to occur when the program was implemented and that were designed to meet the needs identified in the disciplined process of needs assessment did occur.

We also pointed out, however, that the function of evaluation can be emphasized at different stages of a program. It is not uncommon for administrators to request progress reports—formative evaluations—that involve evaluation of milestones that lead to ultimate results. This is especially true when the stakes are high. All managers should know the costs and penalties for failing to hit the target. All managers should also know that timely program adjustments can be the difference between success and failure. Evaluators are called upon to assist in making this adjustment as well as to report final findings. It should be noted that this role is often expressed through use of the term *formative and summative evaluation.*

The following types of reports are based on the requirement to report findings at differing points in the life cycle of a program. The term *program*

**Figure 7.1**    Evaluation Report Language Impact Questionnaire for Use by
Evaluators

---

1. Which course of action would the evaluation report best support?

   a. Increase funding for this program.
   b. Continue the funding at its current level.
   c. Reduce funding for the program.
   d. Revision of the program.
   e. Eliminate funding for the program.

2. Based on the evaluation report, how would you describe the effectiveness of the program evaluated?

   a. Completely successful—meets all program goals.
   b. Partially successful—meets some program goals. Achievement of remaining goals cannot yet be determined.
   c. Partially successful—meets some program goals. Remaining goals were definitely not achieved and will not be achieved with the current approach.
   d. Unsuccessful—none of the program goals have been achieved.

3. In comparison to other programs with the same general purposes, how would you rate this program, based on the evaluation report?

   a. Clearly superior
   b. Somewhat better
   c. About the same
   d. Less effective
   e. Definitely worse

4. Other programs with the same general purposes, how would you rate this program, based on the evaluation report?

5. According to the evaluation report, the program's main goals are (list as many as apply):

   a. _____
   b. _____
   etcetera.

6. According to the evaluation report, the program's important strengths or accomplishments are (list as many as apply):

   a. _____
   b. _____
   etcetera.

7. According to the evaluation report, the program's important limitations or deficiencies are (list as many as apply):

   a. _____
   b. _____
   etcetera.

8. According to the evaluation report, the program's important side effects are (list as many as apply):

   a. _____
   b. _____
   etcetera.

*(Continued)*

**Figure 7.1** (Continued)

9. According to the evaluation report, the program is perceived positively overall by what percentage of the users:

   a. 90% or higher
   b. 80% to 89%
   c. 70% to 79%
   d. 60% to 69%
   e. 50% to 59%
   f. 30% to 49%
   g. 0% to 29%

10. According to the evaluation report, which statement best describes the likelihood that the program will positively impact organizational performance:

   a. Virtually certain—positive impact is already evident.
   b. Probable—trends so far are positive.
   c. Possible—basic program design is sound, but no trends or evidence is available at this time.
   d. Unlikely—trends so far are negative and basic program design is flawed.
   e. Program will not positively impact performance: No impact or negative impact is already evident.

is used here in the most general sense that a course of action or solution strategy has a beginning and an end that can be managed. In the course of real events in time, many programs coexist, start, and stop in a complex context of social, economic, and physical forces. Evaluators who can tease out the important facts from background noise and confusion by writing or presenting a clear and well-founded report can contribute a great deal to the educational enterprise.

### Report of Findings Based on Program Evaluation Results

This report is used at the end of a program (or evaluation contract) to present findings relating to the Products, Outputs, and Outcomes of the program under study. This report will include a comparison of the obtained results with the expected results and explanations as to the differences based on observations that occurred during the evaluation study. The report will include recommendations as to a future course of action regarding the program.

### Report of Findings Based on Evaluation of Alternative Courses of Action

This report is used following needs assessment when goals and objectives (the ends) have been derived and are linked to a desired societal condition (Mega) based on needs. At this point, alternative solutions to reach the goals and objectives (the means to be employed to reach desired results) are evaluated based on cost-to-benefit ratio and other criteria related to the specific stakeholders. This report can also be used to report findings and recommendations related to midcourse adjustments. When milestones are missed, some adjustment may be required. Unpredicted events can cause disruption to the tactics. Changes can be required due to a cut in resources, a change in the populations involved, a change in the political situation, and a host of other factors.

### Report of Findings Based on Evaluation of Goals and Objectives

This report is used when the evaluation team has reason to question the legitimacy of goals and objectives. Perhaps a needs assessment was never done. The team may want to recommend that one be carried out and provide guidance.

### Report of Findings Based on Evaluation of Performance Records

This report is used to present findings of an evaluation study that is directed at a perceived deficiency in performance. The report will contain the evidence and arguments stemming from each candidate for causal or contributing factor. The factors are rank ordered. Sometimes, there are recommendations made concerning how the deficiencies might be reduced or eliminated.

## Oral Reports

Evaluators are often called upon to make oral presentations. We include a brief discussion of three situations that are highly likely to be requested in any evaluation study.

### Executive Briefing

The executive briefing should be short and to the point. Pay particular attention to avoid repetition and know the content of previous briefings so as not to cover old ground. A short recap of the previously provided information can begin the brief but limit the points to those that are relevant to the rest of your presentation. In general, the same things listed in the report components below will provide a structure for your presentation. Remember, as an evaluator, you take your lead from the agreed-upon goals and objectives derived from needs assessment and linked to Mega. As such, you are there to brief the facts of the findings. You are not there to make a sales pitch. Many of the public speaking advice books are aimed at making convincing arguments and closing the deal. There is no deal to close in an evaluation. You report the findings relative to the goals of the program and the guidelines of professional ethics. When you jump over to advocacy or spin doctoring, you have moved away from evaluation into a new role.

### Public Forum

Speaking in public can be daunting for some evaluators. Toast Masters is a good forum for practicing, but the presentation of evaluation findings has the added requirement to inform more than entertain. The use of a logical structure in your presentation, clear visual aids that are simple and direct, and notes to keep you on track will help you serve the audience. In a public forum, you must be prepared to answer questions. While it is your duty to be impartial in presenting the findings, your audience will often contain passionate advocates of different views. The evaluation findings presentation is not the proper forum to argue or defend these points of view. If your program was initiated using a disciplined approach to needs assessment, you will be in a position to answer questions, because the societal benefit and the linkage to program goals is made explicit in that process.

### Demonstration

Demonstrations are often more effective than words in presenting evaluation findings. Video and audio recordings can convey the results in cases where the program goals involve the arts and music education for example. Sports education and training also represent areas of performance where seeing the results in action can provide a valuable supplement to other measures of performance.

## Basic Components of Written Evaluation Reports

- Executive summary
- Statement of relevance and purpose
- Statement of evaluation questions and the needs data that support them
- Description of the evaluation scope of inquiry
- Description of methodology
- Observation chronology

- Discussion of relevant factors
- Observation results
- Measurement results
- Findings (that answer each evaluation question)
- Discussion
- Possible threats to the validity of the findings and recommendations
- Recommendations (based on observation and performance data)
- Appendix A: details of methods, statistics, and assumptions that would otherwise "clog up" the main report
- Appendix B: persons involved in the evaluation, including those who facilitated the evaluation process

## NOTES

1. As emphasized in *New Directions for Evaluation,* 2000, Summer, R. Hopson, Ed.

2. Stufflebeam was a pioneer in this orientation to evaluation (Stufflebeam et al., 1971).

# Scenario 3

## *Working Knowledge*

T he school year was at the halfway point in Cobb County. The evaluation team had settled into the schedule (still congratulating themselves for having done a proper needs assessment) and had accumulated a lot of data in the form of notes, interviews, recordings, questionnaire data, and firsthand accounts from the participants and graduate students. The issue for them now was how to make sense out of all of the data. There seemed to be so much.

After forming subcommittees to each take a part of the data, the team realized that the whole evaluation picture would not come together: It would have been splinters of the educational enterprise, not a fabric, where all of the pieces (threads) stayed unique but also related one to the others. They decided to apply evaluation thinking to themselves: to apply what they were using on others to their own tasks.

The team once again listed the questions that the evaluation was to ask and answer, and the nature of the data they had for each, and they listed them down the right-hand side of a huge piece of butcher paper. Then, across the top of the paper, they listed the various statistical tools and techniques that could be used. Next, using their methodology and educational statistics, members selected the best analysis tool for each. (See Table 3.A).

Next, the team set about finding the data for each evaluation question. They obtained the data they had for each evaluation question and then used the best tool for making sense of each item. It took a bit of practice, but soon they had all questions covered and the best statistical tools for each. Next was to actually reduce the data and come up with some observations about each item, making sense of the data they had obtained.

Soon they had a landscape of evaluation with all of the evaluation questions and the data about each. They scanned across all questions to make sure that where there was overlap, they would note the relationships. (After all, they were working with an educational system, not a bunch of individual and unrelated subsystems.)

**Table 3.A**     Fear Building and Trust Building

| Chapters | Fear | Trust |
|---|---|---|
| 4. Identifying Required Data | • Data will be used to place blame.<br>• "They" will find out we don't track the data we should be tracking.<br>• What if we can't get access to the data?<br>• What if we lose funding because "negative" data are found? | • Emphasize that data will be used to improve.<br>• This is an opportunity to derive a sound data-tracking framework.<br>• This is an opportunity to demonstrate why you should have access and how it impacts other areas of the organization.<br>• Better that we find the truth and have an opportunity to fix it than have someone else do it when it's too late. |
| 5. Data Collection | • We don't have the expertise/time/other resources. | • Data collection can be done very effectively and efficiency with limited resources. |
| 6. Data Analysis and Interpretation | • We don't have the expertise.<br>• Statistics are intimidating.<br>• Statistics can be manipulated.<br>• Conclusions and recommendations can be biased. | • There are many user-friendly data analysis software tools available.<br>• Statistics should be presented in a straightforward manner.<br>• Limitations of findings should always be made explicit.<br>• Conclusions should be well supported by the evidence. |

The team methodically listed all findings for each evaluation question and also listed evaluation questions that were linked, having some elements in common. Now, they had the data and conclusions for their first evaluation draft.

Next came a list of observations and recommendations related to the evaluation questions. The evaluation team did one more internal review—making sure what they had was solid and everything was justifiable—and then turned in the draft (clearly marked "DRAFT") to the superintendent for her review. They met, clarified the findings and recommendations, and then made revisions she suggested and with which they agreed.

Finally, the evaluation was turned over to the superintendent, who submitted it to the board for approval and further direction.

The basic component sections of the written report were:

- Executive summary
- Statement of relevance and purpose
- Statement of evaluation questions (and the needs data that support them)
- Description of the evaluation scope of inquiry
- Description of methodology
- Observation chronology
- Discussion of relevant factors
- Observation results
- Measurement results
- Findings (that answer each evaluation question)
- Discussion
- Possible threats to the validity of the findings and recommendations
- Recommendations (based on observation and performance data)
- Appendix A: details of methods, statistics, and assumptions that would otherwise "clog up" the main report
- Appendix B: persons involved in the evaluation, including those who facilitated the evaluation process.

Now, let's turn to lessons learned based on this part of the Scenario.

## TRAPS, ERRORS, AND RULES OF THE ROAD IN THE RESULTS PHASE

### The Analysis Trap and the Action Trap

*Error of Data Reduction Generality, Error of the Ratio*

We use descriptive statistics to provide a better shorthand way of describing data sets. It is often good to know that 100% of a population passed a test. A school district required all of its teachers to be certified based on a new test of teacher competency. Some schools reported a 100% pass rate, one school reported a 0% pass rate, and two schools reported a 75% pass rate.

The district superintendent, a person of action, immediately ordered a study to find out what the 0% school was doing wrong and the 100% schools were doing right to prepare their teachers for the test. The consultant hired to do the study took a look at the raw data. It turned out that all of the schools had scheduled the test with options to take the test on the initial test day or on subsequent days, depending on teacher workload and

> *Fear Builder:* The evaluator, knowing that a particular decision maker has a reputation for wanting to look decisive, warns persons being interviewed that they had better respond to his questions because he is on a tight schedule and the decision maker is a busy man, so get cracking . . . .

self-assessed readiness to take the test. The schools reporting a 100% pass rate had between 1 and 3 teachers take the test. The school reporting 0% had 1 teacher take the test. The schools reporting 75% had 10 teachers and 5 teachers, respectively, take the test. The percentage of passing teachers reflected the test-taking population on that day—not the entire population of the school, as the superintendent had assumed.

The test-taking population did not represent the entire teacher population at each school, so the percentage reported did not represent a true ratio of success or failure based on the entire population. Thus the *error of the ratio* along with the more general *error of using the wrong data generalization statistic* were present in the report presented to a decision maker. Couple these errors generated by the "analysis trap" with an inappropriate response, and you have a case of the "action trap," which occurs when faulty analysis is used for decisions leading to a wrong or damaging action (or lack of correct action).

> *Trust Builder:* The evaluator, knowing that a particular decision maker has a reputation for wanting to look decisive, makes sure that presentations are fully explained and detail is provided to prevent superficial conclusions. In dealing with persons being interviewed, the evaluator is careful not to pass along the anxiety caused by an anxious administrator. The evaluator tries to set the person at ease and gives them plenty of time to answer questions.

Note that the inappropriate response committed by the superintendent had two parts. The first part was the assumption that the data extremes of 100% and 0% automatically showed that schools were doing something right and wrong; and the second was to expend resources based on that assumption. As it turns out, the consultant's effort was not entirely wasted, however, because the schedule factor was discovered and it was learned that one of the schools had used an incorrect version of the test.

### Error in Using Descriptive Statistics

Take care to avoid the *error of the ratio* in the application of a statistical routine by including information on the nature of the population being described. The statistic should capture the entire population. If the statistic describes only a part of the population or a sample from the population, that should be clearly stated.

## The Intervention Trap

*Errors of Fidelity*

The "intervention trap" occurs when educational programs do not achieve desired results because of low fidelity in three key areas. Evaluation of an educational practice is influenced by the way that practice is broken down into its components to gain a practical insight into what is going on and why. The term *intervention* is the correct word for describing the active part of these components. Evaluators must decide how much to consider in planning an evaluation.

Most educators who design interventions of one kind or another would argue that interventions are designed from the outset to bring about a change that is positive. But anyone who has observed the history of educational movements knows that all interventions are not equally successful in obtaining desired ends. Some interventions succeed where others fail. It is not always enough to identify what you want to achieve, create a plan, and then just press the "Start" button to get guaranteed results. The difference between a plan on paper and the activity of plan implementation is often the difference between success and failure; one must be faithful to the plan. This difference requires a focus on the logic of and rationale for the intervention.

Evaluators must consider three key dimensions of an intervention in order to make meaningful judgments about the results.

1.  The plan or model correctly reflects a course of action that will achieve a desired result, correctly matching the solution to the problem. If it doesn't, the plan or model is flawed from the outset. The design alone will not achieve a desired result. We refer to this dimension as *situational fidelity*. In other words, plan what you do, and do what you plan.

2.  Doing what was planned brings up a second dimension, *execution fidelity*, in which the plan can be carried out well or might be corrupted in the execution by unplanned events and interruptions or by failure to follow the plan.

3.  A third dimension consists of the human element, such as teachers, students, administrators, and other players who behave as predicted and planned. This is *behavioral fidelity*. This last dimension can include social forces generally outside of the planned area of engagement but capable of imposing change by supporting or undermining the effort. Included here might be educational politicians and the politics of the board or community.

Evaluators fall into the "intervention trap" when they overgeneralize the value of an intervention, by condemning a good plan that was poorly executed or praising a poor plan that was saved by outside help. To avoid this trap, we suggest the use of the Intervention Cube (see Figure 3.A). The three conceptual dimensions of the cube are *situational fidelity, executional fidelity,* and *behavioral fidelity.* The following list gives examples of the high and low ends of these dimensions.

*Situational Fidelity High*

Clear valid goals and objectives
Problem matched to solution
Appropriate choice of means

*Situational Fidelity Low*

No goals and objectives
Problem unrelated to solution
Poor choice of means (quick fix)

*Executional Fidelity High*

Objectives are operational
Following the plan well
Stable situation

*Executional Fidelity Low*

Objectives are overgeneralized
Deviating from the plan
Unstable situation with distraction

*Behavioral Fidelity High*

Teachers competent
Students motivated
Community supportive

*Behavioral Fidelity Low*

Teachers less than competent
Students distracted
Community nonsupportive

Using the three dimensions of fidelity: The "high/high/high" corner is the "corner of success," and the "low/low/low" corner is the "corner of failure" (see Table 3.B).

**Figure 3.A**   The Fidelity Cube

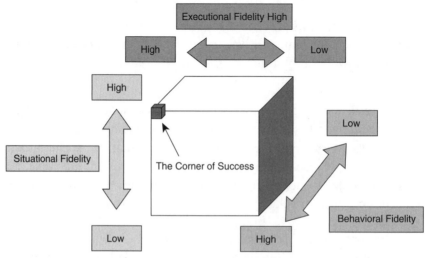

**Table 3.B**  Fidelity Cube Assessment Table

| The Corner of Success | The Corner of Failure |
|---|---|
| Situational Fidelity High | Situational Fidelity Low |
| Executional Fidelity High | Executional Fidelity Low |
| Behavioral Fidelity High | Behavioral Fidelity Low |

Evaluators may incorrectly assess an intervention by not looking in the right place, drawing the wrong conclusion by not having looked at all of the important factors, and not collecting the complete and required data.

**The Validity Trap**

*The Terminology Error*

The "validity trap" results from a confusion of substituting one type of validity for another and then acting on the conclusion. It is changing horses in midstream and not letting anyone know. There are several types of validity, and they are not interchangeable and should not be confused with one another. This is an *error of terminology* that can lead to serious problems in judging the quality of programs. The term *validity* is frequently used with multiple or misleading meaning.

The test and measurement conception of validity is the degree to which an instrument measures what it purports to measure (i.e., "predictive validity" is firmly established in test construction methodology). Valid tests are used and have been used with great success since World War II in personnel selection. Fitting the person to the job was important in the selection of pilots and specialty fields to maximize the efficient use of personnel resources. However, effective prediction in the case of a pilot, for example, does not address the desirability of having pilots in the first place. In times of war, pilots are important and fill a societal requirement: peace and protection of life and livelihood. In some cases, useful data may be collected by "pilotless" aircraft without risking lives.

The social consensus based on the values—perceptions of what is important—of the community at large made having pilots desirable, in short, a valid goal. When the term *validity* is used in this context, it is different from the predictive validity of a test. After all, the methodology of test construction is open for all to use to effectively screen personnel. It is up to the professional to decide the ethics of what is being done. For example, a terrorist organization could construct a test that was a valid predictor of candidates who would commit suicide in an attack. Having a valid predictive test does not in any way relate to the validity of the test purpose or acceptance in the light of larger societal values; an assessment instrument can be valid and subtract societal value. Yet examples of the mixture and confusion of the two are common in society.

Here is an example from the field of education. We use development models for educational material that call for validation of the material. In some cases, this may mean having valid and reliable tests, and in other cases, it may mean that the material is effective in causing learning to take place. But it usually does not mean that the materials have been vetted against a valid societal requirement. When educationists and the public at large blur the difference between the two validity types, the validity trap can occur. Consider the following case: School district officials take great pains to select a sex education program that has been proven to reduce teen pregnancy. They buy and implement the program only to find that half of the parents in the district refuse to let their children attend the program. When it is used, only part of the population shows a reduction in teen pregnancy, while another part shows no decline. The instrument selected might have not been validated on the full population in the school district.

## The Conclusion Trap

### Error of False Conclusion

When we offer a conclusion regarding a program that is really unsupported by the facts of the case or influenced by one or more errors in our data collection or data analysis, we are making an important error: the *error of false conclusion.* Recommendations to decision makers that are based on these defective conclusions may harm stakeholders, waste resources, or at the very least embarrass school officials.

### Causality Error

Most of the time, we teach and we observe the effects of teaching directly, and we are likely correct in assuming the direct link between the teaching (or other instructional tactics) and the results. In one-on-one coaching and mentoring, this is usually a safe assumption. But what happens when we try to apply the direct causal linking to whole programs, to too many students, and to averaged scores on tests? The larger and more complex the program and the longer the time frame, the more we have to consider a wide range of variables that may or may not influence the results of our programs. What if a onetime disruption contributed to low test sores in an otherwise sound program? What if extra effort on the part of one teacher influenced the results of a weak program? Educational administrators could make a bad decision. Scrapping a good program and supporting a weak program are two *errors of causal path,* the roadway to results.[1]

### Error of Misattribution

In the work place of today, managers tend to think in terms of problems and solutions. Most of the time, that is a helpful way of approaching a situation. But occasionally, a complex problem is combined with a simplistic solution that does more harm than good. This is usually accompanied by a *misattribution* of causes and effects or problems and solutions. For example, the Chicago school board once set out to improve academic performance in a certain school. They perceived that a lack of progress in one school reflected the lack of will or ability on the part of the local principal. The solution was to replace the principal. It took a wise evaluator, Bob Stake,[2] to point out that the school was in a drug neighborhood, most of the students were from single family homes, the one good meal the children got each day came from the school, and much mentoring of troubled youth was encouraged by the local principal, who had created a safe harbor each day for the students. Academic progress was not at the standard set by the board, but in light of the other accomplishments relating to fundamental survival, the local principal had done a remarkable job. Replacing her would not have improved academic performance and may have made things worse.

### Error of Wishful Thinking

When we reach a conclusion that is based not on the facts of the case, but on the expectations and desired objectives, that is the *error of wishful thinking.* It is here that if you are not careful, you will force the data to fit your preconceived notions.

### Error of the Faulty Construct

When observing behavior, we have a tendency to explain it in terms of motivation and other constructs, like hunger or social forces striving for success and so forth. All of these are in fact just hypotheses, which must be verified, grounded with other observations, and tested against alternative explanations. That is acceptable if it is open and done in the proper context. Occasionally, however, we treat these abstractions as if they could be directly observed and manipulated. Constructs like mathematical aptitude, hunger, and so on are labels that are placed on behavior after the fact of some event or series of tests. The concepts allow for discussion and theory, but they must always be grounded in real behavior at some point. When we start using the terms independent of this grounding, the meaning can drift away and the resulting plans and ideas that are based on the interaction of constructs are suspect.

## RULES OF THE ROAD FOR THE ANALYSIS PHASE

*Rule 1.* Time and resources must be devoted to sensible and sensitive analysis. If you cut corners, you jeopardize the whole evaluation.

*Rule 2.* Select an analysis approach that can answer the questions based on the collected data.

*Rule 3.* Review the results relating to the goals and objective, and examine the results in light of targets and the fulfillment of the identified needs before trying to make sense of the data on process.

*Rule 4.* Look for cause-and-effect relationships that can explain deviations from target results.

*Rule 5.* Look for contextual issues starting from the core educational process first and then expand to cultural and environmental factors.

*Rule 6.* Form tentative conclusions, and subject these to formal review by the team and outside reviewers if possible.

*Rule 7.* Divide the finding and analysis conclusions into one part that can be firmly supported by the data of the study and one part that cannot be firmly supported but is worth checking with additional investigation.

*Rule 8.* Don't ever allow politics to enter into the evaluation.

## NOTES

1.   You may see a parallel here to the well-known Type I and Type II errors talked about in statistical hypothesis testing.

2.   Personal communication, 2003, between Professor Stake and Bill Platt.

# Part IV

# Action and Adjustment

**Figure IV**   A Phased Evaluation Plan for Evaluation

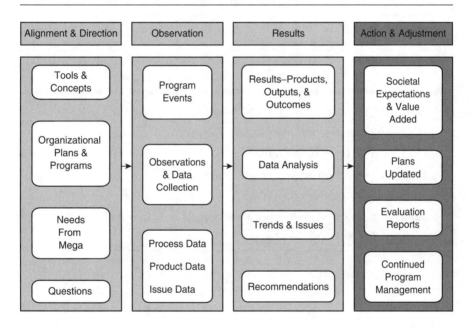

E valuations serve a purpose to support the management of the educational enterprise. The action and adjustment phase is the realization of that purpose through the meaningful presentation of findings, conclusions, and recommendations to decision makers and to stakeholders who are served by the educational system. It is important to ask and get answers to the right evaluations. It is equally important to put those answers to good use. What you do in the action and adjustment phase will determine what follows; inaction and procrastination are always possible even in the face of valid data. It is your job to present those data in support of your recommendations, to preserve what is good, and change what is not.

---

*Prime Questions for Action and Adjustment Section*

Did we achieve the results that were intended?

Do the results line up with valid needs?

If not, why not?

What should we keep, what should we adjust, and what should we discard to start new? This applies to the needs-driven solution set at organization and program level.

How should change and continuous improvement be managed?

---

*Secondary Questions for Action and Adjustment Section*

Who will get evaluation reports?

How will the report be presented?

How will evaluation be carried on into the future?

Do we require professional help?

Which stakeholders are in a position to assist or hold up the implementation of change?

# Evaluating for Continuous Improvement

# 8

The entire point of our approach to educational evaluation is to serve the long-term interests of society, using our educational system as the vehicle. An evaluation process that assesses the current value of an educational enterprise is both vital and practical. Using that data for growth and continuous improvement is key . . . the evaluation itself may have been conducted well, but if the data are not used for improving, the time, effort, and other resources used to conduct the evaluation will have been spent in vain. We have set the stage for continuous improvement by providing you with data collection tools that gather the type of information required to answer your evaluation questions, as well as some methods for summarizing, analyzing, and interpreting such data. Furthermore, we have reiterated on numerous occasions that means and ends must be considered together: The effectiveness of the former is dependent on the achievement of the latter. In this chapter, we offer you the most critical concept of evaluation: Evaluation and the use of the data it produces for improvement must be continuous.

## USING THE DATA ABOUT *WHAT WORKED* AND *WHAT DID NOT* TO MEASURABLY IMPROVE OUR EDUCATIONAL ENTERPRISE

Continuous improvement is dependant on asking the right questions, collecting useful data, and then applying that data to make decisions about what to continue, modify, and change. There is much talk about continuous improvement, but in practice, it is rarely done. The norm in organizations is to maintain the status quo, and it will be challenging to persuade some individuals to put this data to good use. After all, change is perceived as painful by many, though in many cases, it would be far more painful to remain in the current state.

The increasing responsibilities of professional educators for the results, consequences, and payoffs of their activities have magnified the importance of valid and useful evaluation. For the evaluation professional, this era requires a renewed commitment and focus on:

- Value added
- The research basis—asking and answering the "right" questions—for decision making
- The *system approach* to individual and organizational performance improvement
- Consistency in language that leaves no confusion regarding the value added for individuals, organization, and society

In the world of business, industry, and government, continuous improvement is an accepted concept that is built into many organizations. It is becoming accepted in education. It is sensible: Why would anyone not want to know whether things are on target and getting useful results and use those data to decide what to keep and what to change?

The benefit of continuous improvement can have great payoffs in any endeavor, educational or otherwise. The ideal educational process is one that can be controlled to define, deliver, and then maintain quality and to adjust at the earliest sign that something is out of tolerance. While quality control measures keep things on track, all parts of the organization are encouraged to look for ways to improve the educational enterprise by adjusting design specifications and altering the educational process to include any new improved features and/or changing that which will not deliver measurable success.

This is a three-part enterprise:

- The goals of education must be aligned with the *needs*—gaps in results and their consequences—of society.
- The Processes of education must be capable of efficiently and effectively reaching the goals and objectives.
- All elements must deliver success by continuously revising as required (based on sound data), any time that change is required. There is no sense in moving blindly toward the end of a program or project without tracking whether this will be the end you expected.

In education, the Process-Product relationship is complex; human learning in a group setting introduces an enormous set of variables. And teachers, administrators, parents, and community members add to the richness. But even within the limitations of existing learning and organizational theories, the *system approach* works because it allows for continuous adjustment to reach the target, a target that has been validated by *needs assessment* data. Of course, this benefit of the *system approach* is illusive when the target is not well-defined, which is why our approach to evaluation places great emphasis on setting clear goals and objectives that are valid in the context of society at large.

## USING EVALUATION TO BUILD CONTINUOUS IMPROVEMENT IN EDUCATIONAL SYSTEMS

What does it take to improve an educational program, school, or school system? There are three fundamental components:

1. The stakeholders and their attitudes

2. The language system that makes possible or prevents the possibility of change

3. The tools of evaluation, including evaluation of goals and objectives (initial planning), evaluation of Process (observation), and evaluation of results (planning and adjusting to implement change), so we can continuously improve

An important distinction must be made, however, between continuous improvement and turmoil created when whole programs are scrapped or new ones employed in a trial-and-error effort. This can result when evaluation has not captured sufficient detailed information to allow isolation of appropriate parts of programs that can be fixed or discarded without wholesale disruption of the entire enterprise.

An atmosphere of constant change is just as detrimental to a school system as sticking with a bad program to avoid turbulence. It is our assertion that good evaluation can allow the preservation of the solid parts of a program that produce required results and add the well-controlled and well-managed changes that gradually reduce the gap between required results and actual results. This point brings us full circle to the importance of asking the right questions in the first place.

So much of useful evaluation depends on asking and answering the "right" questions in the first place. The basis for this lies in how we find out what we should be accomplishing and how we know that is worth accomplishing and that we have useful data for initial planning and implementation, as well as for evaluation and continuous improvement.

Let's turn to each of the four components that play a role in continuous improvement.

### Stakeholders and Their Attitudes: The Societal Value-Added Perspective and Frame of Mind

The required frame of mind, your guiding paradigm, is simple, straightforward, and sensible: a primary concern for adding value for external clients and our shared society. From this societal value-added frame, everything one uses, does, produces, and delivers is linked to achieving positive societal results. A central question that each and every organization should ask and answer is: *If Your Organization Is the Solution, What's the Problem?*

This fundamental proposition is central to thinking and planning strategically. It represents a shift from the usual focus only on oneself and one's organization to making certain you also add value to external clients and society—yes, external clients and society. This basic question, directly or indirectly, should reappear through your thinking and work, for it keeps ends and means in perspective. It better ensures you will be successful through making a useful contribution outside of your organization where you and your clients live and work.

### The Language System of Logical Planning and Correct Perspective: Thought Into Action

The culture of an organization is usually expressed in the language used and accepted in the organization. Culture may be defined as "How we do things around here," and what the language communicates and then how things do get done are vital. So, let's look at an appropriate language for finding what worked and what did not, revising as required. Here, then, is a glossary of terms to review and use as we approach evaluation that will define what worked and what did not, based on Kaufman and Watkins (2000).

### System, Systems, Systematic, and Systemic: Related But Not the Same

To set the framework, let's define these basic terms, relate them, and then use them to put other vocabulary in context.

*System Approach:* Begins with the sum total of parts working independently and together to achieve a useful set of results at the societal level, adding value for all internal and external partners. We best think of it as the "large whole," as shown in Figure 8.1.

*Systems Approach:* Begins with the parts of a system–subsystems that make up the "system," as shown in Figure 8.2.

It should be noted here that the *system* is made up of smaller elements, or subsystems, in the figure shown as "bubbles" imbedded in the larger system. If we start at this smaller level, we will start with a part and not the whole. When someone says they are using a "systems approach," they are really focusing on one or more subsystems, unfortunately focusing on the parts and not the whole. When planning and doing at this level, they can only assume that the payoffs and consequences will add up to something useful to society and external clients, and this is usually a very big assumption.

**Figure 8.1**   System Approach

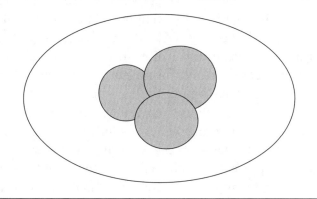

**Figure 8.2**   Systems Approach

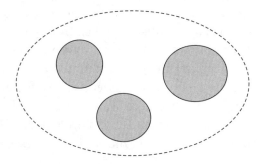

*Systematic Approach:* An approach that does things in an orderly, predictable, and controlled manner. It is a reproducible process. Doing things, however, in a systematic manner does not ensure the achievement of useful results.

*Systemic Approach:* An approach that affects everything in the system. The definition of "the system" is usually left up to the practitioner and may or not include external clients and society. It does not necessarily mean that when something is systemic, it is also useful.

*Change Creation:* The definition and justification, proactively, of new and justified as well as justifiable, in that it waits until change requirements are either defined or imposed and then moves to have the change accepted and used.

*Comfort Zones:* The psychological areas, in business or in life, where one feels secure and safe (regardless of the reality of that feeling). Change is usually painful for most people. When faced with change, many people will find reasons (usually not rational) not to make modifications. This gives rise to Tom Peter's (1997) observation that "it is easier to kill an organization than it is to change it."

*Costs-Consequences Analysis:* The process of estimating a return-on-investment analysis before an intervention is implemented. It asks two basic questions simultaneously: What do you expect to give, and what do you expect to get back in terms of results? Most formulations do not compute costs and consequences for society and external client (Mega) return on investment. Thus we must prove what has been, or has to be, accomplished. Many educational activities, programs, and projects in place today do not use rigorous indicators for expected performance. If criteria are "loose" or unclear, there is no realistic basis for evaluation and continuous improvement. Loose criteria often meet the comfort test but don't allow for the humanistic $z$, or even a splintered quick fix. Most planning models do not include Mega results in the change process and thus miss the opportunity to find out what impact their contributions and results have on external clients and society. The other approaches might be termed "superficial change" or "limited change" in that they focus only on an organization or a small part of an organization.

*Desired Results:* Ends (or results) identified through *needs assessments* that are derived from soft data relating to "perceived needs." "Desired" indicates these are perceptual and personal in nature.

*Ends:* Results, achievements, consequences, payoffs, and/or impacts. The more precise the results, the more likely that reasonable methods and means can be considered, implemented, and evaluated. Without rigor for results statements, confusion can take the place of successful performance.

*Evaluation:* Compares current status (what is) with intended status (what was intended) and is most commonly done only after an intervention is implemented. Unfortunately, "evaluation" is used for blaming and not fixing or improving. When blame follows evaluation, people tend to avoid the means and criteria for evaluation or leave them so loose that any result can be explained away.

*External Needs Assessment:* Determining and prioritizing gaps, then selecting problems to be resolved at the Mega-level. This level of *needs assessment* is most often missing from conventional approaches. Without the data from it, one cannot be assured that there will be strategic alignment from internal results to external value added.

*Hard Data:* Performance data that are based on objectives and is independently verifiable. This type of data is critical. It should be used along with "soft" or perception data.

*Ideal Vision:* The measurable definition of the kind of world we, together with others, commit to help deliver for tomorrow's child. An Ideal Vision defines the Mega-level of planning. It allows an organization and all of its partners to define where they are headed and how to tell when they are getting there or getting closer. It provides the rationality and reasons for an organizational mission objective.

*Inputs:* The ingredients, raw materials, physical, and human resources that an organization can use in its Processes in order to deliver useful ends. These ingredients and resources are often the only considerations made during planning, without determining the value they add internally and externally to the organization.

*Internal Needs Assessment:* Determining and prioritizing gaps, then selecting problems to be resolved at the Micro- and Macro-levels. Most *needs assessment* processes are of this variety (Watkins, Leigh, Platt, & Kaufman, 1998).

*Learning:* The demonstrated acquisition of a skill, knowledge, attitude, and/or ability.

*Learning Organization:* An organization that sets measurable performance standards and constantly compares its results and their consequences with what is required. Learning organizations use performance data related to an Ideal Vision and the primary mission objective to decide what to change and what to continue, and they learn from their performance and contributions. Learning organizations may obtain the highest level of success by strategic thinking—focusing everything that is used, done, produced, and delivered on Mega results: societal value added. Many conventional definitions do not link the "learning" to societal value added. If there is no external societal linking, then it could well guide one away from the new requirements.

*Macro-Level of Planning:* Planning focused on the organization itself as the primary client and beneficiary of what is planned and delivered. This is the conventional starting and stopping place for existing planning approaches.

*Means:* Processes, activities, resources, methods, or techniques used to deliver a result. Means are useful only to the extent that they deliver useful results—at all three levels of planned results: Mega, Macro, and Micro.

*Mega Planning:* Planning that starts with the central focus on society and an agreed-upon definition, in measurable terms, of the kind of world we want to create for tomorrow's child. This, then, is focused on external clients, including parents/citizens, learners, and the community and society that the organization serves. This is the usual missing planning level in most formulations. It is the only one that will focus on societal value added: survival, self-sufficiency, and quality of life of all partners. It is suggested that this type of planning is imperative for getting and proving useful results.

*Mega Thinking:* Thinking about every situation, problem, or opportunity in terms of what you use, do, produce, and deliver as having to add value to external clients and society (same as "strategic thinking").

*Methods-Means Analysis:* Identifies possible tactics and tools for meeting the *need* identified in a "system analysis." The *methods-means analysis* identifies the possible ways and means to meet the *need* and achieve the detailed objectives that are identified in this Mega plan, but it does not select them. Interestingly, this is a comfortable place where some operational planning starts. Thus it either assumes or ignores the requirement to measurably add value within and outside the organization.

*Micro-Level Planning:* Planning focused on individuals or small groups (such as desired and required competencies of associates or supplier competencies). Planning for building-block results. This also is a comfortable place where some operational planning starts. Starting here usually assumes or ignores the requirement to measurably add value to the entire organization as well as to outside the organization.

*Mission Analysis:* Analysis step that identifies: (1) what results and consequences are to be achieved, (2) what criteria (in interval and/or ratio scale terms) will be used to determine success, and (3) what are the building-block results and the order of their completion (functions) required to move from the current results to the desired state of affairs. Most mission objectives have not been formally linked to Mega results and consequences, and thus strategic alignment with "where the clients are" is usually missing (Kaufman, Watkins, Triner, & Stith, 1998).

*Mission Objective:* An exact, performance-based statement of an organization's overall intended results that it can and should deliver to external clients and society. A mission objective is measurable on an interval or ratio scale, so it states not only "where are we headed" but also adds "how we will know when we have arrived." A mission objective is best linked to Mega-levels of planning and the Ideal Vision to ensure societal value added.

*Mission Statement:* An organization's Macro-level "general purpose," a mission statement is measurable only on a nominal or ordinal scale of measurement, states only "where are we headed," and leaves off rigorous criteria for determining how one measures successful accomplishment.

*Need:* The gap between current results and desired or required results. This is where a lot of planning "goes off the rails." By defining any gap as a "need," one fails to distinguish between means and ends and thus confuses what and how. If "need" is defined as a gap in results, then there is a triple bonus: (1) It states the objectives (what should be); (2) it contains the evaluation and continuous improvement criteria (what should be); and (3) it provides the basis for justifying any proposal by using both ends of a *need*, "what is" and "what should be" in terms of results. Proof can be given for the costs of meeting the *need* as well as the costs of ignoring the *need*.

*Needs Analysis:* Taking the determined gaps between adjacent organizational elements and finding the causes of the inability for delivering required results. A needs analysis also identifies possible ways and means to close the gaps in results—*need*—but does not select them. Unfortunately, *needs analysis* is usually used interchangeably with *needs assessment*. They are not the same. How does one "analyze" something (such as a need) before one knows what should be analyzed? First, assess the need; then analyze it.

*Needs Assessment:* A formal process that identifies and documents gaps between current and desired and/or required results, arranges them in order of priority on basis of the cost of meeting the *need* as compared to the cost of ignoring it, and selects problems to be resolved. By starting with a *needs assessment*, justifiable performance data and the gaps between "what is" and "what should be" will provide the realistic and rational reason for both what to change as well as what to continue. When the *needs assessment* starts at the Mega-level, then the "+" is appropriate.

*Objectives:* Precise statement of purpose, or destination to which we are headed and how we will be able to tell when we have arrived. The four parts to an objective are (1) What result is to be demonstrated? (2) Who or what will demonstrate the result? (3) Where will the result be observed? And (4) What interval or ratio scale criteria will be used? *Loose or Process-oriented objectives will confuse everyone* (cf. Mager, 1997). *A Mega-level result is best stated as an objective.*

*Outcomes:* Results and payoffs at the external client and societal level. Outcomes are results that add value to society, community, and external clients of the organization. These are results at the Mega-level of planning.

*Outputs:* The results and payoffs that an organization can or does deliver outside of itself to external clients and society. These are results at the Macro-level of planning, where the primary client and beneficiary is the organization itself. It does not formally link to Outcomes and societal well-being unless it is derived from Outcomes and the Ideal (Mega) Vision.

*Paradigm:* The framework and ground rules individuals use to filter reality and understand the world around them (Barker, 1992). It is vital that people have common paradigms that guide them. That is one of the functions of the Mega level of planning and Outcomes, so that everyone is headed to a common destination and may uniquely contribute to that journey.

*Performance:* A result or consequence of any intervention or activity, including individual, team, or organization. An end.

*Performance Accomplishment System* (PAS) (system approach, systems approach, systemic approach): Any of a variety of interventions (such as "instructional systems design and development," quality management/ continuous improvement, benchmarking, reengineering, and the like) that are results oriented and are intended to get positive results. These are usually focused at the Micro/Products level. This is my preferred alternative to the rather sterile term "performance technology" that often steers people toward hardware and premature solutions (Kaufman, 2000; Kaufman & Watkins, 1999).

*Processes:* The means, activities, procedures, interventions, programs, and initiatives an organization can or does use in order to deliver useful ends. While most planners start here, it is dangerous not to derive the Processes and Inputs from what an organization must deliver and the payoffs for external clients.

*Products:* The building-block results and payoffs of individuals and small groups that form the basis of what an organization produces and delivers, inside as well as outside of itself, and the payoffs for external clients and society. Products are results at the Micro-level of planning.

*Quasi-Need:* A gap in a method, resource, or Process. Many so-called "need assessments" are really "quasi-needs assessments," since they tend to pay immediate attention to means (such as training) before defining and justifying the ends and consequences (Watkins et al., 1998).

*Required Results:* Ends identified through *needs assessment* that are derived from hard data relating to objective performance measures.

*Results:* Ends, Products, Outputs, Outcomes—accomplishments and consequences. Usually misses the Outputs and Outcomes.

*Soft Data:* Personal perceptions of results. Soft data are not independently verifiable. While people's perceptions are reality for them, they are not to be relied on without relating to hard, independently verifiable data as well.

*Strategic Alignment:* The linking of Mega/Outcomes, Macro/Outputs, and Micro/Product-level planning and results with each other and with Processes and Inputs. By formally deriving what the organization uses, does, produces, and delivers to Mega/external payoffs, strategic alignment is complete.

*Strategic Planning Plus:* Mega planning five steps or elements for defining and delivering a preferred future that include (1) deriving the tactical and operational plans; (2) making/buying/obtaining resources; (3) implementation; and simultaneously (4) continuous improvement/formative evaluation; and then (5) determining effectiveness and efficiency. While not strictly planning, this is the part that puts all of the previous planning to work to achieve positive results.

*Strategic Thinking:* Approaching any problem, program, project, activity, or effort noting that everything that is used, done, produced, and delivered must add value for external clients and society. Strategic thinking starts with Mega.

*System Analysis:* Identifies and justifies *what* should be accomplished based on an Ideal/Mega Vision and is results focused. It is a series of analytic steps that include mission analysis, function analysis, and (if selected) task analysis. It also identifies possible methods and means (methods-means analysis) but does not select the methods-means. This starts with rolling down (from outside to inside the organization) linkages to Mega.

*Systems Analysis:* Identifies the most effective and efficient ways and means to achieve required results. Solutions- and tactics-focused. This is an internal (inside the organization) process.

*Tactical Planning:* Finding out what is available to get from "what is" to "what should be" at the organizational/Macro-level. Tactics are best identified after the overall mission has been selected based on its linkages and contributions to external client and societal (Ideal Vision) results and consequences.

*Wants:* Preferred methods and means assumed to be capable of meeting *needs.* Unfortunately, most so-called educational needs assessments are actually "wants assessments."

*What Is:* Current operational results and consequences; these could be for an individual, an organization, and/or for society.

*What Should Be:* Desired or required operational results and consequences; these could be for an individual, an organization, and/or society.

*Wishes:* Desires concerning means and ends. It is important not to confuse "wishes" with "needs."

If you use these terms consistently and so do your educational partners, you will help create an educational culture and environment that does several valuable things:

- Puts learners and our shared society in central focus
- Makes things rigorous and precise
- Aligns what the educational system uses, does, produces, and delivers to measurable societal value added
- Allows for really finding out what worked and what did not so we can revise as required

## THE TOOLS OF CHANGE: AN OVERVIEW OF THE BASIC CONCEPTS AND TOOLS FOR MEGA PLANNING

### Three Basic Guides

There are three basic tools, guides, or templates, actually, that will be helpful to you as you define and achieve organizational success. Each is defined in much greater detail in several books (see the references), but for our entry into Mega planning and strategic thinking, here is a short introduction to these three guides.

#### Guide 1

The Organizational Elements Model (OEM) defines and links/aligns what any organization uses, does, produces, and delivers with external client and societal value added. For each element, there is an associated level of planning. Successful planning links and relates all of the organizational elements, for each organization has external clients for which they must add value—measurable value.

Table 8.1 shows the *organizational elements*, along with the levels of planning to which each relates, and a brief example of each element.

These elements are also useful for defining the basic questions every organization must ask and answer (as provided in Table 8.2 later in this section).

#### Guide 2

A six-step problem-solving model shown in Figure 8.3 includes (1.0) identifying problems based on *need*; (2.0), determining detailed solution requirements and identifying (but not yet selecting) solution alternatives; (3.0), selecting solutions from among alternatives; (4.0), implementation; (5.0), evaluation; and (6.0), continuous improvement (at each and every step).

Each time you want to identify problems and opportunities and systematically progress from current results and consequences to desired ones, use the six-step process.

**Table 8.1**    The Organizational Elements Model: The Five Levels of Results, the Levels of Planning, and a Brief Description

| Name of the Organizational Element | Name of the Level of Planning and Focus | Brief Description | Example |
|---|---|---|---|
| **Outcomes** | **Mega** | Results and their consequences for external clients and society | Graduate or complete being on welfare, in jail, and all earning at least as much as it costs them to live |
| **Outputs** | **Macro** | The results an educational organization can or does deliver outside of itself | At least 95% of all learners graduate or complete with licenses or entry-level skills |
| **Products** | **Micro** | The building-block results that are produced within the educational organization | At least 95% of all learners master the state basic skills test at or above grade level |
| **Processes** | **Process** | The ways, means, activities, procedures, and methods used internally | A validated reading skills program |
| **Inputs** | **Input** | The human, physical, and financial resources an educational organization can or does use | Budget from the county and state that meets planning requirements |

**Figure 8.3**    The Six-Step Problem-Solving Process

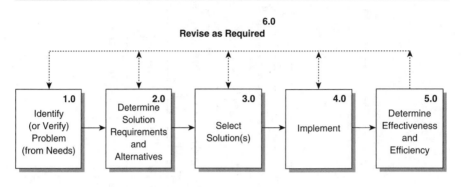

SOURCE: Kaufman (1998, 2000).

*Guide 3*

There are the Six Critical Success Factors that set a vital framework of this book and for Mega planning. Unlike conventional "critical success factors," these are factors for successful planning, not just for the things that an organization must get done to meet its mission. These are for Mega planning, regardless of the organization.

Six Critical Success Factors (CSFs) for Mega planning for any organization[1] (not targeted for any one organizational business, but only for the planning process and concerns) are shown in Figure 8.4. Note that these are critical success factors for strategic thinking and planning, not the usual "critical success factors" for an educational organization.

## New Realities for Organizational Success

To be successful—to do and apply Mega planning—you have to realize that yesterday's methods and results often are not appropriate for tomorrow. Most planning experts agree that the past is only a prologue and tomorrow must be crafted through new patterns of perspectives, tools, and results.[2] The tools and concepts for meeting the new realities of society, organizations, and people are linked to each of the Six Critical Success Factors.

The details and how-to's for each of the three guides are also provided in the referenced sources. The three basic guides, or templates, should be considered as forming an integrated set of tools—like a fabric—instead of each one only on its own.[3]

**Figure 8.4**   The Six Critical Success Factors

---

CRITICAL SUCCESS FACTOR 1

Move out of your comfort zone—today's paradigms—and use new and wider boundaries for thinking, planning, doing, evaluating, and continuous improvement.

CRITICAL SUCCESS FACTOR 2

Differentiate between ends (What) and means (How).

CRITICAL SUCCESS FACTOR 3

Use all three levels of planning and results (Mega/Outcomes, Macro/Outputs, Micro/Products).

CRITICAL SUCCESS FACTOR 4

Prepare all objectives—including the Ideal Vision and mission—to include precise statements of both where you are headed as well as the criteria for measuring when you have arrived. Develop "Smarter"[a] objectives.

CRITICAL SUCCESS FACTOR 5

Use an Ideal Vision (what kind of world, in measurable performance terms, we want for tomorrow's child) as the underlying basis for planning and continuous improvement.

CRITICAL SUCCESS FACTOR 6

Defining "need" as a gap in results (not as insufficient levels of resources, means, or methods.

---

SOURCE: Based on Kaufman, Oakley-Browne, Watkins, and Leigh (2003).

a. "Smarter" objectives are: S: Specific targeted result; M: Measurable; A: Audacious; R: Results to be achieved (excluding methods means or resources); T: Target time; E: Encompassing all aligned results, and R: Reviewed and evaluated.

## Mega Planning

To apply the guides and concepts provided early in the book, a Mega-planning framework is provided later. This framework, in turn, has three phases: *scoping, planning,* and *implementation/continuous improvement.* From this framework, specific tools and methods are provided to do Mega planning. It is not complex, really. If you simply use the three guides, you will be able to put it all together. When doing Mega planning, you and your associates will ask and answer the questions shown in Table 8.2.

A "yes" to all questions will lead you toward Mega planning and allow you to prove that you have added value, something that is becoming increasingly important. These questions relate to Guide 1. They define each organizational element in terms of its label and the question each addresses.

**Table 8.2**    Key Questions for Mega Planning

| Questions | Self-Assessment | | Organizational Partners | |
|---|---|---|---|---|
| | NO | YES | NO | YES |
| 1. Do you commit to deliver organizational results that add value for your external clients AND society? (Mega/Outcomes) | | | | |
| 2. Do you commit to deliver organizational results that have the measurable quality required by your external clients? (Macro/Outputs) | | | | |
| 3. Do you commit to produce internal results that have the measurable quality required by your internal partners? (Micro/Products) | | | | |
| 4. Do you commit to having efficient internal processes? | | | | |
| 5. Do you commit to acquire quality human capital, information capital, and physical resources? (Inputs) | | | | |
| 6. Do you commit to evaluate/determine:<br><br>6.1 How well you deliver products, activities, methods, and procedures that have positive value and worth (Process Performance)<br><br>6.2 Whether the results defined by your objectives in measurable terms are achieved? (Evaluation/Continuous Improvement) | | | | |

### Mega Planning is Proactive

Many approaches to organizational improvement wait for problems to happen and then scramble to respond. Of course, like true love, the course of organizational success hardly ever runs smoothly. But there is a temptation to react to problems and never take the time to plan so that surprises are fewer and success is defined (before problems spring up) and then systematically achieved. Figure 8.5 provides a job aid to consider any time you start organizational planning.

## THE SIX CRITICAL SUCCESS FACTORS IN BRIEF

Let's look at each of the Six Critical Success Factors (Guide 3) briefly to get a feel for the frame of mind (or paradigm) Mega planning provides.

### Critical Success Factor #1

*Use new and widest boundaries for thinking, planning, and doing and evaluating/continuous improvement.* Move out of today's comfort zones.

Look around our world. There is evidence just about everywhere we look that tomorrow is not a linear projection—a straight-line function—of yesterday and today, such as car manufacturers that squander their dominant client base by shoving unacceptable vehicles into the market and airlines that focus on shareholder value and ignore customer value. A lot of "conventional paradigm" organizations are "history," as noted by futurist Alvin Toffler in his early classic *The Third Wave* and his more recent *War and Anti-War.*[4] An increasing number of credible authors have said, and continued to tell us, that the past is at best prologue and not a harbinger of what the future will be. In fact, old paradigms can be so deceptive that Tom Peters (1997) suggested that "organizational forgetting" must become conventional culture.

Times have changed, and anyone who doesn't also change appropriately is risking failure. It is vital to use new and wider boundaries for thinking, planning, doing, and delivering. Doing so will require getting out of current comfort zones. Not doing so will likely deliver failure (Peters, 1997).[5]

### Critical Success Factor #2

*Differentiate between ends and means.* Focus on "What" (Mega/Outcomes, Macro/Outputs, Micro/Products) before "How."[6]

**Figure 8.5**  Mega-Planning Algorithm

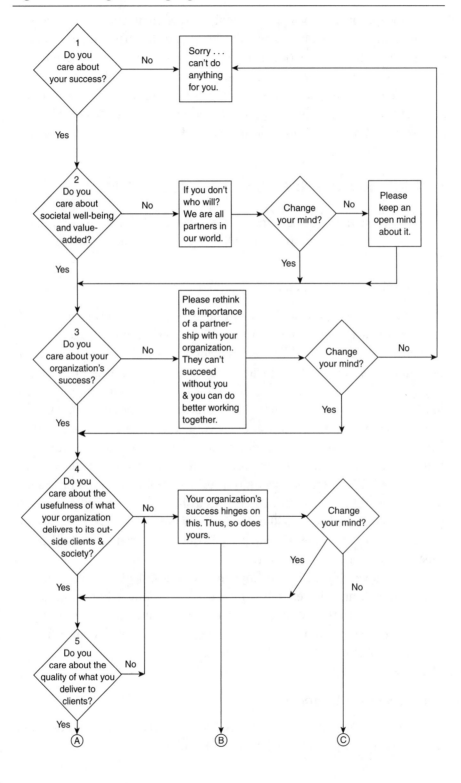

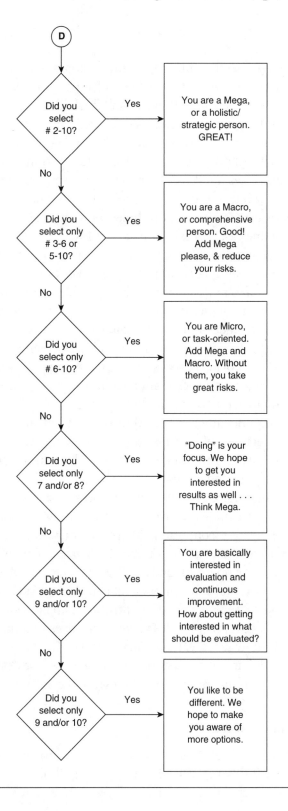

People, especially in our U.S. culture, are "doing-type people." We hate delay and detest not swinging right into action. We want to get going. In this dash to doing, we often jump right into *solutions*—means—before we know the *results*—ends—we must deliver. Writing and using measurable performance objectives is something upon which almost all performance improvement authors agree. Objectives correctly focus on ends and not methods, means, or resources.[7] Ends—"What"—sensibly should be identified and defined before we select "How" to get from where we are to our destinations. If we don't base our solutions, methods, resources, and interventions on what results we are to achieve, what do we have in mind to make the selections of means, resources, or activities?

Focusing on means, Processes, and activities is usually more comfortable as a starting place for conventional performance improvement initiatives. Doing so can be seductive, but dangerous. For example, imagine that you are in a novel area and then are provided with a new automobile, keys in the ignition and fully fueled—but there are no maps for navigation to your destination to guide your journey after you start out. This situation would be similar if for any organization and performance improvement initiative, you were provided Process tools and techniques without a clear map that included a definite destination identified (along with a statement of why you want to get to the destination in the first place). Also, a risk for starting a performance improvement journey with means and Processes would be that there would be no way of knowing whether your trip was taking you toward a useful destination or the criteria for telling you whether you were making progress.[8]

It is vital that successful planning focuses first on results—useful performance in measurable terms—for setting its purposes, measuring progress, and providing continuous improvement toward the important results and for determining what to keep, what to fix, and what to abandon.

It is vital to focus on useful ends before deciding "How" to get things done. It also sets the stage for another related Critical Success Factor #3 (Use and link all three levels of results) through application of the OEM and for Critical Success Factor #4 (Prepare objectives that have indicators of how you will know when you have arrived). The OEM relies on a results focus because it defines what every organization uses, does, produces, and delivers and the consequences of that for external clients and society.

## Critical Success Factor #3

*Use all three levels of planning and results.* As we noted in Critical Success Factor #2 (above), it is vital to prepare all objectives that focus only on ends—never on means or resources. All objectives. Three levels

**Table 8.3** Three Levels of Planning and Results

| Primary Client and Beneficiary | Name for the Level of Planning | Name for the Level of Result | Level of Planning |
|---|---|---|---|
| Society and external clients | Mega | Outcomes | Strategic planning |
| The organization itself | Macro | Outputs | Tactical planning |
| Individuals and small groups | Micro | Products | Operational planning |

of results, shown in Table 8.3, are important to target and link during planning and doing and evaluation and continuous improvement.

As will be discussed in greater detail later, there are three levels of planning and results, based on who is to be the primary client and beneficiary of what gets planned, designed, and delivered. For each level of planning, there are three levels of associated results (Outcomes, Outputs, Products).[9]

There are three levels of planning (Mega, Macro, Micro) and three levels of results (Outcomes, Outputs, Products) and how to ensure that there is strategic, tactical, and operational alignment among what you and your organization uses, does, produces, and delivers and the value added for external clients.

When one begins planning at the Mega-level, that is *strategic planning;* at the Macro-level, it is *tactical planning;* and at the Micro-level, it is termed *operational planning.* These terms and purposes of planning are usually blurred, both in the literature as well as in operational education.

### Critical Success Factor #4

*Prepare objectives, including those for the Ideal Vision and mission objectives, that have indicators of how you will know when you have arrived (Mission Statement + Success Criteria).*

It is vital to state, precisely and rigorously, where you are headed and how to tell when you have arrived.[10] Statements of objectives must be in performance terms so that one can plan how best to get there, how to measure progress toward the end, and how to note progress toward it. (Note that this also relates to Critical Success Factor #2).

Objectives at all levels of planning, activity, and results are absolutely vital. And as we will note later, everything is measurable, so don't kid yourself into thinking you can dismiss important results as being "intangible" or "nonmeasurable." It is only sensible and rational to make a commitment to measurable purposes and destinations. Organizations throughout the world are increasingly focusing on Mega-level results (Kaufman et al., 1998).

## Critical Success Factor #5

*Define "need" as a gap between current and desired results (not as insufficient levels of resources, means, or methods).*

Conventional English language usage would have us employ the common word *need* as a verb (or in a verb sense) to identify means, methods, activities, and actions and/or resources we desire or intend to use.[11] Terms such as *need to, need for, needing,* and *needed* are common, conventional, and destructive to useful planning. What? Semantic quibbling? Absolutely not.

As hard as it is to change our own behavior (and most of us who want others to change seem to resist it the most ourselves!), it is central to useful planning to distinguish between *ends* and *means.* We have already noted this as Critical Success Factor #2. To do reasonable and justifiable planning, we have to (1) focus on *ends* and not *means,* and thus (2) use *need* as a noun. *Need,* for the sake of useful and successful planning, is used only as a noun—a gap between current and desired results.

If we use *need* as a noun, we will be able to not only justify useful objectives but also to justify what we do and deliver on the basis of costs-consequences analysis. We will be able to justify everything we use, do, produce, and deliver. It is the only sensible way we can demonstrate value added. It really is. Also provided are the tools for *needs assessment* and *needs analysis:* what they are and how to do them.

## Critical Success Factor #6

*Use an Ideal Vision as the underlying basis for all planning and doing (don't be limited to your own organization).*

Here is another area that requires some change from the conventional ways of doing planning. Again, we have to buck the conventional wisdom.

An Ideal Vision—which is the measurable statement of Mega—is never prepared for an organization, but rather identifies the kind of world we want to help create for tomorrow's child. From this societal-linked Ideal Vision, each organization can identify what part or parts of the Ideal Vision we commit to deliver and move ever closer toward. If we base all planning and doing on an Ideal Vision of the kind of society we want for future generations, we can achieve "strategic alignment" for what we use, do, produce, and deliver and the external payoffs for our Outputs.

But we have to change some paradigms, change some old habits—even, as Peters (1997) suggested, "forget" Processes and paradigms that will hamper our success.[12] Get out of our current comfort zones.

So? Mega thinking and planning means defining a shared success, achieving it, and being able to prove it. It is a focus not on one's organization alone, but upon society now and in the future. It means adding value to all stakeholders. It is responsible, responsive, and ethical to add value to all.

Sensible and practical evaluation will ensure that you and your educational partners will ask and answer the right questions and will provide the basis for continuous improvement of everything that is used, done, produced, and delivered and will be able to demonstrate the value added to individuals, the organization, our communities, and our shared society.

It is worth the trouble.

## NOTES

1. Please realize that unlike many other presentations of critical success factors, these relate to any organization and should be generalized to any organization, public or private. Most "critical success factors" discussed in the management literature refer to organization-specific factors related to their unique business. These apply to any organization and are "above" any organizational-specific factors.

2. Lately and increasingly, planning experts now agree. Kaufman first proposed using a societal frame of reference as the primary focus for individuals and organizations in 1968 and 1969 (which brought alarm and suspicion on the part of many "old paradigm" thinkers). He has recently been joined in this call for new paradigms by many future-oriented thinkers, including (but not limited to) those included in the references in this chapter.

This shift in thinking to new paradigms—frames of reference that are radically different from the "conventional wisdom"—are sprouting, as Joel Barker (1992) suggested they would, when seen by the "Paradigm Pioneers" of our world.

3. Of course, each one is valuable. But used together, they are even more powerful.

4. See Toffler's interview with Peter Schwartz in the November 1996 issue of *Wired* (Schwartz & Kelly, 1996). In this interview, Toffler suggested that the failure to pay attention and respond to changed realities, such as the "information age," is a "failure in imagination." Instead, most people seem to rely on experts who are usually trapped in old paradigms themselves. He points to some consensus assessment techniques such as Delphi studies, which build on old paradigms instead of imagining new ones.

5. Again, Peters (1997) stated that it is easier to kill an organization than it is to change it.

6. It might seem as if there are a bunch of new words—jargon—flowing at you now. And there are. Please be patient. Each will be defined, justified, and related to the others. The distinctions are important.

7. Bob Mager set the original standard for measurable objectives. Later, Tom Gilbert made the important distinction between behavior and performance (between actions and consequences). Recently, some "Constructivists" have had objections to writing objectives because they claim it can cut down on creativity and impose the planner's values on the clients. This view, I believe, is not useful. For a detailed discussion on the topic of Constructivism, please see the analysis of philosophy professor David Gruender (1996). Also, a withering critique of Constructivism is provided by Professor Dale Brethower (2005).

8. Jan Kaufman provided this insight.

9. It is interesting and curious that in the popular literature, ALL results tend to be called "outcomes." This failure to distinguish among three levels of results blurs the importance of identifying and linking all three levels in planning, doing, and evaluating/continuous improvement.

10. An important contribution of strategic planning at the Mega-level is that objectives can be linked to justifiable purpose. Not only should one have objectives that state "where you are headed and how you will know when you have arrived," they should also be justified on the basis of "why you want to get to where you are headed." While it is true that objectives deal only with measurable destinations, useful strategic planning adds the reasons why objectives should be attained.

11. Because most dictionaries provide common usage, not necessarily correct usage, they note that *need* is used as a noun as well as a verb. This dual conventional usage doesn't mean that it is useful. Much of this book depends on a shift in paradigms about "need." The shift is to use it only as a noun . . . never as a verb or in a verb sense.

12. Tom Peters (1997) suggested that "organizational forgetting" can be a vital element in success. He noted that the successful organization will "forget" the conventional wisdom of the past—erase it from the corporate reality—in order to use new thinking. Good advice.

# Contracting for Evaluation Services   **9**

This chapter provides tips for contracting, for when you want an external organization to conduct the evaluation. The checklists and statement of work provided, however, can be used as guides for planning your own evaluation. A challenge in any evaluation is completing the study as planned without letting extraneous issues consume too much of the time and resources.

The set of evaluation questions is the main controlling device in a contract. You can use it to make sure that a contractor addresses each question and delivers on those evaluation questions. Likewise, the evaluation questions are the anchor for an in-house evaluation process and all associated activities.

What you cannot do is control what the contractor provides in the way of answers. The credibility of the findings of an evaluation, internal or external, rests on the objectivity and independence that is granted and respected. There are ways to guide evaluation teams to stay on track in terms of answering the evaluation questions, but we do not dictate the answers as part of the package.

## THE NATURE OF CONTRACTS

A contract is an agreement between two parties to provide something in exchange for a consideration (usually payment in money in exchange for goods and services). In principle, a handshake can seal the deal, but prudent people have recognized the value of written contracts that are clear and are executed in front of a witness. This proves valuable if the parties begin to argue over something and one claim or another ends up having to be settled in the courts. In fact, a written contract may prevent any differences from ending up in legal confrontations at all, or at the least, it provides a clearer basis for settling the dispute.

Contract law is a field that is complex and will not be covered here. Instead, we are going to concentrate on helping you develop a clear description and specifications of the tasks and deliverables you want accomplished in the evaluation and come to mutual understanding about what will and will not be delivered. This is the part that a contracting officer or procurement official cannot do for you. We will include controls to guide the contractor, writing proposals, a sample statement of work, and suggestions for types of contract mechanisms for payment. For example:

- Fixed price
- Cost plus fixed fee
- Time and materials
- Consulting retainer

## Fixed Price

A *fixed-price contract* means that all of the work is done for a preset amount of money that is set at the time of the contract award (usually based on a contractor proposal). This type of contract payment works best when proposals are accepted from a set of contractors who are in competition and the work is clear and rigorously specified in the contract. Contractors who know the field can plan work efficiently and figure a price that will be adequate given their technical approach to the work. Note however, that if after the award, the party asking for the work starts to add things to the list of contractor tasks, the contractor has every right to ask for renegotiation of the fixed-price contract to add more money for more work. After the award, the contractor is not faced with any competition, so there is less pressure to keep costs down in the change proposal. If no technical innovation or discovery is required and both parties know the field, the risk is about equal to both parties. An evaluation study that was very tightly constructed could use this form of contract. It is well to keep in mind, however, that some evaluation studies are more in the nature of problem identification studies as opposed to confirmation of results in an experimental setting. A study that is to have some latitude can include additional work tasks in the statement of work that are separately priced options, but this requires some anticipation of the nature of the option tasks. Therefore a different form of contract may be more suitable.

## Cost Plus Fixed Fee

A *cost-plus-fixed-fee contract* means that the contractor must keep track of all expenses and bill for the actual cost of doing the work (subject to audit). At the end of the contract, the contractor is paid a fixed fee, which can be a flat, preagreed amount or some formula that is acceptable to both parties. In this arrangement, the contractor is able to accept some work variations or take time to investigate emerging issues as long as cost records are maintained and the work variation is acceptable to both parties. Note that change orders must be accepted before work variations are initiated. A contractor who goes out of scope without permission can be forced to absorb the cost of the misadventure. However, by the same rule, any overexuberant guidance from anyone on the staff of the school district could mean that the contractor will get paid for any resulting work. It is a good idea to set up a clear paper trail for any change orders and to make sure that both parties know who can authorize a change. This contract type allows risk associated with unknown discovery to be shared as long as good control is maintained.

### Time and Materials

A *time-and-materials contract* means that the contractor gets paid for the hourly rates for each of the workers engaged in providing direct or indirect support to the contract. The contractor also gets paid for expenses such as travel and materials used. A time-and-materials contract is used when the scope of work and the statement of tasks include analysis, discovery, or experimentation that may have to be repeated many times before getting the desired results. Redirection of work activity simply results in more time and material consumption. It is still wise to maintain control over work change orders, but the flexibility offered is greater. However, the risk to the school district is that work could be expended and funds exhausted before the contractor produces any desired product. Upper dollar limits can be placed on a time-and-materials contract. Reaching that limit without a final resolution of the work is a possibility, but that possibility can be made less likely by attentive management using periodic program reviews.

### Consulting Retainer

The most flexible type of contract is an agreement with a *consultant* or consulting firm to provide evaluation services. Consultants can do entire evaluations or provide guidance as you plan and implement your own study. Each consultant will have his or her own way of arranging for payment. This can range from honorarium acceptance to flat daily fees. The use of consultants can be extremely beneficial to a school system, or they can be provocative and drain resources. It is best to consider the use of a consultant only after first checking all internal resources and then doing a thorough background search of candidates.

## CONTRACTING CONTROLS

Contracting for evaluation service (and results) is more than a simple matter of hiring a contractor and then turning them loose while you do other business. It is more like getting on a horse that you must ride to the end of the road. The "quality of the ride" is up to you. You can magnify what you can get done with the proper use of a contract, but it will require an investment in time and attention to detail. Some of the management burden can be eased if you start with a good contract that is clear and provides a framework for you and the contractor to advance through the stages of the work and complete the tasks you want done, with a desired set of results.

Here are some contract features that will assist you (and the contractor) by clearly stating what you want done and the limits of the work.

### The Scope of Work

The scope of work is a statement that you will include in your contract that clearly defines what the work is to be done and what the limits of the work effort will be. This is particularly important, because issues of payment may hinge on the determination that a given bit of work is either in scope or not. A sample scope statement is provided in the sample "Statement of Work," later in this chapter.

### The Statement of Work

The statement of work is a type of specification. This does require commonality of understanding on the part of contractors and school administrators regarding certain tasks and what will be delivered. For example, the simple phrase "conduct an evaluation" does not include enough detail. But the phrase "conduct analysis of variance" may be too specific, especially if another statistic would better serve the study. In evaluation studies, we have found that the contract can be based on the evaluation question set, and this set should be firm and mutually understood. The two main provisions of any statement of work are a list of tasks to be performed and the deliverable associated with each task (see sample "Statement of Work").

### Other Contract Clauses

It is often useful to include clauses in your contract to cover expectations in the area of rights to any data-based products that are produced in the evaluation. The publication of findings in reports may include restrictions on distribution or specify distribution requirements. Specifications on the printing of reports, number of copies, shipping costs, and format may be included. A clause can also be inserted to cover the development of special instruments like standardized tests. These works are often the type of product that is eligible for copyright protection. The clause should make clear that any such rights are covered or not covered by the contract. (Copyright law does provide that the rights to "works made for hire" go to the party that did the hiring.)

### Management Plan

You can require a contractor to submit a management plan that describes how they will proceed with the work and what in-process deliverables will be available for review and feedback. In cases where some negotiation is required to adjust the statement of work, this is one way to include details not possible in the statement of work (often, you have to start work to find out what you are dealing with). The management plan should include provision for progress review, reports, evaluation schedule, and mechanisms for change, quality control, and personnel replacement approval.

### Program Review

We recommend that formal monthly reviews take place in which the contractor is required to show progress on all tasks, show financial accountability for all funds expended, and discuss all possible change or redirection in light of any problems or unusual events that affect the evaluation study.

### Schedule and Work Breakdown Structure

Each task in the statement of work becomes an item that must have a start and end date on a program schedule. Many excellent project management tools now make using a project schedule a relatively easy task.

### Delivery and Acceptance

Each deliverable should have a due date and the conditions of acceptance spelled out in the contract. Many contractors use a cover letter with a place for an acceptance signature for each delivered item. Make sure that the contract specifies who will sign for each deliverable. In most organizations, the contracting officer or the contracting officer's technical representative (COTAR) are designated as the official with signature authority.

Often vital is a provision for timeliness of acceptance of what has been submitted. One way to assure the contractor that there will be a response that will not hold up the progress of the evaluation is a clause that notes what happens when response is not made on a timely basis: "If there is no response from the school district, the submission will become 'accepted and approved.'"

## Ethics and Professionalism

Don't ever be a "liar for hire." Tell the truth about what you did, how you did it, why you did it, and what you found. Report all assumptions and limitations. Don't add or omit anything that is not justified. Don't change anything simply because the client wants it. Never.

Now let's look at a responsive and responsible sample of an evaluation contract statement of work. The following is an example only. You should replace the example items with what is appropriate for your educational organization and evaluation.

## STATEMENT OF WORK (SOW)

GENERAL INFORMATION

1. *Title of Project:* Evaluation of the Teacher Training Program of the Peach County School District.

2. *Scope of Work:* The contractor shall provide all material and personnel to accomplish the deliverables described in this statement of work (SOW), except as may otherwise be specified. The scope of this task order and associated deliverables include (a) performing literature review using university-based search tools, (b) analysis of conceptual/theoretical basis of instructional tactics, methods, and activities, (c) evaluation of alternative approaches to teacher training, (d) preparation of agreed-upon evaluation questions that will drive and guide the evaluation, (e) creation and administration of a database for data collected in this evaluation, (f) data collection using methods and techniques that ensure valid and reliable data that relate directly with the agreed-upon evaluation question, (g) preparation of reports and briefing documents and revising as required, and (h) travel to specified educational locations for briefings and meetings.

The contractor shall be competent in all phases of educational evaluation with a proven ability in evaluation of educational systems and education programs. References are required to confirm this.

## WORK STEPS

Work steps shall include the following: (a) analyze school district regulations and other state and county requirements and list evaluation requirements, (b) conduct literary database search relative to the type of program being evaluated and tools and techniques used elsewhere in similar projects, (c) develop and obtain approval of evaluation questions that will drive data collection and findings, (d) prepare an evaluation work flow and schedule, (e) identify evaluation methods, means, processes, and techniques and relate each with evaluation questions, (f) identify and document data collection methods selected, (g) define data collection sites, sample, and resources required, (h) collect data, (i) reduce and analyze data using valid and reliable analysis statistics and tools, (j) provide initial findings with sponsors and revise as required, (k) prepare and submit draft final reports, and (l) revise as required.

## FIELD VISITS

All fieldwork and on-site observations shall be coordinated with the office of the superintendent and/or the evaluation project director.

## PROJECT MANAGEMENT

Throughout the performance period of the delivery order executed by this SOW, the contractor shall keep the office of technical training and evaluation fully informed as to issues and progress.

1. *Background:* This contract is a follow-up to a quick-response, short-term effort to investigate trends and concepts in teacher training and education that impact or will potentially impact training and associated learning in the Peach County School District.

2. *Performance Period:* The work shall begin within 10 calendar days of award, unless otherwise specified. Work at the site shall not take place on school holidays or weekends unless directed by the contracting officer. Report delivery items and schedule to be set at kickoff meeting.

3. *Type of Contract:* Time and materials. With fixed-price limit.

## CONTRACT AWARD MEETING

The contractor shall not commence performance on the tasks in this SOW until the contracting officer has conducted a kickoff meeting or has advised the contractor that a kickoff meeting is waived.

GENERAL REQUIREMENTS

1. The contractor shall confirm work assignments by telephone with the evaluation project manager. A brief outline of work approach shall be reflected in the technical proposal.

2. All written deliverables shall be phrased in acceptable terminology of the field. Words shall be defined in layperson language. Statistical and other technical terminology shall be defined in a glossary of terms and referenced for validity and usefulness.

3. Unless otherwise specified, where a written deliverable is required in draft form, the school district office shall complete their review of the draft deliverable within 10 calendar days from date of receipt. If there is no response from the district within 10 calendar days, it shall be automatically deemed "approved." The contractor shall have 10 calendar days to deliver the final deliverable from date of receipt of the government's comments.

4. This contract shall not require access to student files.

5. All deliverables, except where specified otherwise, shall be provided in one electronic copy via e-mail to the project manager. All deliverables shall be delivered via software compatible with the school district office.

6. The school district reserves the right to review resumés of personnel the contractor proposes to assign to each task or subtask and to approve or disapprove personnel assignments based on the resumés provided.

7. The contractor shall provide via e-mail minutes of all school distict-contractor meetings, within 3 calendar days after completion of the meeting.

SPECIFIC MANDATORY TASKS AND ASSOCIATED DELIVERABLES

**Description of Tasks and Associated Deliverables**

The contractor shall provide the specific deliverables described below.

*Task 1:* The contractor shall conduct evaluation studies and data in accordance with the evaluation management plan and the agreed-upon evaluation questions. The school district shall review the draft review and provide written comments to the contractor no later than 10 calendar days after receipt of the draft review. The contractor shall then submit the revised review no later than 20 calendar days after receipt of comments. If there is no response from the district within 10 calendar days, it shall be automatically deemed "approved." The contractor shall update the review as required by guidance from the contracting officer or designated representative. The deliverable shall be in electronic form transmitted via e-mail, using software compatible with software available at the school district office.

*Deliverable 1: Evaluation Report*

*Task 2:* The contractor shall provide detailed analysis of selected topics and issues identified in the evaluation report number, and type of topics shall be in accordance with guidance from the project manager. Work shall proceed on a time-and-material basis not to exceed specific financial limitations of the purchase order. The contractor shall present significant and timely findings to the project management team using an appropriate contractor-developed format in paper and electronic form.

*Deliverable 2: Draft and Final Evaluation Report*

SCHEDULE FOR DELIVERABLES

1. The contractor shall provide all deliverables to the project manager as stated in the schedule established at the kickoff meeting.

2. Unless otherwise specified, the number of draft copies and the number of final copies shall be the same (i.e., one electronic copy delivered via e-mail).

3. If for any reason, any deliverable cannot be delivered within the scheduled time frame, the contractor is required to explain why in writing to the contracting officer, including a firm commitment of when the work shall be completed. This notice to the contracting officer shall cite the reasons for the delay and the impact on the overall project. The contracting officer shall then review the facts and issue a response in accordance with applicable regulations within 10 days.

CHANGES TO STATEMENT OF WORK

Any changes to this statement of work shall be authorized and approved only through written correspondence from the project manager. A copy of each change shall be kept in a project folder along with all other products of the project. Costs incurred by the contractor through the actions of parties other than the project manager shall be borne by the contractor.

## REPORTING REQUIREMENTS

4. The contractor is required to provide the project manager with weekly telephone or e-mail progress reports.

5. The progress reports shall cover all work completed during the preceding week and shall present the work to be accomplished during the subsequent week. This report shall also identify any problems that arose and a statement explaining how the problem was resolved. This report shall also identify any problems that have arisen but have not been completely resolved with an explanation. The progress reports shall also provide cost data, schedule data, cost variance data, and schedule variance data, as required by each task order.

## TRAVEL AND SITE VISITS

Travel and on-site visit shall be authorized by the project manager; limited travel is envisioned.

## SCHOOL RESPONSIBILITIES

The schools shall provide access to technical and procedural information. The schools shall provide a copy of the required confidentiality statement at contract award or upon request by the contractor.

## CONTRACTOR EXPERIENCE REQUIREMENTS

The contractor shall have experience with educational evaluation research and analysis. Additional relevant knowledge is desirable in research, theoretical literature, and practical application of the following areas: needs assessment, learning development and implementation, criterion-referenced testing development and validity and reliability assessment, formative evaluation, summative evaluation, data collection, data analysis, data and results summary, and evaluation results reporting.

## CONFIDENTIALITY AND NONDISCLOSURE

It is agreed that:

6. The preliminary and final deliverables and all associated working papers and other material deemed relevant by the school district that have been generated by the contractor in the performance of this task order are the exclusive property of the school district and shall be submitted to the project manager at the conclusion of the evaluation initiative.

7. The project manager shall be the sole authorized official to release verbally or in writing any data, the draft deliverables, the final deliverables, or any other written or printed materials pertaining to this task order. No information shall be released by the contractor. Any request for information relating to this task order presented to the contractor shall be submitted to the project manager for response.

8. Press releases, marketing material, or any other printed or electronic documentation related to this project shall not be publicized without the written approval of the project manager.

---

Now you have it. Practical Education Evaluation.

Educational evaluation is a sensitive, sensible, and serious activity. It pays to be very clear about what is to be done, what is to be delivered, and when it should be delivered. Evaluation. What worked and what did not. Now it would be good to ask yourself the same question about this book and what was provided: "What worked and what did not."

Once again, please complete the "self-assessment" at the beginning of this book. Note the differences from the first time you took it as to *What Is* and *What Should Be.* This will let you evaluate how effective the content has been in enhancing your abilities to find "what works and what doesn't."

# Scenario 4

## *Actions That Work*

---

The school year was nearing an end in Cobb County. The evaluation team had worked hard and produced a draft of a final report that had been reviewed by an external consultant from the local university. Superintendent Anita Jackson got her team together to talk about putting their evaluation findings in a form that would ensure action on the part of the school board. Several suggestions were made about who should share in the knowledge gained during the evaluation. Anita decided to do the following:

- She formed a presentation team to brief the school board and superintendent on the finding and recommendations prior to release of the hard-copy report. She alerted the team that there was a possibility that some people might want an electronic copy of the final report.
- She provided the board and superintendent with a possible press release and offered to arrange an appearance on local TV after they had reviewed the evaluation report.[1]
- She requested that the board and superintendent be given approval to:
  - Schedule a separate briefing for her staff and the teachers at each school
  - Provide a special report for students
- She prepared a proposal for future evaluation in the school district.
- She prepared a contract statement of work for professional independent evaluation and consulting support for the future.

The presentation of findings to the school board included charts and graphs of results and a short description of the methods that were used and the issues that emerged during the year. Each team member was allocated 5 minutes to make their presentation, and Anita followed up with a summary and took questions.

The superintendent organized her findings around the goals, objectives, and methods that formed the strategy for the past year.

## FINDINGS RELATING TO THE NEW CURRICULUM

The community and the school board wanted to avoid cutting things out (art, music, a full line of sports activities). The core curriculum did consist of Mathematics, English, General Science, Biology, Chemistry, Personal Health, American History, Spanish, and French. Much of these changes were based on the requirements for learners to be successful in school, as well as in later life.

There would also be several types of Industrial Arts class and Home Economics, and three new subjects were added: Computer Science; a combination Reading, Literature, and Library course; and a course that was simply called "Tutorial."

Findings data included:

- The cost impact for each class on the yearly budget.
- The cost impact for each sport and special offering.
- The reaction of the students, including enrollment in each of the classes, the popularity of the class, and standard scores on tests during the classes.
- The academic progress of each student was recorded and cross-referenced with athletics and special offerings like art and music.
- The community reactions were gathered at each event, like recitals, shows, and academic competitions with other schools.
- It was a bit early to tell what impact the curriculum would have on students after graduation, but a special letter was provided to each graduate asking whether they would check back with the school at the end of 1 year. There was also a suggestion for a formal and proactive placement and follow-up study of completers, leavers, and graduates in order to determine the effectiveness of the curriculum on each learner's self-sufficiency, survival, and quality of life.

## FINDINGS RELATING TO THE NEW
## APPROACH TO TEACHING AND LEARNING

Anita realized that some of the innovations that she had put in place might take some time to take root, but she also knew it would be important to see what happened in the first year. (She remembered that when controversy about school performance originally appeared, she swung into action with a "new program" that now seemed to her to be premature.)

Data were collected on each of the innovations as follows:

• There would be "tracks" for the college-bound and job-market-bound students, but the old way of separating the children early and branding them as "smarties" (or nerds) and "dummies" was scrapped. Now, all children had to take the basic core. Data on this innovation consisted of teacher feedback, student interviews, academic records, standardized test scores, and parent and possible employer interviews.

• Students who progressed rapidly were required to tutor students who were having difficulty. This was done in the tutorial session, which was the last period of the school day, and the tutoring was done with the help of the entire faculty, who were required to be at this class. Data on this innovation consisted of interviews with tutors and monitors, coaches, students, and parents; academic records; and standardized test scores. The impact on the community of the longer school day was also discussed with community leaders, parents, and staff, including bus drivers, maintenance personnel, and district financial managers.

• Volunteers from the community, who were qualified based on years in the workplace, were asked to mentor students.

• To teach the large class selection, Anita was able to hire some qualified part-time teachers from the private school, who came 1 day a week for their special subjects.

• To get into the college track, students had to earn their way by completing the core and by participating successfully in the tutorial program.

• All students were required to play one sport. Varsity players would tutor the less gifted athletes (who may be the very same students tutoring the athletes in algebra or biology). Data on this innovation included interviews with students, parents, and coaches, and a cross-check with academic records and a national database on health and fitness by age group.

• Homework assignments were changed. Students were not assigned homework to take home; instead, they were given practice exercises and assignments that had to be completed in supervised study hall. Each student was, however, required to visit the town library and write an independent paper each term. Every student had to do this, no exceptions. Data on this consisted of teacher, student, and parent interviews, academic records, and standardized test scores.

• A strict-yet-sensible dress code was adopted. Data for this consisted of school attendance records, detention records, referrals for conduct, student, teacher and parent interviews, and interviews with visitors and members of the community who interacted with the school system on a regular basis.

## ANITA'S EVALUATION TEAM FOLLOW-THROUGH

Anita asked Dr. Mackenzie, head of the Center for Curriculum Development and Evaluation at State University, to meet again with her team to help with the organization and analysis of the data. Together with team leader John Quick and the two graduate assistants, they provided a framework for the evaluation report and made team assignments for continuing analysis of the data and for reviewing the findings and preparing the report with recommendations. Assignments were:

• As team leader, John Quick prepared a schedule and checklist to make sure that each evaluation question was answered and that the answers were supported by data and checked by the entire group. John asked for daily reports during the analysis, and he shared these with Anita, especially when trends and findings were unexpected as well as clear confirmation of the expected results.

• Shirley Lopez, the Spanish teacher and participant observer co-ordinator, was tasked with preparing a report based on the inputs of the observers. As a second duty, she was assigned to the review panel to review findings and conclusions and recommendations prior to the issuance of the final report.

• The English teacher, Myrna Grey, was assigned duty as the editor and "book boss" to make sure each submission by each writer was accounted for and on schedule.

• Anita's deputy, Fred Bliss, was put in charge of the financial records and the use of financial data at various points in the analysis. Fred also prepared a subreport on the resources and costs of the evaluation.

• The two graduate students, William DuPont and Judith Andrews, would be outside observers and do most of the interviews and data collection in general.

• Dr. Mackenzie would meet regularly with the group to lead weekly meetings in which trends and issues of the developing study would be discussed. He assisted John in making data collection assignments.

• Anita rounded out the team with the school computer/audiovisual specialist, who documented events using audio and video recording.

## THE SET OF EVALUATION QUESTIONS—DATA COLLECTION PLAN AND SCHEDULE

Now the team was ready to report findings and make presentations. Each team member was assigned writing duties based on their roles during the data collection/observation. Dr. Mackenzie suggested that everything they had so far should be cross-checked against the original goals and objectives stated in the newly published plan, titled "The New Approach to Schooling in Cobb County: Defining and Delivering Useful Results."

The published goals were:

- Every student will graduate from high school.
- Every school in the district will achieve an "A" rating from the state.
- Graduating students will be qualified for entry-level jobs or to enter military service or to enter college.
- The school system will be drug free, gang free, and premature-pregnancy free
- Teachers will "love their jobs."
- Students will be motivated.
- The schools rating based on standardized national testing will rank in the upper third of the nation's schools.
- Learners will be successful in school and in later life.

Dr. Mackenzie prepared an outline that included findings relating to each of the goals,[2] recommendations relating to changes, and issues that were generated from the observations. Some of the issues related to unplanned events that had direct bearing on the teaching-learning environment or on the stakeholders. Not all of the findings were positive. He provided the following guidance.

## HOW TO HANDLE POSITIVE AND NEGATIVE FINDINGS FOR EACH EVALUATION QUESTION

A well-designed evaluation study will have questions dealing with the legitimacy of the goals and objectives (Were they based on valid *needs?*), the effectiveness of the tactics and methods for realizing the goals and objectives, and the results (Were the goals and objectives obtained?). An overall program for a school system will become a complex mix but not an unmanageable one if evaluation is approached with integrity, independence, discipline, and determination.

Using the examples created for our scenario, here are some hypothetical findings, some positive and some negative:

- Regarding the curriculum, the students, parents, and community at large showed approval for the new curriculum and a positive correlation to academic achievement based on grades and standardized testing.
- Data on student morale, teacher morale, and parental approval were positive.

The cost of obtaining this result, however, was a longer school day and higher short-term cost of instruction. Not all of the community supported the longer school day and higher cost. In particular, one feature of the new approach to school caused a very vocal segment of the community to complain. The idea of doing what was previously called "homework" in the tutorial period, using mentors and fellow students, proved to be more effective for learning but unpopular with some parents. Anita developed data to show that about two thirds of the parents did not participate in the homework process. On the other hand, the one third that did felt that a valuable part of their parenting role had been usurped by the school. It turned out that this third was highly organized and vocal. The data on improved student learning was not relevant to this group if it meant a loss of parental authority and prerogative.

Anita was faced with a situation that is not uncommon for innovators. She had a good idea that achieved a desired objective, but it had a negative side effect that she could not ignore. After consulting with parents, teachers, mentors, and other school officials, a recommendation for modification of the tutorial was prepared as one of the recommendations in the evaluation report.

## THE FORMAT AND SECTIONS OF THE FINAL PUBLISHED REPORT

Following the advice of Dr. Mackenzie, Anita and the report-writing team prepared a draft report, which was reviewed by her entire team and an outside reviewer, who was invited to read the draft and ask questions relating to the following:

- Clarity of ideas and expression?
- Do conclusions follow from the analysis?
- Support of findings by data?
- Points of controversy?

The review caused some adjustment to the draft, which was made under the supervision of the editor and the team leader. The final included the following sections:

- Executive summary
- Statement of relevance and purpose
- Statement of evaluation questions (and the needs data that support them)
- Description of the evaluation scope of inquiry
- Description of methodology
- Observation chronology
- Discussion of relevant factors
- Observation results
- Measurement results
- Findings (that answer each evaluation question)
- Discussion
- Possible threats to the validity of the findings and recommendations
- Recommendations (based on observation and performance data)
- Appendix A: details of methods, statistics, and assumptions that would otherwise "clog up" the main report
- Appendix B: persons involved in the evaluation, including those who facilitated the evaluation process

### Evaluation Contract

On the basis of the final report and the reactions from all stakeholders, Anita decided to prepare a contract for consulting services with the university, so that the valuable assistance that was provided this year could be a continual effort of the evaluation programs for the school district.

## CONSEQUENCES OF EVALUATION AS SUGGESTED IN THIS BOOK

Here is a capsule of what happened when the report was ready to be delivered:

The board and superintendent met and opened a dialogue with the evaluation team. They went over each and every evaluation question—carefully. They complimented the team on their completeness, openness, and competence. And then the questions began.

## Not Everything Was Clear Sailing

In some cases, the evaluation team was asked to clarify the real implications of its findings, noting that there were some with some political ramifications. Especially troubling were some findings on discipline, teacher performance, and links to learner performance and learner success in further education and as they became good citizens.

The evaluation team carefully explained that politics was not in their portfolio for evaluation—they were not there to "spin" results or even be sensitive to the politics, but to simply supply clear information on what worked and what did not. They noted if politics were going to enter into the use of the evaluation information, the board and superintendent would bear the complete responsibility for how the evaluation results were to be used.

This did not sit well at first, but the evaluation team persevered. Politics, they carefully noted time and time again, was not in the evaluation process, questions, or reports.

Still, the evaluation team owed it to the board and superintendent to justify everything: processes, methods, and findings. And they did. At one point, some of the data on teacher performance and links to learner accomplishment were reanalyzed to confirm the findings and recommendations. And that was as it should have been. Evaluation is open and objective and can always continuously improve.

The dialogue continued, and all questions were resolved. The evaluation team went away a bit tired but very much exhilarated by making a unique contribution.

The board and superintendent went into executive session and hammered out their findings and recommendations based on the evaluation information. They were pleased to have solid evidence based on performance, something that had not previously been a part of their educational landscape.

## Going Public

The evaluation findings and board recommendations were made public. After careful review and re-review, the board and superintendent made public their actions based on the evaluation data. They announced the major findings and the changes that they were making as a result of the findings.

The media were called in (actually briefed in advance as well), and parents and community members were informed. The decision was made to break the public into small groups to respond to each set of recommendations and the bases upon which the recommendations were made.

There were some single-issue groups represented, and it was up to all attending the meeting to hear the issues and respond but not be bullied by one political faction or another. Performance and data were the basis for everything.

The evaluation team was asked to serve as "expert resource consultants" at the meeting, and they did. In a few instances, the community groups asked for (and once demanded) to have justification for the evaluation results that affected them. The evaluation team found that in some ways, the preconceived notions of the public concerning means and ends mirrored their early ones.

Patience, calmness, and data served all very well. Most went away with a clear understanding of what the decision makers had decided, and why. All were not completely happy, but all knew that everything was done on the bases of both good faith and good data.

### But That Was Not the End of the Evaluation Story

As a result of the evaluation experience, the citizen's group recommended that this evaluation process continue and be at least an annual reporting event. The board and superintendent ratified that recommendation and modified the budget to "institutionalize" evaluation to find out what worked and what didn't: to allow useful decisions to be made and justified so that all stakeholders perceived that they were not only being well served, but being served well.

The work of the evaluation team was over—at least until the next phase brought them together again to find out what worked and what did not. Let's look at lessons learned.

## TRAPS, ERRORS, AND RULES OF THE ROAD FOR THE ACTION AND ADJUSTMENT PHASE

The evaluation team has done its work and even obtained some wonderful insight on how the school system relates to the community. Sound findings are well documented in the report, but it could all lead nowhere if this final phase is not carried out with the same energy and attention to detail that was given to the first three. Here are three more traps to avoid in this critical phase.

### The Communication Trap

Excellent planning, detailed observation, and insightful analysis can be of no use if the findings are not clearly and properly presented to decision makers and stakeholders. When the evaluation team presents the findings of the study, including recommendations for change, it is important that all who receive the report understand the intent of the study team. That is not always the case, however, if the following errors are committed.

### Error of Inflammatory or "Loaded" Language

Many words in the general vocabulary carry pejorative and negative connotations, including those with negative racial stereotypes and off-color terms. Most writers will avoid the more obvious of these. However, some words carry meaning for certain populations that are not in general use. If accidentally inserted into reports, these can upset people without that being the intension of the writers. Other terms to be avoided if not fully justified include:

*All*

*None*

*Absolutely*

*Totally* (and other words that convey absolutes that are not justified by data)

Technical terms can also have confusing layers of meaning. Everyone has a general idea of what the terms *validity* and *validation* mean. But the technical meaning of these terms is complex and linked to certain procedures. A curriculum, for example, may be considered a valid part of the school offerings (because it meets a need identified in needs assessment), but tests provided as part of that same curriculum to measure Products in terms of learning may not be valid predictors of future activity or transfer of training. A chance comment in a report about the invalid test may be taken as a challenge to the curriculum in general.

The use of words is vital. For example, throughout this book, you have been exposed to many terms that are different from common usage. (And we thank you for your careful consideration.) You should maintain the rigor of your language even when others do not; model the language and behavior you want others to adopt. Just for the sake of acceptance, don't "go native" and use common words that are different from what you intend to communicate. Maintain the rigor you worked so hard to create, but don't get antagonistic about it. Just do what's right, not what is acceptable.

### Error of Audience

Language must be matched to the audience in several ways. The tone of a report should never be patronizing or arrogant. There should be no

"We told you so" paragraphs or excessive pontification in evaluation report writing. Technical terms should be explained for general audiences. Technical terms should never be inserted just to impress or confuse an audience.

Lofty rhetoric is not for evaluation reports. Reports must speak directly to every audience, school administrators, school boards, parents, teachers, and students. Each audience will have a special set of concerns and questions regarding the results and findings of an evaluation study. The wise writer will make sure that the special concerns of each audience are addressed in any reports that will be accessed and read. Reports should not be "one size fits all" or too technical for a particular segment of readers.

The *error of the audience* is to do one of the following: (1) dumb down a report due to holding an audience in low esteem; (2) overemphasize technical content in order to impress the general audience and, by association, create the impression that everything must be right in the report because the technical experts must know what they are talking about ("Because I sure don't understand what they are saying"); and (3) fail to include specific sections that address the concerns of each stakeholder.

### Error of the Secret

Evaluation should have no secrets, and all findings should be a matter of public record. This is true even when the findings are disappointing and bound to upset some stakeholders. It is far better to publish negative findings than later fight the battle that will surely come related to accusations of a cover-up.

Realize that many people will suspect the evaluation team, and indeed the administration, of having "hidden agendas." Be sure to dispel any suspicions of this.

## The Action Trap

School systems get into trouble when they fail to take correct action or when they take action that fails to get desired results. Only correct action leads to desired results. It is unfortunate that the vast array of action choices does not come with convenient labels telling decision makers what to expect from each choice. There are, however, some common errors that if avoided will help reduce the number of wrong turns.

### Error of the Expert

When we rely on the advice of experts who operate outside of their area of expertise or when we see experts as infallible even when their opinions fly in the face of the facts, that is the *error of the expert.*[3] There are some common examples that occur in school systems. Teachers who have trained in one field are asked to step in and teach a course outside of their special area. This may help ease one problem, but will it create another? When consultants are used, their advice should be limited to the area of their expertise. When teachers have great success with a given method (in a particular setting with particular students), do we rush to copy that success regardless of the special circumstances that led to the original good result? Do we hold to certain ideas put forward by "experts" even when the facts do not support the ideas?

All of these are habits of behavior that tend to be exhibited in and around experts. Why? Because expert knowledge is highly valued in our culture and because of what has been called the "halo effect." That is overgeneralization from one good thing to all things or one good act to all acts.

### Error of the Quick Fix

When we base our actions and conclusions on the desire to look effective and decisive but in fact put in place quick-fix or "fad" programs in order to say we did something, we commit the *error of the quick fix.*

Quick fixes are form without function, and they are usually easy actions to take, but even the ease of the action does not keep you from wasting resources on efforts that will not produce effective or long-lasting results that are in line with valid goals and objectives. Quick fixes produce superficial results. It is much better to fend off the critics than to let them pressure you into actions that have no good or long-lasting results.

### Error of Looking Busy

We all know someone who makes a practiced art of "looking busy." These persons are always up to their necks in Process, but the Process never seems to lead anywhere. They attend lots of meetings and are almost always late for meetings or unavailable due to other assignments. Time and resources are consumed, but to no particular end in view.

There are two main causes of this error: First, there are people who cover up a lack of skill and knowledge with a superficial routine calculated to keep others at bay, especially supervisors and management personnel. When asked to do something, the superficially busy will respond with a host of reasons why they do not have the time, and list a dozen or so unfinished tasks (the same tasks they have been using for years). The second cause stems from a legitimate concern with Process and the value of the experience as a worthwhile activity. While the first cause stems from laziness or incompetence, this cause is harder to deal with because there is great value to Process, and it can be rewarding in and of itself. The problem is that the two cannot be divorced. Education must serve an end that goes beyond the enjoyment of process. That is true of the educational system because it is conceived and funded to serve the needs of the community. This is much different than a casual activity. This is serious building of the infrastructure of community and nation.

### Error of Tunnel Vision

Just as a Process-only approach usually leads to error, so can an exclusive focus only on results with no understanding of the wider context in which the results flow.

For example, we have emphasized a results-centered approach to evaluation, but not in the narrow sense. Suppose improved reading scores was an objective of the school board and several schools in the district were not showing progress on that particular Output of the educational programs. If the school board decided to change the programs and fire all of the staff who could not produce results, that could be an error depending on some other factors. Suppose the staff in question had to cope with terrible teaching conditions, drugs in the schools, students who had poor conditions at home, and the influence of gangs. Suppose the staff in question was the only reliable and solid mentoring support in the lives of the children and it was a minor miracle that the students were still in school. Changing the staff and discarding the curriculum might do more harm to an already-suffering population of students. The school board might look like they were making an executive decision based on facts. But in this case, they would not be acting on all of the facts, just the limited concept of results.

Results are important and should be the driving force in decision making. But results must also be taken in context so the overall situation can be improved. In our approach, we want evaluation to identify what works so that we can build on a solid baseline to keep what works and build on that. In short, the old saying "throwing out the baby with the bathwater" should not be the result of a narrow bathwater evaluation. This leads to the next action error.

### Error of Turmoil

Turmoil results when systems are in a constant state of unproductive change. Unproductive change results when entire programs are thrown out and new ones put in place after each evaluation. The results are not what you want, so you start over from scratch instead of keeping the good parts and building on them. This places the organization into a constant state of stress on resources, personnel, and students. In short, this is *turnover turmoil*.

In this context, the staff never has time to learn the new processes and procedures, students do not know what to expect, and the cost of each new program stresses the budget.

The error of turmoil occurs when a lack of sensible evaluative and contextual information turns decision making into a black-and-white, go/no-go choice between keeping a failing program or starting a new one from scratch. Few programs are 100% failures, and few are 100% success stories. It is that space in between that should be filled by good evaluation data. That happens only when the evaluation team is gathering contextual and process information on all aspects of the programs, and that happens only by design.

## The Testing Trap

### The Relevancy Error and the Error of the Instrument

Testing is such a predominant feature of education, it is taken for granted as being useful, important, and valid. Casual use of testing can, however, lead to problems.

Whenever we test things that do not matter and fail to test things that do matter, we fall into the "testing trap." The testing trap occurs because of two errors, the *error of the instrument* and the *error of relevancy.* The first of these includes testing that is unreliable or without construct validity. This wastes time and resources because the results of the test are either of no consequence or lead to false conclusions about the skills and abilities of those taking the test. The error of relevancy can occur because it is possible to make a reliable and valid test that measures only a subset of required behavior. We tend to simply test the things that are easy to test. We might test for knowledge of sentence construction and assume that people will communicate successfully. The rules of use and a set of signals from sentence structure must be learned and practiced, especially if the use of the language is to communicate successfully. Responding to this challenge, there have been a number of suggested hierarchies of learning and educational objectives.

Tests must reflect the level of objective-related performance required for mastery of an entire skill or an entire task. How many courses have you taken in your educational experience that seemed to be a random collection of bits that did not add up to any unified system of ideas or lead to any mastery of a skill or a useful performance competence? The tests for the course were always hard. The test was hard because you did not know what to expect or how to prepare. The professor was happy with the reputation for having a difficult course. His tests were always a surprise, seemingly a random sample of items selected from all the odd bits of the course, with a few new items that were not even covered in the course. His pleasure mounted as he always had a nice normal curve of student performance on his tests. A dangerous assumption, but one that is unleashed on learners almost worldwide.

The normal curve is a naturally occurring phenomenon that occurs in natural events. Any group of students selected at random will tend to fall into a normal distribution on a host of nature-allocated attributes (height and weight will fall into a normal distribution unless some prior selection activity intervenes). If a random group of students were to be given our professor's test without taking his course, they would probably fall into a normal distribution. What does that say about the course and the test? If an instructional intervention is effective and the objective is mastery of a subject (as opposed to tests that are designed to screen), the results of the test should not be normal, but strongly skewed to the positive. Our professor has committed the *error of relevancy.*

Another way to fall into the testing trap is to start with a test and then construct a course of instruction to satisfy the test. Tests should be constructed to measure attainment of objectives that flow from a coherent curriculum that contributes to the larger goals of the school system.

## RULES OF THE ROAD
## FOR THE ACTION AND
## ADJUSTMENT PHASE

> *Scenario Teaching Point:*
> A simple description of results is not evaluation of results. Results are valued according to the goals and objectives of the educational system and larger society that supports that system. Results may be as planned or not, depending on the success of the program or methods used to achieve them. Fully meeting the wrong goals is not a success.

*Rule 1.* Time and resources must be sensibly and sensitively devoted to action and adjustment.

*Rule 2.* Make sure there is evaluation in your evaluation report (remember this point from Scenario 2).

*Rule 3.* Say something to every stakeholder in language they can understand, while maintaining the rigor of your approach and findings.

There are two points to Rule #3: First, make sure you address every stakeholder. Every person should at least have access to everything that was provided by the evaluation—secrecy is not allowed. The second point here is that you must speak in language that is understood. Many terms are hot buttons for certain issues. Be sure you have vetted your language for the intended audience.

*Rule 4.* Render guidance and advice only in areas where the evaluation data supports your conclusions and recommendations. Make recommendations to change, alter, or scrap the programs and supporting organizational establishment only in terms of a continuing understanding of the valid needs of the community. Use the Mega approach.

*Rule 5.* If the results are not as planned, the evaluator may or may not be in a position to provide evaluation data to support the decisions to change, adjust, or start over. If you have supporting data, use them to get the program on track. But if you do not have supporting data, do not substitute wishful thinking in place of weak data. Just because you have done some evaluation activity, you are not free to comment on any and all things in the name of evaluation. The guidance that the evaluator can render is a function of the understanding of what went on, which, in turn, is a function of the information gathered. If very little understanding was gained, then "very little" should also be the operant phrase for your conclusions and recommendations.

*Rule 6.* Don't stop now. Evaluation should be continuous. Part of your report should outline areas for future evaluation. Be sure to include cost and schedule in your proposal.

The next section is a checklist for an evaluation proposal.

## LIST FOR EVALUATION PROPOSAL

As part of your evaluation report, you may want to include a proposal to make sure that resources are available in the future to identify, document, and report gaps between what the organization set out to accomplish and what was actually delivered. Here is a simple checklist:

*Checkpoint 1.* Include the What, Why, and How in your proposal.

A proposal—regardless of who issues it or what it is seeking—is a request to get something accomplished. The "something" might be to evaluate a program or project, evaluate an entire organization, or to ensure needs assessment continues to take place from a Mega perspective.

*Checkpoint 2.* Communicate your capability.

A proposal is a communication document with which you want to convince someone that you can do what you propose to do,

you can do it well, and

the results will be worth their confidence in you that you will deliver useful results within the time and cost required.

*Checkpoint 3.* Focus on evaluation questions.

You should answer these questions in your document:

Why this evaluation question versus all other questions that could be addressed?

Why this approach to answering versus all other approaches that might be employed?

How will you know when you have accomplished that which you set out to accomplish?

*Checkpoint 4.* Include an Evaluation Management Plan.

How will it be managed?

What is the budget?

What is the schedule?

> *Costs-consequences analysis:* the comparison of what you give to what you get. Costs include expenditures, budgets, foregone opportunities, outlays of people, and/or resources (Watkins & Kaufman, 1996).

If the proposal requires a budget and its justification, one more question should be answered: How much will it cost?

Here are some cost drivers:

- Salaries for project staff
- Related fringe benefits
- Other personal services
- Travel
- Supplies
- Equipment
- Postage
- Data processing/computing
- Word processing
- Copying, duplicating, printing
- Telephone/e-mail/FAX
- Graphics

- Editorial
- Overhead (or list the items of overhead separately, such as rent, utilities, janitorial, etc.)

*Checkpoint 4.* Writing style (Keep it simple)

> Write clearly, simply, and format it for understanding. Write it in such a way that you would want to read it, and in such a manner that you would fund the effort.

Again, the basic purpose of writing a proposal is to get someone to support an activity in order to get useful results and payoffs. That "someone" is critical and must be convinced of both the merit of the idea as well as the procedures to implement the idea and meet the *needs* you have identified and justified. Find out, if possible, who will review the proposal and what they might be looking for. This approach to writing proposals has emphasized *needs assessment,* planning, and purposive activities. While it is tempting to write in an intricate, complex style, you should avoid the tendency to "sound scientific." Simple words and sensible short sentences have a higher probability of being read and understood than long, complex ones.

Keep sentences short. Keep ideas basic. Keep facts in focus. Remember who your reviewer is, and try to include content, words, and references that will be understood and accepted by that person. Make sure that your proposal is complete and shows exactly what you want to do, and why. Don't "waffle" or be vague. If something is unknown, say so, but don't try to "fake it." Reviewers might not ultimately accept your proposal, but help make any decision they make be an informed one. Be objective. Be professional. Be right.

## NOTES

1.   While it might be tempting to provide independent reporting to all of the stakeholders, this should not be done unless specifically negotiated in advance with those who funded the evaluation. This does not mean that the results of the evaluation will be distorted or abused, because education is public and everything that goes on is open to public scrutiny.

2.   *Goals* are measurable on a nominal or ordinal scale, while *objectives* are measurable on an interval or ratio scale.

3.   Often, in training, curriculum developers and instructional designers rely on "subject matter experts." Unfortunately, these so-called experts often are not (Kaufman, Oakley-Browne, Watkins, & Leigh, 2003) and might be more accurately termed "subjective matter experts."

# References

Adler, P., & Adler, P. (1994). Observational techniques. In N. K. Denzin & Y. S. Lincoln (Eds.), *The handbook of qualitative research* (pp. 377–392). Newbury Park, CA: Sage.

Astin, A. W., & Panos, R. J. (1971). The evaluation of education programs. In R. L. Thorndike (Ed.), *Educational measurement* (2nd ed.). Washington, D.C.: American Council on Education.

Banathy, B. H. (1991). *Systems design of education: A journey to create the future.* Englewood Cliffs, NJ: Educational Technology.

Banathy, B. H. (1992). *A systems view of education: Concepts and principles for effective practice.* Englewood Cliffs, NJ: Educational Technology.

Barker, J. A. (1992). *Future edge: Discovering the new paradigms of success.* New York: William Morrow.

Barker, J. A. (2001). *The new business of paradigms* (21st Century ed.). [Video-cassette]. St. Paul, MN: Star Thrower Distribution.

Berk, R. A. (Ed.). (1980). *Criterion-referenced measurement.* Baltimore: Johns Hopkins University Press.

Berk, R. A. (1981). *Educational evaluation methodology: The state of the art.* Baltimore: Johns Hopkins University Press.

Bernardez, M. (2004). *The Refinor case. Integrating sound business practice with societal-based objectives and ethics: Lessons learned from applying Mega planning and thinking.* ISPI 2004 Conference Proceedings.

Bertalanffy, L. Von. (1968). *General systems theory.* New York: George Braziller.

Branson, R. K., Rayner, G. T., & Cox, J. L. (1975, August). *Interservice procedures for instructional systems development (Phases I, II, III, IV, V, and Executive Summary)* (U.S. Army Training and Doctrine Command Pamphlet 350). Fort Monroe, VA.

Brethower, D. M. (2005). Yes we can: A rejoinder to Don Winiecki's rejoinder about saving the world with HPT. *Performance Improvement, 44*(2), 19–24.

Campbell, D. T., & Stanley, J. C. (1966). *Experimental and quasi-experimental designs for research.* Chicago: Rand McNally. American Council on Education.

Churchman, C. W. (1969). *The systems approach.* New York: Dell. (2nd ed.)

Cook, W. J. Jr. (1990). *Bill Cook's strategic planning for America's schools* (Rev. ed.). Birmingham, AL, & Arlington, VA: Cambridge Management Group & the American Association of School Administrators.

Cooley, W. W., & Lohnes, P. R. (1976). *Evaluation research in education.* New York: John Wiley.

Converse, J., & Presser, S. (1986). *Survey questions: Handcrafting the standardized questionnaire.* Newbury Park, CA: Sage.

Corrigan, R. E., & Corrigan, B. O. (1985). *SAFE: System approach for effectiveness.* New Orleans, LA: R. E. Corrigan.

Corrigan, R. E., & Kaufman, R. (1966). *Why system engineering?* Palo Alto, CA: Fearon.

Corrigan, R. E., et al. (1975). *A system approach for education (SAFE).* Garden Grove, CA: R. E. Corrigan.

Daniel, R. (1995). Revising letters to veterans. *Technical Communication* (69). See also references and discussions on assessment of the effectiveness of communication in documents on the Plain Language website (www.plain language.gov).

Davis, R., Stake, R., Chandler, M., Heck, D., & Hoke, G. (2000). *VBA appeals training module: Certify a case to the Board of Veterans Appeals, Phase II.* Champaign: University of Illinois, CIRCE.

Davis, R., Stake, R., Ryan, K. E., Heck, D., Hinn, D. M., & Guyn, S. (1999). *VBA appeals training module: Certify a case to the Board of Veterans Appeals, Phase I.* Champaign: University of Illinois, CIRCE.

Dick, W., Carey, L., & Carey, J. (2001). *The systematic design of instruction* (5th ed.). New York: Addison-Wesley.

Drucker, P. F. (1973). *Management: Tasks, responsibilities, practices.* New York: Harper & Row.

Drucker, P. F. (1992, September/October). The new society of organizations. *Harvard Business Review,* pp. 95–104.

Drucker, P. F. (1993). *Post-capitalist society.* New York: Harper Business.

Drucker, P. F. (1994). The age of social transformation. *The Atlantic Monthly, 274*(5), 53–80.

Dumas, J. S., & Redish, J. (1999). *A practical guide to usability testing.* Bristol, UK: Intellect.

Garratt, B. (1987). *The learning organization.* London: HarperCollins. (2nd ed. 1994)

Garratt, B. (Ed.). (1995). *Developing strategic thought: Rediscovering the art of direction-giving.* London, McGraw-Hill.

Gilbert, T. F. (1978). *Human competence: Engineering worthy performance.* New York: McGraw-Hill.

Glass, G. V., & Ellet, F. S. (1980). Evaluation research. *Annual Review of Psychology, 31,* 211–228.

Gruender, C. D. (1996). Constructivism and learning: A philosophical appraisal. *Educational Technology, 36*(3), 21–29.

Guba, E. G. (1978). *Toward a methodology of naturalistic inquiry in educational evaluation* (Monograph No. 8). Los Angeles: UCLA Center for the Study of Evaluation.

Guerra, I. (2003a). Asking and answering the right questions: Collecting relevant and useful data. *Performance Improvement, 42*(10), 24–28.

Guerra, I. (2003b). Key competencies required of performance improvement professionals. *Performance Improvement Quarterly, 16*(1), 55–72.

Harless, J. (1998). *The Eden conspiracy: Educating for accomplished citizenship.* Wheaton, IL: Guild V.

House, E. R. (1977). *The logic of evaluative argument* (CSE Monograph Series in Evaluation No. 7). Los Angeles: University of California, Center for the Study of Evaluation.

Isaac, S., & Michael, W. B. (1971). *Handbook in research and evaluation.* San Diego, CA: Knapp.

Kaufman, R. (1992a). *Mapping educational success.* Thousand Oaks, CA: Corwin.

Kaufman, R. (1992b). *Strategic planning plus: An organizational guide* (Rev. ed.). Newbury Park, CA: Sage.

Kaufman, R. (1995). *Mapping educational success* (Rev. ed.). Thousand Oaks, CA: Corwin.

Kaufman, R. (1998). *Strategic thinking: A guide to identifying and solving problems* (Rev. ed.). Arlington, VA, & Washington, D.C: Jointly published by the American Society for Training & Development and the International Society for Performance Improvement. (Also published in Spanish: *El Pensamiento Estrategico: Una Guia Para Identificar y Resolver los Problemas*, Madrid, Editorial Centros de Estudios Ramon Areces, S.A.).

Kaufman, R. (2000). *Mega planning.* Thousand Oaks, CA. Sage.

Kaufman, R., & English, F. W. (1979). *Needs assessment: Concept and application.* Englewood Cliffs, NJ: Educational Technology.

Kaufman, R., & Grise, P. (1995). *Auditing your educational strategic plan: Making a good thing better.* Thousand Oaks, CA. Corwin.

Kaufman, R., Grise, P., & Watters, K. (1992). Needs assessment summary forms. In K. L. Medsker & D. G. Roberts (Eds.), *ASTD trainer's toolkit: Evaluating the results of training.* Arlington, VA: American Society for Training & Development.

Kaufman, R., & Lick, D. (2000). Mega-level strategic planning: Beyond conventional wisdom. In J. Boettcher, M. Doyle, & R. Jensen (Eds.), *Technology-driven planning: Principles to practice* (chap. 1). Ann Arbor, MI: Society for College and University Planning.

Kaufman, R., & Lick, D. (2000/2001, Winter). Change creation and change management: Partners in human performance improvement. *Performance in Practice*, pp. 8–9.

Kaufman, R., Keller, J., & Watkins, R. (1995). What works and what doesn't: Evaluation beyond Kirkpatrick. *Performance and Instruction, 35*(2), 8–12.

Kaufman, R., Oakley-Browne, H., Watkins, R., & Leigh, D. (2003). *Practical strategic planning: Designing and delivering high-impact results.* San Francisco: Jossey-Bass/Pfeiffer.

Kaufman, R., Rojas, A., & Mayer, H. (1993). *Needs assessment: A user's guide.* Englewood Cliffs, NJ.: Educational Technology. (Winner of the 1994 ID Tools AWARD, Division of Instructional Development, The Association for Educational Communications & Technology).

Kaufman, R., & Thomas, S. (1980). *Evaluation without fear.* New York: New Viewpoints Division, Franklin Watts.

Kaufman, R., & Unger, Z. (2003). Evaluation plus: Beyond conventional evaluation. *Performance Improvement, 42*(7), 5–8.

Kaufman, R., & Watkins, R. (1999). Needs assessment. In D. Langdon (Ed.), *The resource guide to performance interventions* (pp. 237–242). San Diego, CA: Jossey-Bass.

Kaufman, R., & Watkins, R. (2000). Getting serious about results and payoffs: We are what we say, do, and deliver. *Performance Improvement 39*(4), 23–32.

Kaufman, R., Watkins, R., & Leigh, D. (2001). *Useful educational results: Defining, prioritizing, accomplishing.* Lancaster, PA: Proactive Press.

Kaufman, R., Watkins, R., Sims, L., Crispo, N., & Sprague, D. (1997). Costs-consequences analysis. *Performance Improvement Quarterly, 10*(3), 7–21.

Kaufman, R., Watkins, R., Triner, D., & Stith, M. (1998). The changing corporate mind: Organizations, visions, mission, purposes, and indicators on the move toward societal payoff. *Performance Improvement Quarterly, 11*(3), 32–44.

Kirkpatrick, D. (1967). Evaluation. In R. L. Craig & L. R. Bittel (Eds.), *Training & development handbook* (American Society for Training & Development). New York: McGraw-Hill.

Kirkpatrick, D. L. (1994). *Evaluating training programs: The four levels.* San Francisco: Berret-Koehler.

Leigh, D., Watkins, R., Platt, W., & Kaufman, R. (2000). Alternate models of needs assessment: Selecting the right one for your organization. *Human Resource Development Quarterly, 11*(1), 87–93.

Levin, H. M. (1983). *Cost effectiveness: A primer (New Perspectives in Evaluation).* Beverly Hills, CA: Sage.

McMillan, J. H. (1992). *Educational research: Fundamentals for the consumer.* New York: HarperCollins.

Mager, R. F. (1997). *Preparing instructional objectives: A critical tool in the development of effective instruction* (3rd ed.). Atlanta: Center for Effective Performance.

Miles, M. B., & Huberman, A. M. (1994). *Qualitative data analysis: An expanded sourcebook* (2nd ed.). Newbury Park, CA: Sage.

Mohr, L. B. (1992). *Impact analysis for program evaluation.* Newbury Park, CA: Sage.

Muir, M., Watkins, R., Kaufman, R., & Leigh, D. (1998). Costs-consequences analysis: A primer. *Performance Improvement, 37*(4), 8–17, 48.

Peters, T. (1997). *The circle of innovation: You can't shrink your way to greatness.* New York: Knopf.

Peters, T. J., & Waterman, R. H. Jr. (1982). *In search of excellence: Lessons learned from America's best run companies.* New York: Harper & Row.

Platt, W. (1982). *Toward a general theory of evaluation.* PhD Dissertation, Indiana University.

Popcorn, F. (1991). *The Popcorn report.* New York: Doubleday.

Popham, W. J. (1966). *Educational objectives.* Los Angeles: Vimcet.

Popham, W. J. (Ed.). (1974). *Evaluation in education.* Berkeley, CA: McCutchan.

Popham, W. J., & Husek, T. R. (1969). Implications of criterion-referenced measurement. *Journal of Educational Measurement, 6*(1), 1–19.

Rea, L., & Parker, R. (1997). *Designing and conducting survey research: A comprehensive guide.* San Francisco: Jossey Bass.

Richards, T. J., & Richards, L. (1994). Using computers in qualitative analysis. In N. K. Denzin & Y. S. Lincoln (Eds.), *The handbook of qualitative research* (pp. 445–462). Newbury Park, CA: Sage.

Robinson, W. (1951). The logical structure of analytic induction. *American Sociological Review, 16,* 812–818.

Rummler, G. A. (2004). *Serious performance consulting: According to Rummler.* Silver Spring, MD: International Society for Performance Improvement and the American Society for Training and Development.

Schwartz, P., & Kelly, K. (1996). The relentless contrarian. *Wired, 4*(8). [Online Journal]

Scriven, M. (1967). The methodology of evaluation. In R. Tyler, R. M. Gagne, & M. Scriven (Eds.), *Perspectives of curriculum evaluation* (AERA Monograph Series on Curriculum Evaluation). Chicago: Rand McNally.

Scriven, M. (1973). *Goal free evaluation.* In E. R. House (Ed.), *School evaluation: The politics and process.* Berkeley, CA: McCutchan.

Stake, R. (1974). Program evaluation, particularly responsive evaluation. *New Trends in Evaluation* (Report No. 35, pp. 1–20). Gothenburg, Sweden: University of Gothenburg, Institute of Education.

Stake, R. (2004). *Standards-based and responsive evaluation.* Thousand Oaks, CA: Sage.

Steel, L. E. (2004). *Teacher evaluation works.* [CD-ROM]. Thousand Oaks, CA: Corwin.

Stufflebeam, D. L., Foley, W. J., Gephart, W. R., Guba, E. G., Hammon, R. L., Merriman, H. O., & Provus, M. M. (1971). *Educational evaluation and decision making.* Itasca, IL: Peacock.

Stufflebeam, D. L., & Webster, W. J. (1980). An analysis of alternative approaches to evaluation. *Educational Evaluation and Policy Analysis, 2,* 5–20.

Triner, D., Greenberry, A., & Watkins, R. (1996). Training needs assessment: A contradiction in terms? *Educational Technology, XXXVI*(6), 51–55.

Tyler, R. W. (1966). Assessing the process of education. *Science Education, L*(3), 239–242.

Watkins, R., & Kaufman, R. (1996). An update on relating needs assessment and needs analysis. *Performance Improvement, 35*(10), 10–13.

Watkins, R., & Kaufman, R. (2002). Assessing and evaluating: Differentiating perspectives. *Performance Improvement, 41*(2), 22–28.

Watkins, R., Leigh, D., Foshay, R., & Kaufman, R. (1998). Kirkpatrick plus: Evaluation and continuous improvement with a community focus. *Educational Technology Research and Development Journal, 46*(4), 90–96.

Watkins, R., Leigh, D., Platt, W., & Kaufman, R. (1998). Needs assessment: A digest, review, and comparison of needs assessment literature. *Performance Improvement, 37*(7), 48–53.

Weiss, C. H. (1972). *Evaluation research: Methods of assessing program effectiveness.* Englewood Cliffs, NJ: Prentice Hall.

Weitzman, E. A., & Miles, M. B. (1995). *Computer programs for qualitative data analysis, a software sourcebook.* Thousand Oaks, CA: Sage.

Witkin, B., & Altschuld, J. (1995). *Planning and conducting needs assessments.* Thousand Oaks, CA. Sage.

Wolf, R. L. (1979). The use of judicial evaluation methods in the formulation of educational policy. *Educational Evaluation and Policy Analysis, 1,* 19.

Worthen, B. R., & Sanders, J. R. (1973). (Eds.). *Educational evaluation: Theory and practice.* Worthington, OH: Charles A. Jones.

# Index